Communicating Social Support

When stresses and hassles challenge our abilities to cope, we frequently turn to family, friends, and partners for help. Yet social support from close relational partners does not uniformly benefit recipients or their relationships. By probing the communication processes that link enactments of social support to participants' reactions, this book provides new explanations for when and how receiving social support will be evaluated as helpful and relationally satisfying. The author's research addresses a variety of types of relationships and stresses, including young adult friends and romantic partners coping with the stresses of university life; adult friends, family, and spouses responding to everyday hassles; and married couples coping with chronic health conditions. This innovative program of research combines qualitative and quantitative methods to develop a distinctive communication-based framework for understanding why the content, form, style, and sequence of talk matter for our evaluations of the help we receive from others.

Daena J. Goldsmith (Ph.D.) is Associate Professor of Speech Communication at the University of Illinois at Urbana–Champaign. Her teaching and research span a variety of topics, including social support, communication theory, gender issues, and personal relationships. She is widely published in national and international journals in the areas of communication and personal relationships.

T0384521

ADVANCES IN PERSONAL RELATIONSHIPS

HARRY T. REIS
University of Rochester

MARY ANNE FITZPATRICK
University of Wisconsin-Madison

ANITA L. VANGELISTI
University of Texas, Austin

Although scholars from a variety of disciplines have written and conversed about the importance of personal relationships for decades, the emergence of personal relationships as a field of study is relatively recent. *Advances in Personal Relationships* represents the culmination of years of multidisciplinary and interdisciplinary work on personal relationships. Sponsored by the International Association for Relationship Research, the series offers readers cutting-edge research and theory in the field. Contributing authors are internationally known scholars from a variety of disciplines, including social psychology, clinical psychology, communication, history, sociology, gerontology, and family studies. Volumes include integrative reviews, conceptual pieces, summaries of research programs, and major theoretical works. *Advances in Personal Relationships* presents first-rate scholarship that is both provocative and theoretically grounded. The theoretical and empirical work described by authors will stimulate readers and advance the field by offering up new ideas and retooling old ones. The series will be of interest to upper division undergraduate students, graduate students, researchers, and practitioners.

OTHER BOOKS IN THE SERIES
Attribution, Communication Behavior, and Close Relationships
Valerie Manusov and John H. Harvey
Stability and Change in Relationships
Anita L. Vangelisti, Harry T. Reis, and Mary Anne Fitzpatrick
Understanding Marriage: Developments in the Study of Couple Interaction
Patricia Noller and Judith A. Feeney
Growing Together: Personal Relationships Across the Life Span
Frieder R. Lang and Karen L. Fingerman

Communicating Social Support

DAENA J. GOLDSMITH
University of Illinois at Urbana-Champaign

CAMBRIDGE UNIVERSITY PRESS
Cambridge, New York, Melbourne, Madrid, Cape Town, Singapore, São Paulo, Delhi

Cambridge University Press
32 Avenue of the Americas, New York, NY 10013-2473, USA

www.cambridge.org
Information on this title: www.cambridge.org/9780521066860

First published 2004
First paperback edition 2008

Printed in the United States of America

A catalog record for this publication is available from the British Library.

Library of Congress Cataloging in Publication Data

Goldsmith, Daena J., 1964–
    Communicating social support / Daena J. Goldsmith.
      p. cm. – (Advances in personal relationships)
    Includes bibliographical references and index.
    ISBN 0-521-82590-3
    1. Social networks – Psychological aspects. 2. Interpersonal relations.
    3. Interpersonal communication. 4. Stress (Psychology) I. Title.
    II. Advances in personal relationships (Cambridge, England)
    HM741.G65   2004
    302 – dc22   2003069661

ISBN 978-0-521-82590-0 hardback
ISBN 978-0-521-06686-0 paperback

For Michael and Graehm

Contents

Acknowledgments

I suspect that writing a book on the topic of social support has heightened my awareness of how others' encouragement and aid have helped bring this project to completion. Leslie Baxter and Mac Parks have been mentors and friends who encouraged my interest in relational contradictions and my desire to combine different approaches to communication study. As my research program was first taking shape, Robert Gaines and Brant Burleson encouraged my interest in close attention to the strategic value of message features. Barbara O'Keefe and Bruce Lambert influenced my thinking about how messages are adapted to task, identity, and relational purposes. My book shares its title with an earlier volume by Teri Albrecht and Mara Adelman – their book served as my introduction to research in this area and Teri has been a wonderful supporter of my research. I hope my own book will be as useful to others as Teri and Mara's work has been for me.

Dale Brashers, Dan O'Keefe, and John Caughlin have served as conversation partners, statistical consultants, and stalwart supporters. This book is better for their hand in it. Kristine Fitch has been my sounding board, faithful friend, and encourager. Virginia McDermott was my right hand for several years – the conversation data would not have been collected if not for her – and she continues to help me think and laugh out loud. Grants from the University of Illinois Campus Research Board supported the Community Conversation Study and the Illinois Heart Care Project.

Several individuals encountered my work in graduate courses or in research collaborations with me and have served as readers, discussants, and/or collaborators, including Susan Dun, Kristen Bauer, Elaine Hsieh, Stewart Alexander, Thom Bovino, Erina MacGeorge, Lance Rintamaki, Josh Barbour, Gwen Costa, Michelle Gabris, and Mei Kuan Huang.

Finally, my friends and family teach me to value my work while keeping it in perspective and provide instrumental aid in getting it done. Nancy, Virginia, Cheryl, Risa, Brigitte, and Heather encourage me and remind me of what I can do. Mom, Dad, and Laurie have always had unwavering confidence in my abilities. This book is dedicated to my husband, Michael, and my son, Graehm, who believe in me, love me, put up with me, and make it all worthwhile.

Introduction

In an interview with a 49-year-old woman, the interviewer asked what advice she would give to friends or family members of persons with cancer. The woman replied, "let them talk about it and face the fears together. That I think is a measure of a true friend or a true relative, is they're willing to walk along that road with you."[1]

In a study of conversations about everyday problems and stresses, a 28-year-old man explained his definition of a supportive person: "[They] give you feedback on your work or your actions. Also they are able to be honest with you and realize that the more we communicate our feelings and thoughts, the more our relationship will rest on a strong, passionate, and profound sense of intimacy."

In a letter to Dear Abby, "Hurting Friend" explains how she turned to a friend for support during a time of stress only to be rejected. She says that her friend's unwillingness to provide emotional support "was a slap in the face and one that hurt much worse than a physical blow. Abby, I feel hurt and betrayed."

Several decades of research reinforce the observation common to these examples from everyday life: Talking about problems with family and friends is important to individual and relational well-being. This book is about those conversations: what they look like, how and why they matter, and what are more and less effective ways of doing them. These conversations and their success or failure are important because they are the beginning of a chain of processes that can influence coping, relationship satisfaction, and individual health and well-being.

In the interdisciplinary literature relevant to these issues, concepts such as *enacted social support* and *troubles talk* capture some of what goes on in these conversations. Yet the research literature associated with each of

---

[1] I am grateful to Virginia McDermott for sharing with me this quotation from her interviews with members of a cancer recovery support group.

these concepts provides an incomplete picture. Those who study enacted social support have usually focused on how much of it a person reports and have overlooked the give and take of conversations in which it occurs. In contrast, those who study troubles talk have typically been concerned with the internal structure and organization of these conversations, without systematic attention to the import of these conversations for their participants' individual and relational well-being. There are exceptions to this generalization, scholars who share my interest in understanding how the features and processes of talk about troubles are evaluated by participants and how these evaluations translate into coping, well-being, and relational satisfaction.[2] Moreover, although much of the social support individuals receive comes from close relational partners, and although close relationships are often the setting for troubles talk, talk about stresses and problems has received less attention from scholars of close relationships than have other types of talk, such as conflict or self-disclosure. Consequently, there is much that we don't know about the contours and landmarks of troubles talk in close relationships, how partners navigate it, and the effects of this on their journey through the stresses and hassles of daily life. My goal in this book is to map some of the unexplored territory that lies at the intersection of research on social support, troubles talk, and personal relationships.

   The research relevant to this book is spread across various disciplines, and the approach I take differs from that taken in most previous work, so it may be useful to explain my focus, its relevance to various audiences,

---

[2] For example, a number of researchers have examined messages or conversations in which comfort or support is provided. Burleson and his colleagues (see Burleson, 1994, for a review) have shown how students' reactions to comforting messages (and message producers) depend on the degree to which the message acknowledges, legitimates, and elaborates on the other person's feelings. Barbee and Cunningham (see Barbee & Cunningham, 1995, for a review) have examined how different ways of seeking help (i.e., directly or indirectly, verbally or nonverbally) are related to the kind of support one receives (i.e., problem-solving or emotion-focused support, approach or avoidance of problem/emotion). Cutrona and colleagues (e.g. Cutrona, 1996b; Cutrona & Suhr, 1992, 1994) have examined how different types of support (e.g., problem-solving, nurturant, or esteem support) may be more or less effective and satisfying depending on features of the problem situation (e.g., how controllable the problem is) and the recipient (e.g., personality, gender, and marital satisfaction). Pistrang and her colleagues (Pistrang & Barker, 1998; Pistrang, Barker, & Rutter, 1997; Pistrang, Clare, & Barker, 1999; Pistrang, Picciotto, & Barker, 2001; Pistrang, Solomons, & Barker, 1999) have identified the particular behaviors that are perceived as more and less supportive from different sources and by different raters. For reviews, see Burleson and Goldsmith (1998) and Burleson and MacGeorge (2002). There are other studies that do not examine social support per se, but nonetheless focus on conversations in which troubles are discussed, including the features of these conversations and their interpretations and consequences. For example, there are programs of research focused on how elderly and nonelderly individuals talk about problems faced by the elderly and what implications different styles of speaking may have for identities and stereotypes of the elderly (e.g., Coupland, Coupland, & Giles, 1991; Hummert & Ryan, 2001).

and how it complements work undertaken from other perspectives. This book focuses on *enacted social support* that is communicated in *troubles talk* conversations between *close relational partners*. Enacted support is but one facet of the broader social support construct and enacted social support can occur in contexts other than troubles talk in close relationships. Similarly, troubles talk is not limited to close relationships. However, the processes of enacted support are distinctive and the troubles talk conversations of close relational partners are a frequent and significant site for these processes.

THE IMPORTANCE OF ENACTED SUPPORT

As shown in the next chapter, *social support* is an umbrella construct used to refer to several related yet conceptually distinct social phenomena and processes. I study *enacted social support* (the things people say and do for one another) and how it can *buffer* individuals from the negative effects of stress by facilitating coping.

Enacted support is central to the broader social support construct. Prominent researchers in a wide variety of academic disciplines have defined social support in ways that state or imply it is conveyed through the actions of one person in interaction with another. For example, in his classic volume on social support and work stress, House (1981, p. 39) stated that researchers and laypersons alike conceive of social support as an "interpersonal transaction" that yields emotional concern, instrumental aid, information, or information relevant to self-evaluation. In a review of research on social support among the elderly, Antonucci (1985, p. 96) concluded, "most definitions assume that social support is based on supportive social interactions...." In a discussion of the significance of social support in personal relationships, Gottlieb (1985b, p. 361) stated that "in the coping process, it is the behavioural manifestations of support expressed by my close associates – its materialization in interpersonal transactions – that has greatest significance for the course and outcomes of my ordeal." Enacted social support is also central to research on interventions. Many support interventions are designed to provide or improve the interactions stressed individuals have with their relational partners, peers who have experienced a similar stressful condition, or healthcare professionals (Gottlieb, 1996; Heller & Rook, 1997; Wortman & Conway, 1985). In a review of research on social support interventions, Heller and Rook (1997, p. 650) suggested the social transactions through which support is expressed are "important building blocks" of relationships and of support interventions.

Given the conceptual centrality of social interaction to the social support construct, it is perhaps surprising that most researchers who study social support focus on other, related phenomena. The most common measures tap an individual's perception that support is available, and there is evidence these perceptions reflect a relatively stable and global sense of acceptance rather than a summary report of what goes on in actual interactions (Sarason, Pierce, & Sarason, 1990). Similarly, even studies of supportive interactions more often enumerate their frequency rather than model their processes. For social support researchers, then, this book fills an important gap. Interactions in which individuals discuss their problems and communicate various kinds of support are a central feature of the multifaceted social support construct and yet these interactive processes are among the least studied components of social support.

TROUBLES TALK AS A KEY LOCATION FOR ENACTED SUPPORT

Troubles talk is one important type of conversation in which social support is enacted. The term was coined by Jefferson (1980, p. 153), who described it as "a conversation in which troubles are reported." In research I have conducted with my colleagues (Goldsmith & Baxter, 1996; Goldsmith & McDermott, 1998), we have found that troubles talk episodes are recognized by many U.S. Americans not only by their topical focus on a trouble but also by the presumed purpose of the conversation, which is to assist in coping with the problem. Troubles talk is distinct from conversations in which participants discuss problems in their relationship. For example, it is different from complaining or arguing about the other's behavior (e.g., "I'm stressed out because you and I don't communicate very well" or "It's a problem for me that you smoke in the house") or from having a relationship talk with the hearer (e.g., "I'm worried about where our relationship is headed"). However, troubles talk may include stresses or problems external to the relationship that affect both partners (e.g., when one's spouse is ill, it is likely to be a concern for both; financial difficulties, moving, or changing jobs may be stressors faced together). Everyday conversations that are not focused on troubles are no doubt important to global perceptions of the supportiveness of a partner or relationship (Barnes & Duck, 1994; Gottlieb, 1985b; Leatham & Duck, 1990; Rook, 1990). However, my focus is on one particularly important and prototypical type of conversation in which social support is enacted: conversations in which individuals talk about problems, from the hassles of daily life to the major life events that pose stressful challenges, threats, or losses.

Understanding how support is enacted in the context of troubles talk is important theoretically. One of the ways social relationships facilitate well-being is by providing access to this kind of interaction, in which individuals can receive assistance with coping (Thoits, 1986). Many measures of social support include items that measure the availability of someone with whom you can talk about problems, someone who will listen to you talk about your feelings, or someone to console you when you are upset. Evidence of the importance of troubles talk as a context for social support is also found in studies of the positive effects of access to a confidant. Having at least one person with whom you can talk about personal problems or troubles is consistently associated with individual well-being (for a review, see Cohen & Wills, 1985; see also Uchino, Cacioppo, Malarkey, Glaser, & Kiecolt-Glaser, 1995).

There are also practical reasons for seeking to better understand troubles talk. Conversations in which one participant discloses a problem and seeks assistance can be challenging, both for the person who makes him- or herself vulnerable by disclosing and for the partner searching for words that can bring insight, comfort, and solidarity. Jefferson's (1980, 1984a, 1984b) conversation analytic studies showed how talk about a trouble poses special problems for the organization and coordination of conversation. Metts, Backhaus, and Kazoleas (1995) explained how troubles talk conversations depart in significant ways from the usual topics and structures of everyday talk: One person may take more than his or her share of the floor time to tell an extended narrative, the topic of the narrative may focus on negative emotions rather than the positive emotions that are preferred, and the hearer of the narrative will eventually feel a need to generate some contribution to the conversation that is topically relevant and yet sensitive to the potential for the other person to be embarrassed and vulnerable. In short, talking about a trouble initiates a type of conversation that differs from "business as usual." Hearing about another person's difficulties can create discomfort and anxiety and this, in turn, can lead hearers to say things that are insensitive and potentially hurtful (Lehman, Ellard, & Wortman, 1986). For these reasons (and others I explore in Chapters 1, 3, 4 and 5), enacting support in troubles talk conversations is often experienced as highly salient and meaningful and yet potentially difficult to do well. Showing individuals how to participate more effectively in troubles talk empowers them to take better advantage of the assistance close relationships can offer.

CLOSE RELATIONSHIPS AS A PRIMARY CONTEXT FOR SUPPORT AND TROUBLES TALK

The literature on social support emphasizes benefits to individual health and well-being, but troubles talk also contributes to relational functioning and satisfaction (Acitelli, 1996). For example, Cutrona (1996a) suggests that social support contributes to marital satisfaction by preventing emotional withdrawal or depression during times of stress, by preventing conflicts from escalating in intensity, and by strengthening the intimate bond between partners. Burleson, Albrecht, Sarason, and Goldsmith (1994) note that supportive interactions are a defining feature of healthy family interaction and crucial to friendships and amicable work relationships.

Among North Americans, close relationships are a primary context for social support in general and for talking about problems in particular (Wade, Howell, & Wells, 1994). Wellman and Wortley (1990) interviewed adults in a residential area just outside Toronto who provided various kinds of support. Talking about problems was significantly more likely to occur in relationships that were intimate and voluntary and spanned more than one context (e.g., two friends who interact in one another's homes, talk over the phone, and work in the same organization). Seventy-two percent of these "strong ties" provided emotional aid and the authors concluded that "respondents appear to get most of their social support – of all kinds – through their small number of strong ties" (Wellman & Wortley, 1990, p. 566). Young, Giles, and Plantz (1982) reached similar conclusions in their study of social networks in rural communities in the eastern United States.

Further evidence of the importance of close relationships as a context for troubles talk comes from the Americans View Their Mental Health studies. These large nationwide representative surveys of adults in the United States were conducted in 1957 and 1976 (see Veroff, Douvan, & Kulka, 1981). In response to a question about what you do "if something is on your mind that is bothering you or worrying you and you do not know what to do about it," 86% of the respondents reported talking about their worries and most of these conversations occurred in close relationships. About half of those who reported talking about worries said they talked only to their spouse. In addition, family, friends, and neighbors were mentioned more often than formal sources of support such as clergy, doctors, and mental health specialists. In a follow-up study, Swindle, Heller, Pescosolido, and Kikuzawa (2000) examined data from the Americans View Their Mental Health surveys as well as similar data from the 1996 nationwide General Social Survey. They focused on responses to the more serious circumstance in which individuals reported having felt an impending nervous breakdown. Across the forty-year period represented in their data, there was a strong increase in reliance on family and friends as partners in troubles talk. This trend remained even after controlling for demographic characteristics and perceived reason for the breakdown.

Troubles talk is a strong expectation of close relational partners. Caughlin (2003) asked college students to describe the communication patterns of people in families with "good communication." The ability to share problems with one another and count on family members for support were among the most frequently mentioned and strongly endorsed standards students used for evaluating good family communication. Similarly, a study that asked students to tell stories about their families found talking about problems and responding with instrumental or emotional support were prominent themes (Vangelisti, Crumley, & Baker, 1999).

The ability to talk about problems and respond supportively not only is an abstract relational ideal but also serves as a strong predictor of relational satisfaction. Young adults' satisfaction with their family relationships are strongly correlated with their perceptions that family members share problems with one another and respond supportively (Caughlin, 2003). In a sample of women juggling work, home, and childcare demands, Erickson (1993) found emotional support from one's husband was a key predictor of marital well-being and protected against the risk of marital burnout. Dehle, Larsen, and Landers (2001) asked married students to report daily for one week on the support they received and desired from their spouses. When expectations for support were met in day-to-day interactions, spouses had higher levels of marital satisfaction. In another survey of young married couples in a university community, Sprecher, Metts, Burleson, Hatfield, and Thompson (1995) compared the relative importance of companionship, supportive communication, and sexual expression. They found that supportive communication (which included items about "listening when I need someone to talk to," "helps me clarify my thoughts," and comfort with "having a serious discussion") was the best predictor of marital satisfaction. Conversely, in a sample of individuals drawn from divorce court records, not having "someone to talk things over with" headed a list of marital complaints (Kitson & Holmes, 1992). Even when partners were acknowledged to fulfill instrumental roles in the marriage (e.g., providing for a family or keeping house), the failure of spouses to achieve satisfactory communication, support, and concern was seen by many as sufficient reason to end a relationship. Observational studies confirm that patterns of giving and receiving social support are associated with concurrent and prospective marital satisfaction (e.g., Collins & Feeney, 2000; Cutrona & Suhr, 1994; Pasch & Bradbury, 1998). The links between giving and receiving social support and marital satisfaction are particularly poignant in studies of couples coping together with health problems (e.g., Abbey, Andrews, & Halman, 1995; Dunkel-Schetter, Blasband, Feinstein, & Herbert, 1992; Lydon & Zanna, 1992; Peyrot, McMurry, & Hedges, 1988; Rankin, 1992; Revenson & Majerovitz, 1990; Swanson-Hyland, 1996).

Responding supportively to a partner in need is a strong expectation of close relationships and yet one that may be difficult to fulfill. At first glance, we might predict that troubles talk would be less difficult in close relationships because of the trust and concern that define our notions of "close." However, some of the same attributes that make a relationship close (e.g., interdependence, strong emotion, past history, and obligations) can complicate our ability to seek, give, and receive support. Sometimes, the dynamic is one of empathy: When those we love hurt, we hurt, and we want more than anything to make the hurt go away. This desire to "fix" the other's problem can actually interfere with the provision of effective support (Burleson & Goldsmith, 1998). In other instances, we may struggle with conflicting feelings of frustration at the other for being in trouble (again!) and guilt for not having more altruistic impulses. The strong expectation (and obligation) to help may be tried by a history of troubles talk in which the assistance provided brings about no apparent improvement in the recurring trouble (e.g., Coyne, Wortman, & Lehman, 1988). Thus, the close relational context for support enacted in troubles talk is distinctive in ways that merit close attention.

OVERVIEW OF THE BOOK

The social support literature is the source of much of what we know (and don't know) about how talking about problems can help people cope. Researchers in this tradition have amassed a vast array of data pointing to the importance of personal relationships for individual well-being and one of the primary explanations for these beneficial effects is that social support improves coping with stress. However, only a small portion of this body of research focuses on what people say and do (enacted support) and the findings that emerge from these studies raise as many questions as answers. Chapter 1 describes several problems in the study of enacted support and proposes that attention to communication processes provides an explanation for these difficulties.

Chapter 2 summarizes the theoretical underpinnings of a communication-based approach. I discuss my assumptions about the nature of enacted support and the social, cultural, and relational processes that link enactments of support to evaluations of support. I also show how my approach is distinct from but complementary to other ways of studying enacted social support. Then, in Chapters 3, 4, and 5, I show how my framework explains several puzzles in the literature.

Chapter 3 addresses the question: Why isn't advice a more helpful form of enacted support? When close relational partners talk about troubles, they frequently give advice and yet advice often goes unappreciated. Attention to *what* people actually advise and to *how* they communicate it helps to differentiate episodes in which advice is seen as helpful from those in which it is seen as unhelpful or even harmful.

Chapter 4 examines matching models of enacted social support. It is widely assumed (and quite reasonably) that effective social support must be matched to the problem for which it is offered (e.g., for a controllable problem, it is helpful to offer advice about how to improve the situation, but for an uncontrollable loss, it is better to offer comfort). However, matching models have had only limited success in predicting the circumstances under which support will have beneficial effects. I propose an alternative model in which close relational partners adapt the support they offer to external constraints on coping as well as modify and coordinate their views of the environment to facilitate coping.

Chapter 5 examines how studying support in the context of close relationships challenges implicit assumptions about the provision and receipt of support. The effects of a stressor on both partners, and the challenge of coordinating each person's preferred way of coping, can complicate partners' abilities to support one another. In these situations, partners may adopt roles as provider and recipient, they may join in coping together with a stressor they define as shared, or they may disagree about their orientation to the problem and its amelioration. These roles are worked out in the ways partners talk about problems – sometimes explicitly and sometimes between the lines. Some of the most successful ways of coordinating coping may rely on shared relational routines that disguise social support.

Chapters 3 through 5 are based on studies I have conducted over a ten-year period. The studies employ a range of research methodologies, including participant observation, ethnographic interviewing, observation of troubles talk between partners in ongoing relationships, solicitation of monologues in response to hypothetical situations, and questionnaire responses to carefully manipulated messages. Some of the results of these studies have been reported in previously published reports but other analyses are provided here for the first time. In presenting various forms of data in this book, my goal is to illustrate and develop a theoretical framework that is broader than any of the particular studies. Consequently, I have relegated some information about participants and procedures to an appendix.

Chapter 6 concludes with implications for theory, method, and practice. Because I am proposing a new way of studying enacted support in the troubles talk of close partners and because this approach has evolved through the course of the research I describe, there is much work left to do. The concluding chapter suggests new directions for research and discusses the practical implications of my findings for helping relational partners improve their ability to assist one another in times of trouble.

1

Puzzles in the Study of Enacted Social Support

Social support is one of the most studied social processes of the last several decades. Entering the term into medical or social science databases yields thousands of citations across dozens of fields of study. This widespread interest is likely due to the variety of important effects that have been associated with social support. Research has linked social support with a longer life, with reduced incidence of various diseases, with better recovery from illness, with improved coping with chronic illness, and with better mental health (for reviews, see Albrecht & Goldsmith, 2003; Berkman, 1985; Sarason, Sarason, & Gurung, 1997; Schwarzer & Leppin, 1989). Social support is also an expectation of personal relationships and predicts perceived interpersonal competence and reported satisfaction with friends, family, and romantic partners (e.g., Abbey et al., 1995; Buhrmeister, Furman, Wittenberg, & Reis, 1988; Cauce, 1986; Cutrona, 1996b; Pasch & Bradbury, 1998; Sprecher et al., 1995).

Through these effects on the individual and on relationships, support also plays a key role in the functioning of various social groups and the prevention or reduction of social problems. Social support can prevent work stress or at least help workers to cope more effectively (e.g., House, 1981; Ray, 1987; Viswesvaran, Sanchez, & Fisher, 1999). Social support can enable individuals to maintain hope and trust in communities wracked by violence (e.g., Berman, Kurtines, Silverman, & Serafini, 1996; Garbarino & Kostelny, 1997; Kliewer, Lepore, Oskin, & Johnson, 1998). Individuals' access to social support may predict or ameliorate the problems of child abuse (e.g., Bishop & Leadbeater, 1999; Moncher, 1995), substance use and abuse (e.g., Fiore et al., 2000; Peirce, Frone, Russell, & Cooper, 1996; Wills, 1990), and homelessness (e.g., Bates & Toro, 1999; Lam & Rosenheck, 2000). Social support plays a role in preventing and responding to public health problems (e.g., Ford, Ahluwalia, & Galuska, 2000; Seeman, 2000). Social support may also influence the success of our education systems; for example, it can reduce burnout and improve morale among teachers (e.g., Greenglass,

Fiksenbaum, & Burke, 1996; Littrell, Billingsley, & Cross, 1994), and it can contribute to achievement on the part of their students (Cutrona, Cole, Colangelo, Assouline, & Russell, 1994; Ma & Kishor, 1997; Okun, Sandler, & Baumann, 1988; Rosenfeld, Richman, & Bowen, 2000).

The vision of close relational partners talking about problems and offering information, aid, reassurance, and comfort is one prototypical way of thinking about social support and many studies implicitly or explicitly subscribe to a model of social support as coping assistance (Thoits, 1986). That is, when individuals confront daily problems or major life stresses, they turn to others in their social network who provide information, comfort, perspective, and aid. These resources (and the symbolic overlay that suggests one is valued and cared for) bolster an individual's ability to cope effectively and thereby buffer him or her from the otherwise deleterious effects of stress. There are ways of conceptualizing social support that do not presume a conversation about a problem and there are ways of modeling the positive effects of social support that don't have to do with coping and stress (for example, Cohen, Gottlieb, & Underwood, 2000, review various models of the effects of support on physical health). However, the stress-buffering properties of enacted social support are one prevalent and powerful way of accounting for the many findings that involvement in personal relationships can enhance individual, relational, and community well-being.

Much of what we know about troubles talk in close relationships is derived from studies in the social support tradition, particularly studies focused on the assisted-coping/stress-buffering model. Consequently, a brief review of the larger social support construct is useful as a backdrop for my focused examination of social support enacted when close relational partners engage in troubles talk conversation. I then review the research specific to the stress-buffering effects of enacted support to bring into focus some puzzles in this body of work. Finally, I propose that attention to communication processes can explain otherwise puzzling findings and improve our understanding of enacted social support.

LOCATING ENACTED SUPPORT WITHIN THE SOCIAL SUPPORT LITERATURE

The term *social support* emerged in the mid-1970s from two influential reviews of research on how life stress predicted mortality and morbidity (Cassel, 1976; Cobb, 1976). Although Cassel and Cobb differed somewhat in their conceptualizations of social support and in their intended audiences, they were motivated by similar research problems: Why do some individuals who are exposed to life stresses and transitions succumb to negative physical and psychological effects, whereas others do not? What is the role of the social environment in protecting individuals from illness and death? *Social support* was the term they used to refer to the ways in which social relationships moderated the influence of stress on health and well-being. Soon, hundreds of studies testing effects of social support and debating the robustness and nature of these effects emerged. For example, one controversy concerned whether benefits of social relationships were due to their stress-buffering effects, whether involvement in relationships had direct positive effects that were independent of one's level of stress, or whether previous measures provided an adequate test of these alternative models.

Over the next decade, a consensus developed that social support had important effects on health and well-being. For example, House, Landis, and Umberson (1988, p. 541) concluded, "social relationships, or the relative lack thereof, constitute a major risk factor for health – rivaling the effects of well-established health risk factors such as cigarette smoking, blood pressure, blood lipids, obesity, and physical activity." In addition, many scholars recognized support might have both stress-buffering and direct effects, depending on how it was conceptualized and measured (for reviews, see Cohen & Wills, 1985; Kessler & McLeod, 1985).

During the 1980s, many reviewers of this rapidly growing research area concluded that progress had been hindered by diverse conceptualizations of social support and lack of theoretical explanation for its effects (e.g., Antonucci & Jackson, 1987; Barrera, 1986; Broadhead et al., 1983; Heller & Swindle, 1983; Shumaker & Brownell, 1984; Thoits, 1985; Vaux & Harrison, 1985). Common use of the term *social support* had obscured the degree to which researchers examined fundamentally different facets of close relationships and their benefits for participants. For example, some studies measured characteristics of social ties or networks (e.g., marital status, involvement in community organizations, frequency of contact with friends and kin, diversity of sources of support, and density of network links), whereas other studies focused on subjective satisfaction with one's network or perceptions that aid would be available if needed. Several reviews pointed out that demonstration of the effects of support had outstripped efforts to provide and test theoretical explanations for these effects (e.g., Depner, Wethington, & Ingersoll-Dayton, 1984; Heller, Swindle, & Dusenberry, 1986; House, Umberson, & Landis, 1988; Wortman & Conway, 1985).

This state of affairs led several authors to distinguish among ways of conceptualizing social support and explaining its effects (e.g., Cohen & Wills, 1985; Heller & Swindle, 1983; House & Kahn, 1985; Sarason & Sarason, 1994; Schwarzer & Leppin, 1991; Vaux & Harrison, 1985; Wethington & Kessler, 1986). Although these authors differed in the ways they parsed the extant literature, they agreed that *social support* is an umbrella term for a variety of pathways linking involvement in social relationships to well-being (Cohen, 1988). For example, involvement in a network of relationships may provide a sense of coherence and meaning that prevents mental illness (e.g., Thoits, 1985) and a source of control or regulation that maintains healthful behaviors (e.g., Rook & Underwood, 2000; Umberson, 1987). In addition, personal relationships may enhance well-being simply by providing companionship and positive affective experiences (Rook, 1990; Rook & Underwood, 2000). Alternatively, one's history of interactions with significant others may produce a cognitive sense of acceptance that leads an individual to appraise life situations with greater confidence in his or her coping abilities and greater flexibility in adapting to the environment (Sarason et al., 1990). Yet another pathway from involvement in relationships to well-being focuses on the resources and information others provide and the ways this improves functioning (Hobfoll, 1989; Holahan, Moos, & Bonin, 1997).

These developments reflect recognition that progress in understanding how social relationships promote well-being is not likely to occur by attempting to integrate all these diverse features and functions of relationships into a single conceptualization of social support. Instead, we are more likely to progress when researchers clearly identify a particular facet of support and then develop and test theoretical explanations for how that facet works. Many of the processes that link relationships to well-being likely occur simultaneously, and so a complete understanding of social support will eventually require considering multiple processes operating in concert. However, at this stage in the development of our understanding, we are well-served by attending to one process at a time.

With that in mind, this book focuses on *enacted social support*,[1] understood as what individuals say and do to help one another. Some commonly recognized types of enacted social support include *emotional support* (expressions of caring, concern, empathy, and reassurance of worth), *informational support* (including not only information but also advice or new perspectives on a problem), and *tangible support* (offers of goods and services). In some schemes, *appraisal support* (providing new perspectives on a problem) is differentiated from other kinds of information support and *esteem support* (giving reassurances of worth) is separated from emotional support. Some taxonomies also include opportunities for socializing or belonging to a group as examples of *network support*.

---

[1] In the research literature, enacted social support is also referred to as received support, supportive behaviors, support transactions, administered support, or objective support. I prefer the term *enacted support* because it focuses attention on the performance of communicative action. The study of social networks focuses on global access to and availability of relational ties and thus studies support as a property of relationships. The study of perceived available support locates support as a property of individual cognitions about the social world. In contrast, support may also be studied as a property of conversation. To locate the study of enacted support in troubles talk is a way of focusing attention on the talk itself as a phenomenon in need of study. This emphasis is one of the distinctive components of the communication approach I offer in this book.

Although there is some variability in how these types of enacted support are differentiated and labeled, enacted support in all its forms is distinct from conceptualizations of social support that focus on the quantity or existence of relationships or the structure of a social network of relationships. It is also distinct from perceived support, which usually refers to the perception that support generally is (or would be) available when needed. Many measures of enacted support rely on self-reports by providers or recipients, so there is a sense in which enacted support is also perceived. However, it is important to differentiate perceptions of what has occurred or is occurring (enacted support) from perceptions of what is generally available or might occur (perceived available support).

We might expect that perceptions of available support would reflect summary judgments of enacted support, but studies comparing measures of enacted support and perceived support have found weak correlations between the two (for reviews, see Dunkel-Schetter & Bennett, 1990; Wills & Shinar, 2000). There is evidence that perceived available support may reflect stable, dispositional views of the social world that are more closely related to personal traits or schemas than to the ebb and flow of social interactions (see Sarason et al., 1990, for a review). In addition, measures of enacted support and perceived available support have different relationships to positive outcomes. Although there is convincing evidence for the beneficial effects of perceived available support, the findings on the effects of enacted support are much less conclusive.

As we have seen in the introduction, enacted social support is central to researchers' (and laypersons') understanding of the social support construct. However, enacted support has been studied less extensively than network ties or perceived available support. In early studies, researchers utilized existing data sets on mortality, morbidity, and life events, deriving measures of support from available information (e.g., marital status, contact with family, and involvement in community organizations). The variables in these large-scale epidemiological surveys were typically most suitable as measures of (or proxies for) social integration or involvement in a social network. As research on social support progressed, several survey measures of enacted support emerged (see Wills & Shinar, 2000, for a review and comparison of measures) and a number of studies used retrospective reports or observations of interactions in which enacted support might occur (see Goldsmith, 1992, for a review). However, most measures and most studies of social support continue to focus on reports of networks or perceptions of available support (Winemiller, Mitchell, Sutliff, & Cline, 1993), perhaps because findings on the effects of enacted support have been problematic. As we turn to a review of research on enacted support, we find some evidence that it has positive effects for recipients but also many studies that show null, weak, mixed, or unexpected effects.

THE BUFFERING EFFECTS OF ENACTED SUPPORT

The buffering effect of social support refers to models that associate social support with reductions in the negative effects of stress on well-being (for discussion of various buffering models, see Barrera, 1988; Lin, Woefel, & Light, 1985; Wheaton, 1985). When stress has negative effects on physical and mental health, social support can reduce or buffer these negative effects. The strongest effects of social support should be observed when individuals experience high levels of stress. Under low levels of stress, the health of individuals with low social support may not differ dramatically or at all from the health of individuals with high social support.

Tests of the buffering effect have produced mixed results. Some studies have reported evidence for buffering effects, whereas some have reported no effects or mixed support (e.g., see Grant, 1990, for a review). These mixed findings may be due, in part, to limitations in measurement, sample, or statistical analysis (Kessler & McLeod, 1985; Veiel, 1992). Also, the failure to differentiate social network involvement, perceived available support, and enacted support contributes to mixed findings. Cohen and Wills (1985) identified studies whose method and statistical analyses provided a reasonable chance of detecting effects of support. They then distinguished among measures of integration in a social network, perceived available support, and enacted support. Within these categories, they further differentiated between global or aggregated measures (i.e., those that combine types of support) and measures of specific functions of support (e.g., informational support, emotional support, and tangible support). They found stress-buffering effects when studies measured the perception that others were *available* to provide the *specific type* of support needed to cope with a stressor (e.g., emotional support for a loss or informational support for a solvable problem). They suggested the belief that stress-specific resources are available and may lead an individual to appraise a stressful situation as less threatening, even if he or she doesn't actually solicit or receive the support that is available.

It is especially difficult to draw conclusions about the buffering effect of enacted support because relatively few studies of the buffering effect have measured enacted support or differentiated it from other facets of support. Several reviews report inconsistent evidence for a buffering effect of enacted support (Cohen & Wills, 1985; Cooper, 1986; Dunkel-Schetter & Bennett, 1990). Some studies even report the counterintuitive finding that individuals who receive more enacted support report *higher* levels of stress and/or *greater* negative effects of stress (Aneshensel & Frerichs, 1982; Barrera, 1981; Cohen & Hoberman, 1983; Coyne, Aldwin, & Lazarus, 1981; Fiore, Becker, & Coppel, 1983; Husaini, Neff, Newbrough, & Moore, 1982; Sandler & Barrera, 1984).

Rather than accepting at face value the null or negative effects of enacted support, many researchers have searched for ways to fashion from
unexpected empirical findings an explanation that retains a beneficial role
for enacted support. Because so many conceptualizations of social support
include a central role for individuals helping one another through social
interaction, many researchers regard the failure to find a simple buffering
effect of enacted support as an anomaly. As Dunkel-Schetter and Bennett
(1990, pp. 285–286) explained, "We have struggled with how to reconcile
the available empirical evidence with our belief, and the arguments of other
researchers, that received support should have buffering effects. . . ." This
search for the buffering effects of enacted support has led in two complementary directions: research on factors that moderate the buffering effects
of enacted support and a recognition that not all attempts at support are,
in fact, experienced as helpful.

Variables That Moderate the Buffering Effects of Enacted Support

One type of refinement is to examine how the stress-buffering effects of
enacted support are contingent on other factors, including the type and
affective tenor of the relationship in which support is offered, the type
and quality of support that is offered, the degree and character of stress
experienced by the support recipient, and the support recipient's own ways
of mobilizing, interpreting, and utilizing support. Analyses that fail to
examine factors such as the timing of support, type of stressor, source of
support, severity of stress, and recipient and provider characteristics may
not reveal these localized buffering effects of social support.

The *timing* of measurement in the course of an individual's coping with
a stressor might affect a researcher's ability to detect stress-buffering effects. Initially, when individuals recognize their need for support and act to
mobilize it, or when network members observe distress and respond to it,
those with the highest levels of stress or distress might be those who seek
or receive the most enacted support. Once support has been mobilized,
we would expect more support to be associated with less distress (Barrera,
1986; Schwarzer & Leppin, 1991).

The buffering effects of enacted support may also be obscured in studies
that aggregate across different *types of stress* or different *sources of support*.
Wethington and Kessler (1986) compared the buffering effects of perceived
available support and total enacted support in a study of distress associated with a recent negative life event. Many scholars cite their classic
study as demonstrating that the perception that support is available is a
more powerful source of buffering effects than actually receiving support.
Wethington and Kessler did find convincing buffering effects of perceived
available support that were independent of the receipt of enacted support;
however, they also found some evidence for a buffering effect of enacted

support when they examined specific types and sources of support for particular kinds of life stresses (e.g., instrumental support from a spouse was associated with emotional adjustment among respondents who had serious physical illness). They recommended that future research on enacted support examine the types of support given by different sources for specific life events.

Studies that have engaged in these types of focused analyses have found buffering effects of enacted support for particular combinations of support type, support source, problem, and outcome. Lin and colleagues (1985) examined support from various sources provided in response to a particular important and undesirable life event. They found buffering effects for support provided by close relational partners who were also similar to the recipient. However, even support from close, similar others did not buffer recipients from the negative effects of marital disruption. Okun, Sandler, and Baumann (1988) found that support from teachers and family (but not from friends) buffered students from the negative effects of negative school events and boosted the positive effects of positive school events.

Lim (1996) studied job insecurity faced by graduates of an MBA program. The greater an employee's sense of job insecurity, the more likely he or she was to express dissatisfaction with the job, to search for another job, and to engage in noncompliant job behaviors. However, support from supervisors and co-workers (but not from family and friends) lessened these negative effects of job insecurity. In contrast, supportive family and friends (but not support from supervisors or co-workers) reduced the degree to which job insecurity affected overall dissatisfaction with life.

Dean, Kolody, Wood, and Ensel (1989) differentiated between the effects of several forms of expressive and instrumental support on depression and disability among the elderly. Expressions of caring and concern, love and affection, social integration, help with daily living, and help with health and medical needs implied different kinds of interactions and occurred in different kinds of relational contexts (e.g., some types of support required proximity of adult children and opportunities for face-to-face interaction). In turn, different types of support had different patterns of association with degree of disability and depression. Studies such as these demonstrate how the positive effects of enacted support may be specific to particular combinations of problem type, support type, support source, and outcome measure.

The buffering effects of enacted support may also depend on the *severity of stress* experienced and the needs for support that result. Pennix and colleagues (1997) studied elderly persons with severe arthritis, with mild arthritis, and with no arthritis. The effects of enacted support depended on the type of relationship and facet of support measured. Regardless of whether one had arthritis, having a partner and regular interaction in close relationships had positive effects. In contrast, the amount of emotional support received and regular interaction with casual acquaintances were most important for those with severe arthritis. Receiving help with daily tasks (instrumental support) had no significant relationship with depression for those with severe arthritis but was associated with increased depression for those with mild or no arthritis, perhaps because for those with severe arthritis, the need for instrumental support was obvious and therefore less likely to create feelings of dependence. Similarly, a meta-analysis of the effects of support on physical health found evidence for a beneficial effect of enacted support in studies of stressed populations but a negative effect of enacted support in studies that included general populations of individuals not selected with reference to some particular stress (Leppin & Schwarzer, 1990).

The effects of enacted support may also depend on characteristics of the *support receiver*. In a study of first- and second-year dental students, Cooper (1986) observed that informational support from peers buffered the harmful effects of problems with faculty and workload demands. However, this occurred only beyond some threshold level of stress: At low levels of stress, peer support had negative effects on distress and well-being. In addition, the stress-buffering effects of peer informational support were different for partnered students (married or involved in a nonmarital romantic relationship) versus unpartnered students. Partnered students under stress benefited from peer informational support, but for students without partners, peer informational support was associated with greater distress. Unpartnered students were also consistently more distressed and had more negative attitudes toward help seeking than the partnered students.

In a review of research on personality characteristics and social support processes, Pierce, Lakey, Sarason, Sarason, and Joseph (1997) explained how individuals may differ in the manner in which they respond to the same social stimulus, in the reactions they evoke from others, and in their proactive efforts to construct a support network. Reis and Collins (2000) described how "interpersonally relevant predispositions" such as social self-esteem, extroversion, sensitivity to rejection, or attachment shape features of supportive interactions. Some early studies showed individuals with an internal locus of control (those who believed they had control over events and their consequences) experienced buffering effects of enacted support, whereas individuals with an external locus of control (those who believed events and their consequences were outside their control) did not (Sandler & Lakey, 1982; Cummins, 1988). More recently, researchers have demonstrated how an individual's attachment style is associated with reactions to receiving social support, perhaps because individuals differ in their needs or preferences for support (Mikulincer & Florian, 1997). Lakey, Adams, Neely, Rhodes, Lutz, and Sielky (2002) found support recipient's ratings of the provider's personality traits were associated with the recipient's positive evaluation of support received. For example, support recipients were more likely to see providers as supportive when they also perceived the providers to be agreeable, emotionally stable, open, and conscientious.

This sampling of findings suggests that the success of enacted support attempts depends on a number of factors. Clearly, the stress-buffering effects of enacted support are contingent on a fit between the support offered and various features of the situation (i.e., *who* does *what* for *whom* with respect to *what problems*? House, 1981, p. 8).[2] Dunkel-Schetter and Bennett (1990, p. 288) went so far as to say that the stress-buffering effects of enacted social support cannot be adequately tested without taking into account the specific needs elicited by a stressor, the timing of support, and how it comes to be activated. Identifying the relevant factors and understanding the processes through which providers and receivers achieve this situational adaptation is an important agenda item in the study of enacted social support.

Differentiating Helpful From Unhelpful Enacted Support

Another reason why the amount of enacted support received may not consistently produce positive results is that not all enacted support actually aids individuals with coping. For example, some pieces of advice may be substantively wiser than others, some emotional support attempts may come across as heartfelt, whereas other attempts are superficial and obligatory, and some offers of aid may be skillful, whereas others may create more burden than they alleviate. An ever-growing body of studies identify helpful and unhelpful behaviors reported by individuals undergoing various kinds of life stresses (for reviews, see Dunkel-Schetter et al., 1992; Goldsmith, 1992; Ingram, Betz, Mindes, Schmitt, & Smith, 2001). Different typologies have been developed for a wide variety of conditions and stresses, ranging from illnesses (including cancer, arthritis, AIDS, and multiple sclerosis) and traumatic life events (including bereavement, unemployment, rape, and divorce) to daily stresses and hassles (including stresses associated with work, school, or the management of ongoing conditions such as disability or a child's chronic illness). Table 1 compiles findings from these studies into a list of commonly identified helpful and unhelpful behaviors.

---

[2] It is interesting to note that House's well-known advice to study who, what, to whom, and for which problems does not include a focus on *how* the support is communicated. This is a useful case in point of how communication processes have been overlooked in attempts to identify the contingencies on which successful support provision depends. I am indebted to Dale Brashers for this insight.

TABLE 1. *Helpful and Unhelpful Forms of Enacted Social Support*[3]

Helpful Forms	Unhelpful Forms
Mere presence, increased attentiveness	Avoided contact, too little concern, wouldn't communicate or listen
Companionship, involved in social activities, did special things	Minimized, questioned severity of condition, didn't recognize difficulty
Opportunity to talk or vent, listened	Encouraged recovery, told about others' positive experiences
Expressed love, concern, empathy, affection	Gave care without emotion or incompetent care, lack of assistance
Showed loyalty	Rude, insensitive remarks
Understood, calmly accepted condition, made accommodations or allowances	Criticism, verbal attacks, hostile acts
Pleasant, kind	Blamed other for condition, lack of acceptance
Reassured, encouraged, praised abilities	Said "I know how you feel"
Respected autonomy	Unhelpful emotional support
Showed honesty	Overly concerned, overprotective, catastrophized consequences, expressed fear, underestimated knowledge or competence
Information, advice	
Contact with similar other, positive role model	Tried to control situation, manipulate, had divided loyalties
Provided philosophical or religious perspective	Unwanted tangible support, interference
Optimistic prognosis	Unwanted discussion of problem or prognosis
Provided practical assistance, competent care, financial support	Patronized, pitied
Engaged in coping, problem solving	Information, advice
Treated normally	Provided too little information
Talked about other topics	Poor role model
Encouraged distance and self-restraint	Negative attitudes or beliefs about condition, disagreed with action
	Seemed uncomfortable
	Provided philosophical perspective

Although these studies are important in demonstrating that not all attempts at enacted support are, in fact, experienced as supportive, they leave us without an overarching framework for explaining why some attempts succeed and others fail (Goldsmith, 1992). The description of

[3] The categories in the table reflect my synthesis of findings reported in studies of persons with cancer (Dakof & Taylor, 1990; Dunkel-Schetter, 1984; Gurowka & Lightman, 1995; Manne & Schnoll, 2001; Meyerowitz, Levin, & Harvey, 1997; Taylor, Falke, Mazel, & Hilsberg, 1988), bereaved individuals (Davidowitz & Myrick, 1984; Lehman et al., 1986; Malkinson, 1987; Range, Walston, & Pollard, 1992; Thompson & Range, 1992; Werner & Monsour, 1997),

behaviors in these typologies is fairly abstract and evaluative. For example, helpful support behaviors include categories such as being a positive role model, showing concern, making helpful accommodations, or recognizing amount of effort to cope. The studies don't indicate what specific features of an interaction led to the respondent's interpretation that modeling, concern, accommodation, or recognition occurred. In addition, some of the same behaviors appear in both helpful and unhelpful categories (e.g., advice, information, showing concern, and telling about positive experiences), making it difficult to discern what features of an interaction differentiate helpful from unhelpful instances of advice, information, concern, and the like. Camille Wortman (whose research with cancer patients provided one of the first detailed accounts of helpful and unhelpful support attempts) has observed the following:

[T]here is a need for more research on transactions between support providers and recipients in natural settings. When people are attempting to provide various forms of support, what do they actually do and how is this perceived by the recipient? For example, specifically how do family members attempt to encourage the patient to adhere to a difficult treatment regimen? When are reminders regarded as supportive, and when are they perceived as nagging, patronizing, or overprotective? When are others' calming, minimizing appraisals of the illness effective in reducing the recipient's distress, and when do they increase distress because they make the recipient feel that his or her concerns are not being heard? (Wortman & Conway, 1985, p. 297)

A related body of work has sought to identify the risks inherent in seeking and providing help. These studies show that even when the support that is provided is helpful, it may come at a cost. Many of these costs arise from the ways in which seeking, receiving, or providing support reflect on individual identities. Those who seek or receive support may appear less competent (Abdel-Halim, 1982; Lee, 1997; Wills, 1983) and in order to receive support, they may have to reveal a stigmatizing condition or undesirable information (Brashers, Neidig, & Goldsmith, in press; Chesler & Barbarin, 1984; DePaulo, 1982; Goldsmith, 1988; Wortman & Dunkel-Schetter, 1979). Support recipients not only risk others' negative impressions but may also suffer negative self-evaluations (Abdel-Halim, 1982; DePaulo, 1982; DePaulo & Fisher, 1980; Newsom, 1999; Tripathi,

women with depression (Harris, 1992), individuals with multiple sclerosis (Lehman & Hemphill, 1990), persons recovering from a stroke (Clark & Stephens, 1996), persons experiencing work stress or unemployment (Pearlin & McCall, 1990; Ratcliff & Bogdan, 1988), nurses in acute care settings (Ford & Ellis, 1998), mentally disabled mothers (Tucker & Johnson, 1989), individuals with rheumatic diseases (Lanza, Cameron, & Revenson, 1995), persons living with HIV/AIDS (Hays, Magee, & Chauncey, 1994; Pakenham, 1998), families of children with chronic conditions (Patterson, Garwick, Bennett, & Blum, 1997), persons living with irritable bowel syndrom or chronic headache (Martin, Davis, Baron, Suls, & Blanchard, 1994), and parents of adults going through a divorce (Lesser & Comet, 1987).

Caplan, & Naidu, 1986; Wills, 1983) and a loss of independence, control, and competence (Brashers et al., in press; Gross, Wallston, & Piliavin, 1979; McLeroy, Devellis, Devellis, Kaplan, & Toole, 1984). Providers may also experience negative evaluations by self and others if they are unable to provide effective assistance (Cheuk, Swearse, Wong, & Rosen, 1998; Clark & Stephens, 1996; Notarius & Herrick, 1988). Empathizing with others in distress may increase one's own risk of distress (Brashers et al., in press; Schieman & Turner, 2001) and significant others may withdraw from expressions of emotional distress (Bolger, Foster, Vinokur, & Ng, 1996).

Other risks and costs arise from the implications of support for relational qualities such as equity, closeness, and respect. Inequity in the provision of support can create individual distress and relational dissatisfaction (Hatfield, Utne, & Traupmann, 1979; Walster, Walster, & Berscheid, 1978; Ybema, Kuijer, Buunk, DeJong, & Sanderman, 2001) and the fear of obligation or the inability to reciprocate can pose obstacles to seeking support or undermine the utility of support that is received (Buunk & Hoorens, 1992; DePaulo, 1982; DiMatteo & Hays, 1981; Greenberg & Shapiro, 1971; Liang, Krause, & Bennett, 2001; Tripathi et al., 1986; Uehara, 1995). Overinvolvement by well-meaning supporters can increase stress and worsen physical and psychological problems (Coyne & DeLongis, 1986). Individual costs can result in relational conflict. If the recipient of support feels threatened by needing help, he or she may react defensively and attribute negative motives to the support provider (Fisher, Goff, Nadler, & Chinskey, 1988; Searcy & Eisenberg, 1992). Support providers whose offers are rejected may react with negative evaluations of their intended recipient and negative attributions about the reasons for rejection (Jung, 1989; Rosen, Mickler, & Collins, 1987). One individual's need for support can produce uncertainty and conflict for both partners as relationship roles and expectations are redefined (Abel, 1989; Robertson, Elder, Skinner, & Conger, 1991).

The studies on the risks and costs of seeking, receiving, and providing support might make us wonder that enacted support ever has positive effects! These pitfalls along the path to successful enacted support must be avoided if partners are to assist one another in coping. Successful support must avoid or minimize undesirable threats to each individual's image as a competent, caring, valued person and to the relational balance of power, resources, and closeness. Although there is a large body of research documenting these hazards, only a few studies have focused on what individuals can do to avoid or minimize them.

Summary

There is a powerful appeal to the idea that enacted support can buffer individuals from the ill effects of stress; however, the search for documentation of these effects has revealed many conditions, costs, and complexities. Enacted social support sometimes demonstrates a buffering effect but in other cases has no effect or even a negative effect. This may be because success in providing social support depends on adaptation to features of the situation in which it is offered and mitigation of some of the risks and costs that often accompany support. Not surprisingly, then, individuals coping with a wide variety of life stresses and daily hassles can recall not only instances when enacted support was appropriate and effective but also times when it was ill-fitted to their needs and not at all helpful.

These features of enacted support are quite consistent with the nature of interpersonal interactions. The notion that effective communication must be adapted to a situation to overcome constraints and obstacles is foundational to the study of communication (Clark & Delia, 1979). Attention to communication processes is essential if we are to understand the conditions under which enacted support has stress-buffering benefits and the features of enacted support interactions that are likely to be judged as helpful by participants.

THE COMMUNICATION OF SOCIAL SUPPORT

Many social support scholars have called for a closer examination of social support interactions. These calls to study the communication of social support are not limited to those in the communication discipline, but instead come from all quarters and from some of the most influential social support researchers. Sandler and Barrera (1984) observed that if we are to understand when enacted support will be helpful rather than harmful, we need to study the "behavioral content" of assistance and how it is perceived, as well as the nature of the relationship between support provider and recipient. Heller and Rook (1997, p. 650) noted that although much has been written about the health-protective benefits of relationships, "a crucial gap in knowledge exists about the effective ingredients of supportive interactions." Hobfoll and Stokes (1988) concluded that few researchers pay attention to the processes of social interactions and called for studies of how people seek and obtain aid and their behavioral, cognitive, and emotional reactions to aid. In the conclusion of their meta-analysis of the effects of social support, Smith, Fernengel, Holcroft, Gerald and Marien (1994, p. 357) remarked that few researchers have attended to the specific interactions or behaviors that individuals view as supportive and they identify as a "promising strategy" research that examines what individuals find valuable about social support provided in a given situation. Gottlieb (1985b, p. 372) pointed out that better understanding of how informal support is mobilized and expressed would enhance theories of social support, interventions to improve social support, and theories of relationship growth and decline.

A major premise of this book is that *many of the problems and disappointments researchers have encountered in studying enacted support have come about because we have tried to understand communicative phenomena without attention to communicative processes*. A close examination of research on enacted support reveals assumptions that are fundamentally at odds with what we know about the processes of interpersonal communication. For example, most survey instruments and coding systems for measuring enacted support focus on frequency of occurrence of various kinds of support. The effect of these measurement approaches is to group together all instances of some type of support, without respect to potential differences in quality of support. Expert advice is weighted no differently than well-meaning but incorrect advice, resources offered with a generous spirt are counted the same as those given begrudgingly, and sincere expressions of concern are considered equal to those that condescend or overprotect. In addition, there is an assumption that more support is necessarily better. In effect, these measurement systems presume that ten instances of mediocre support should have a more positive effect than a single, profound expression of support.

Although the study of how enacted social support is communicated is relatively new, several promising lines of research show that it matters *what* seekers and providers of support say and *how* they say it (for reviews, see Burleson & Goldsmith, 1998; Burleson & MacGeorge, 2002). This book adds to this growing body of research, contributing a distinctive perspective that is grounded in the study of communication processes. In Chapter 2, I describe the assumptions that are entailed in a communication-based approach and the types of questions and issues that are illumined.

CONCLUSION

There is ample evidence that involvement in personal relationships contributes to individual well-being, to relational satisfaction, and to the functioning of social systems. The idea of *enacted support* is central to our intuitions about how involvement in personal relationships brings about these positive effects and there is great conceptual appeal to a theoretical model in which close relational partners talk about problems to cope with stress. However, previous research that has measured the support enacted in personal relationships reveals a confusing array of empirical results. I propose that some of this confusion arises from overlooking the communication processes that link supportive behaviors to participants' evaluations of those behaviors. This book is intended to fill that gap and to provide a communication approach to the study of troubles talk as a complement to extant research on other facets of social support.

2

Conceptualizing Enacted Support as Communication

Chapter 1 explains that although there is great intuitive appeal to the notion that talking about problems with friends and family helps to buffer the
negative effects of stress, the empirical support for this belief is problematic. One conclusion we might draw from this lack of empirical support
is that common sense is wrong – troubles talk has less effect on coping
than we think. Alternatively, studies that have attended closely to the fit
between support and features of the situation, to the risks and benefits of
enacted support, and to the ways in which support is communicated in
conversations suggest that enacted social support *can* assist individuals
in coping with daily hassles, acute crises, and chronic difficulties. However, the conditions under which this occurs and the characteristics of the
behaviors that work appear to be complex.

To understand how and when enacted support may facilitate improved
coping with stress, it is useful to reconceptualize enacted support as a
communication phenomenon. By studying the communication processes
that occur when support is enacted in conversation, it is possible to derive
some baseline predictions about the types of behaviors support recipients
are most likely to judge as positive under various conditions. It is also
possible to develop general principles that can help individuals understand
supportive interactions and improve their abilities to enact and negotiate
social support in their close relationships. The rest of this book is devoted
to elaborating and supporting these claims. In this chapter, I locate the
study of communication processes within a broader set of stress-buffering
processes and I describe the assumptions that underlie my study of how
enacted support is communicated in the troubles talk of close relational
partners.

LOCATING COMMUNICATION PROCESSES WITHIN A
STRESS-BUFFERING MODEL

Figure 1 shows four categories of phenomena involved in one kind of explanation for how enacted support might have beneficial stress-buffering effects. Enacted support occurs in the context of *conversation*, which includes an exchange of messages as well as processes of interpretation and coordination between conversational partners. Conversation, and any support that is enacted during the course of a conversation, are subject to *evaluation* by the participants (e.g., Was the conversation helpful? Did my partner show sensitivity to my emotions? and Did my partner act supportively?). Some of the influences on evaluation are individual, shaped by the evaluator's personality, affective state, and perceptual processes. However, other influences on evaluation are socially based: They are shared to some degree by other members of the social groups with whom the individual uses language, they may be articulated by members of the social group, and they are evident in observable social interactions among group members. Evaluations of the conversation mediate the effects that enacted support might have on individual *coping*. For example, if I judge the advice I receive to be useful and informed, that advice is likely to affect my appraisal of how manageable a problem is and my attempts at problem-solving actions. However, if the support I receive is uninformed, critical, condescending, or aggravating, it may undermine my coping and further reinforce my appraisal that my environment is stressful and threatening.[1] Enacted support that is evaluated as having some positive value is more likely to facilitate coping, whereas enacted support that is evaluated negatively is less likely to assist with coping and could even prove harmful to coping efforts.[2] The

---

[1] In fact, there is an additional complication: A support recipient's evaluation of support may be ill-informed according to some external standard. For example, there are hard truths we may initially judge to be hurtful and then later come to appreciate for the way they helped us alter our own problematic behavior. Conversely, we may welcome information or assurance only to later discover it was inaccurate or unrealistic. I return to this issue in greater detail in Chapter 4.

[2] Several studies have begun to examine the relationships among social support, coping, and well-being (for a review, see Schreurs & DeRidder, 1997). Although there are multiple models of the relationships among social support, coping, and well-being, several studies have found evidence for the path I presume here: Namely, that it is important to understand satisfaction with support because this predicts subsequent coping and well-being. In a study of women with rheumatoid arthritis, a husband's critical or supportive remarks influenced his wife's coping, with subsequent effects on psychological adjustment (Manne & Zautra, 1989). Similarly, cardiac patients' reports of support predicted depressive symptoms 1 year later and this effect was mediated by coping (Holohan, Moos, Holohan, & Brennan, 1997). In an observational study of college dating partners who talked about everyday stressors, Collins and Feeney (2000) documented the linkages between the quality of support provided, the recipient's evaluation of the support, and the recipient's change in mood. In

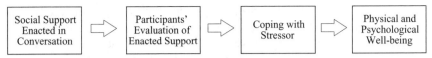

FIGURE 1. One pathway from enacted social support to individual well-being.

degree to which enacted support facilitates or inhibits adaptive coping is pivotal to whether buffering effects on *physical and psychological health* are observed. We might imagine a similar figure in which evaluations of enacted support lead to relational well-being and satisfaction.

Figure 1 is admittedly oversimplified in several ways. It is not intended as a causal model specifying the full range of possible causes and effects. Several likely reciprocal relationships among variables are not represented.[3] In addition, it is possible that social support enacted in a conversation might be linked to well-being through other pathways that are not represented in Figure 1.[4] The model is useful as a visual representation of a subset of relevant phenomena and relationships among phenomena. It helps to locate the different approaches to the study of enacted support that have been prominent in the literature and to differentiate these from the questions I explore in this book. Much of the previous research on enacted support can be characterized as leaping from rather abstract self-reports or codings of conversational phenomena (e.g., amounts of informational, instrumental, and emotional support received) straight to indicators of physical and psychological well-being (e.g., depression, anxiety, and illness). As the brief review of literature in Chapter 1 made clear, attempts to document and explain the link from conversation straight to well-being have not been very successful.

contrast, Savelkoul, Post, de Witte, and van den Borne (2000) examined the relationships among satisfaction with social support, coping, and well-being among a sample of adults with rheumatic disease. They found the best fitting model was one in which social support mediates the effects of coping on well-being (in contrast to the model proposed here, in which coping mediates the effects of social support on well-being). However, their approach aggregated satisfaction with all social support received from all sources, thus obscuring the effects of particular types of support from particular sources that were observed in other studies.

[3] For example, ongoing evaluations of enacted support during the course of a conversation may play a role in shaping the conversation itself and ongoing appraisal and coping processes may also play a role in the unfolding of the conversation and its evaluation. Similarly, one's state of mental or physical health can have effects on the nature of conversation, evaluation, and coping.

[4] For example, a conversation might produce a positive affective experience that directly boosts psychological well-being, or evaluation of a conversation may affect relational satisfaction with implications for one's integration in a network and subsequent effects on health.

In contrast, the approach I take in this book focuses attention on the first two components in Figure 1: detailed examination of conversations and the features and processes that are associated with participants' evaluations of those conversations as helpful, sensitive, and supportive. To illustrate the kinds of questions and issues I address, imagine an interaction between two friends, Liza and Joel. Joel updates his friend on the most recent of his ongoing difficulties in making decisions about caring for his mother, who lives in another state:

> JOEL: This getting lost last week was a real eye-opener. I think I'm going to have to try again to get her to quit driving and if she won't, I may consider the possibility of having her license revoked.
>
> LIZA: Oh. (*Brief pause*) I read somewhere, though, that losing your license can be a real blow to your independence and that it's so important for older people to feel like they still have some control during a time when so many things are changing and they feel they're losing control.
>
> JOEL: Yeah, well anyway, she's agreed that it's not a good idea to drive at night, at least. Her neighbor is retired now and has offered to take her to the store or the doctor when she needs to go but Mom is just stubborn about asking for help.
>
> LIZA: It must be tough to be so far away from family. I know I'm really glad I turned down that Boston promotion – I can't imagine not being able to be there for my Dad when things come up.
>
> JOEL: (*in a defensive tone*) Yeah, well, see Beth and the kids are much better off here than if we'd stayed in Arlington.
>
> LIZA: (*in a sympathetic tone*) Sure. You have to look out for your own family. Will you be able to visit your mom for the holidays?
>
> JOEL: (*shrugs, mumbles*) Up to Bob. The way this project is dragging on. (*pauses, then continues in a businesslike tone*) Have you seen the projections he sent through this morning?

After their interaction, Liza confides to a mutual friend that she feels like she and Joel are really growing close and that she is glad she has been able to offer him advice and encouragement for some of the family stresses he is experiencing. She feels that because she is struggling with some of the same issues in her own family, she is sensitive to what Joel is feeling and better able to give useful information and advice. Conversely, Joel finds himself thinking about the same conversation later that day and decides that maybe he'll stop talking about his mother with Liza. Even though she often gives useful advice and he knows she's trying to be supportive, he so often feels she is judging him or condescending to him and she sometimes makes unfair comparisons between her optimistic and active 65-year-old father and his cantankerous and declining 77-year-old mother. His reflection on the conversation reminds him that he needs to call his attorney to inquire about the logistics of revoking a license.[5]

We could ask a variety of questions about any particular troubles talk conversation or any collection of such conversations. One set of questions might focus on reasons why Joel and Liza behaved as they did. Another set of questions might focus on the effects this conversation had on Joel and Liza. For either set of questions, there could be a number of explanations. We could explain their behavior or reactions with reference to individual personality, cognition, motivation, or emotion. Although research on actual supportive interactions is still relatively rare, those who have studied conversations have typically sought to understand cognitive, motivational, or emotional processes and/or to show how individual mood states or personality traits moderate the operation of these processes. Without denying the utility of these sorts of questions and explanations, I propose an alternative and equally important research agenda that focuses on features of the talk itself and the communicative processes that link features of talk to participant interpretations and evaluations of that talk.

Features of the talk itself are represented in the first box in Figure 1. For example, how does the topic of Joel's mother's health arise – does Joel introduce it or does Liza inquire first? What tone does Joel employ as he describes his mother's situation – does he joke, sigh, and roll his eyes or does he express distress and concern? What features of Joel's response would lead to the description "defensive" or of Liza's response as "sympathetic"? How does Joel go about changing the topic and does this make him appear unappreciative of Liza's help?

The second box in Figure 1 represents participants' evaluations of the conversation, of one another, and of the import this conversation may have for their individual coping and for their ongoing relationship. For example, Liza reaches a positive evaluation of her contributions as supportive and as contributing to the development of a closer relationship, whereas Joel seems less satisfied with the conversation and feels he is being judged. His way of coping with his mother's situation appears not to have been changed by the conversation – he still intends to take the problem-solving action of having her license revoked – and, in fact, the conversation may have given some additional salience and momentum to this plan. In contrast, Joel's evaluation that this and other conversations have been relationally unsatisfying appears to produce some change in his level of openness with his friend.

The arrow linking the first two boxes in Figure 1 represents the social and communicative processes that link features of talk to participant

---

[5] This conversation was constructed for purposes of illustration. In subsequent chapters, I refer to transcripts of messages and conversations produced by participants in various studies I have conducted.

evaluations. Three types of processes are of particular interest. First are the processes of problem appraisal that are displayed in the talk itself. For example, Joel focuses attention on his mother's stubbornness in cooperating with a solution to a problem, whereas Liza redirects analysis of the problem to the long-distance relationship Joel has with his mother. These different emphases suggest different degrees of controllability and different possible options for coping. Similarly, responsibility to family is a value evoked by both speakers, but which family and how to prioritize family are questions raised between the lines. The ways that problems are represented and the coordination between speakers in appraising a problem can contribute to their evaluations of the conversation and its implications for coping.

Another set of processes that link features of talk to participant evaluations are those involved in self-presentation and identity support. Several of Joel's valued identities are displayed in this conversation – a son who cares for his mother, a husband and father who does what is good for his wife and children, a competent and responsible work team member, a friend who trusts Liza, and so on. We might consider how these identities are affirmed or challenged in the conversation and how this may influence Joel's evaluation of the conversation and his options for coping with his mother. We could examine similar processes for Liza.

A third and closely related set of concerns have to do with how features of their talk signal Joel and Liza's power or influence over one another as well as their closeness to and involvement with one another. These processes are clearly intertwined in Liza's positive evaluation of the conversation as enhancing intimacy and Joel's negative evaluation of the conversation as reflecting an uncomfortable asymmetry in power.

These three processes (the definition of the problem situation and coping options, self-presentation and identity support, and the enactment of relational qualities) are the focus of this book. Understanding these processes helps to provide explanations for how and why some observable features of conversation may be systematically linked with common trends in participants' evaluation of troubles talk. These processes are also the basis for recommendations about how participants can engage in troubles talk in a way that maximizes the chances it will be useful for them.

There is much to be gained from studying this first set of the links in the chain of relationships represented in Figure 1 and failure to do so may help to explain why previous attempts to demonstrate a buffering effect of enacted support have been largely unsuccessful. These communication processes are complex and important mediators of any subsequent effects we might observe on individual coping and, more distally, on well-being. To overlook consequential variation in the ways support is enacted introduces noise into the measurements of enacted support. This may drown out what would otherwise be detectable relationships between enacted support and evaluation, coping, or well-being. Similarly, to test relationships between a conversation and distal outcomes such as well-being without attention to more proximate, mediating outcomes such as evaluation and coping is theoretically unsatisfying because we don't specify the intervening processes through which these effects come about.

Further, the phenomena represented by conversation in Figure 1 are of a different type than the phenomena represented by physical health or even individual coping. Conversation is a communicative phenomenon. Certainly, cognition, motivation, emotion, and even physiology may affect and be affected by conversation but conversation cannot be reduced to these processes. Consequently, theories and methods developed to understand cognition, motivation, emotion, and physiology do not shed light on the communicative processes that distinguish *conversation* from thoughts about conversation, motives for engaging in conversation, emotional responses to conversation, or bodily effects of conversation. Elaborating and testing the full set of relationships suggested in Figure 1 calls for the contributions of researchers in different areas of expertise with different theoretical perspectives and methods. This book offers a series of frameworks and findings from communication studies that are useful in understanding some of the processes that go on in conversation and some of the communication features that may account for participants' evaluations of conversation. Although theories of cognition, motivation, emotion, and physiology are well-represented in the interdisciplinary research on social support, theories of communication are less often employed. It is my hope that this book provides a useful and needed complement to the work of researchers who are involved in examining other aspects of the buffering effects of social support enacted in personal relationships.

ASSUMPTIONS OF A COMMUNICATION-BASED APPROACH

Of the various ways to conceptualize social support, enacted support may seem relatively straightforward and its definition commonsensical: It is what people say and do to help one another cope with stress. However, by thinking of enacted support as something that is communicated in social interactions, I bring to bear a number of assumptions about communication behaviors and processes that enrich our understanding of enacted support. These assumptions direct our attention to the meanings of support, to the social resources for arriving at shared meaning, to the situated character of support, and to a rhetorical understanding of effective and ineffective attempts at support (Goldsmith & Fitch, 1997).

Enacted Support Is Meaningful Action

The actions that make up enacted social support have meaning – for participants, for observers, and for researchers – and these meanings are an important component of the processes through which support has effects. The effects of enacted support do not come about mechanistically through the mere issuance of a supportive act but rather through participants' interpretations and evaluations. A communication approach focuses not on behaviors but on meaningful actions.

One type of meaning involves the *interpretation of an act as an instance of "support."* Not all utterances in an interaction are necessarily enacted support, even if the interaction is a conversation about one person's stress. Participants in conversations and researchers alike must differentiate among utterances that count as advice, expressions of concern, offers, tangents, subject changes, jokes, criticisms, and so on (Goldsmith & McDermott, 1998). A second aspect of meaning concerns the broader implications or *evaluations of these actions*. For example, once I recognize advice has been given, is it good advice? Does it signal the other person cares for me? Does it undermine my dignity or autonomy? Does it signal an end of the conversation?

These meanings and their importance are illustrated in the example conversation between Joel and Liza. In that conversation, both parties recognize that she gives advice and other forms of support (agreement on the interpretation of support). They also appear to agree on some aspects of the evaluation of Liza's support (that her advice is often helpful because of her own experiences), but they disagree on other aspects of evaluation (whether the advice is experienced as supportive or judgmental and whether it makes their relationship closer or emphasizes a condescending difference in power). In other conversations, interpretations might differ or evaluations might be more closely aligned; in any case, these interpretations and evaluations – the meanings of supportive acts – are the most immediate results of a conversation and likely to mediate further distal effects that a single conversation or pattern of conversations may have on individuals or their relationships.

To say that the meaning of enacted support is important is not terribly controversial, although how researchers take account of the meanings of support (theoretically and operationally) is varied. For example, several influential reviews of the social support literature have argued for a need to differentiate between the designation or interpretation of a behavior as an example of the phenomenon "social support" and the measurement or evaluation of the impact that behavior has on a person under stress (e.g., Antonucci, 1985; Heller et al., 1986; Thoits, 1985). Similarly, there is recognition that support only works when it is perceived as having value or appraised as useful (Heller et al., 1986; Gottlieb, 1985c).

Although the importance of attending to the meanings of support may be uncontroversial, few have systematically explored the factors that shape interpretations of support. It is common practice for these processes to be implicit in the operationalization or coding of an action as an instance of support. A questionnaire might ask people to report how much advice they get, setting aside the question of how people know advice when they see it or what counts as advice. Similarly, coding schemes allow research teams to differentiate informational support, emotional support, or offers of tangible support that might be present in a conversation, but the principles the coders use and message features to which they attend in reaching those decisions are not typically an object of inquiry, so long as intercoder reliability is sufficiently high.

Just as the interpretation of support has not been systematically studied, most research that has examined providers' or recipients' evaluations has measured those evaluations directly, without seeking the actions or patterns of interaction that gave rise to their judgments. For example, research on helpful and unhelpful support behaviors (summarized in Chapter 1) solicits respondents' evaluations that support was helpful or not but does not tell us much about what behaviors produced those judgments and what about those behaviors led some to be assessed as helpful and others as unhelpful. Similarly, there are a number of measures that tap satisfaction with support (the Arizona Social Support Interview Schedule, Barrera, 1980; the Social Support Questionnaires for Transactions and Satisfaction, Doeglas et al., 1996; the Satisfaction with Social Networks Scale, Stokes, 1983; the Social Support Inventory, Timmerman, Emanuels-Zuurveen, & Emmelkamp, 2000; the multidimensional support measure developed by Vaux & Harrison, 1985). Measures of satisfaction with support tend to be more successful predictors of positive outcomes than measures of the amount of enacted support (Doeglas et al., 1996; Neuling & Winefield, 1988; Power, 1988; Sandler & Barrera, 1984; Wallsten, Tweed, Blazer, & George, 1999). However, measuring satisfaction with support to predict coping or beneficial outcomes does not address the question of what actions produced high or low levels of satisfaction.

To understand meaningful action, a communication approach problematizes what has been taken for granted in survey measures or the coding of interactions. For example, I seek to identify some of the features of a message or conversation that form the basis for participants' and researchers' recognition of actions as instances of support: How do we know an expression of concern or an offer when we see it? And in those instances when it may not be clear whether someone is giving advice or just describing their own past experience, what are ways participants have of attempting to clarify what is occurring? Or what are some of the functions that might be served by leaving such a comment ambiguous? How do variations in the message itself (e.g., the style of language used, the way in which support is introduced into a conversation, and a speaker's confidence or warmth in conveying a message) relate to systematic variation in recipients' interpretations and evaluations of the message?

TABLE 2. *Sample Ratings to Demonstrate Individual and Message Variability*

	Message 1	Message 2	Message 3	Mean by Person
Person 1	1	2	3	2
Person 2	2	3	4	3
Person 3	3	4	5	4
Mean by message	2	3	4	

There Are Social Bases for Shared Meaning

In the communication approach I take, the factors of greatest interest in explaining the meanings of support are features of the talk itself and social processes rather than individual and cognitive processes. There is likely to be individual variability (and even some idiosyncrasy) in how an action is interpreted and evaluated. However, meaning is not completely subjective, nor is it simply correspondence between two subjective individuals. Individual cognitive processes are, of course, involved in the attribution of meaning, but there are also social practices and processes that provide resources for achieving shared meaning.

This emphasis on shared meanings and the social bases for achieving them complements other research that has focused on individual differences in interpretation and evaluation. For example, there are several important lines of research that examine *individual differences* in evaluations of the *same message* due to differences in *cognitive* structures and processes (e.g., Lakey & Drew, 1997; Mankowski & Wyer, 1996; Pierce, Sarason, & Sarason, 1996). In contrast, my research focuses on *similarities* in interpretation of *different messages* that may be attributed to *social* structures and processes.[6] As an illustration of this difference in approach, Table 2 shows hypothetical data that might be examined from two different perspectives. The data are ratings by three individuals of three different support messages using a scale that ranged from 1 to 5, where 1 indicates a message is not very helpful and 5 indicates a message is helpful.

As shown in the last *column*, person 1 consistently perceives these messages to be less helpful than person 3. This type of contrast has been systematically explored in research on the interpretation of support and this body of research suggests that relatively stable individual differences in perceived availability of support can account for some of this variability (Lakey & Cassady, 1990; Lakey & Drew, 1997; Lakey, Moineau, & Drew,

[6] Collins and Feeney (2000) draw a similar distinction between the "bottom up" influences of the objective features of an interaction and the "top down" influences of a perceiver's preexisting schemas. In an observational study of college students discussing everyday problems, they found that although attachment style (an example of an individual difference in cognitive models of relationships) did influence social support interactions, they did not significantly moderate the effects of observed social support on recipients' perceptions of the interaction.

1992; Pierce, Sarason, & Sarason, 1992). However, as the last *row* in the table demonstrates, even when there are individual differences in the interpretation of the same message, there can also be common trends in how individuals rate different messages. In this example, all three raters concur that message 1 is less helpful than message 3. This source of variability has less often been examined and it is this sort of between-message comparison that is the focus of this book.[7]

Although less often studied, these similarities are frequently taken for granted in the methods researchers use to study social support. For example, most of the ways that enacted support has been conceptualized and measured implicitly rely on shared, social bases for meaning. When we use a self-report instrument to measure the frequency with which an individual has received information, offers of aid, or encouragement, we presume that there are common behavioral referents to which these items refer. We do not assume that what counts as tangible aid to one individual might be categorized as emotional support by another and we assume that anyone to whom we administer such an instrument has some basic understanding of these categories of social acts. Even experimental studies designed to illumine individual variability in the evaluation of a supportive message typically take for granted that researchers can generate a message that counts as an instance of support.[8] In studies in which we observe enacted support rather than solicit self-reports, we rely on coders to interpret or evaluate behaviors in similar ways, despite individual differences they bring to the task. Perhaps because we so routinely reach common interpretations in our interactions with one another, meanings that are socially

---

7 In fact, the situation is more complicated than Table 2 suggests. In Table 2, the variability in ratings of enacted support is completely accounted for by consistent differences among perceivers and consistent differences among messages or targets of perception. In a series of studies, Lakey and colleagues (Lakey, Drew, & Sirl, 1999; Lakey, McCabe, Fisicaro, & Drew, 1996) have convincingly demonstrated that there is also substantial variability in ratings of support that is due to the statistical interaction of perceiver and target effects. I address this research later in this chapter.

8 For example, Mankowski and Wyer (1996) and Lakey and Cassady (1990) use a research protocol in which participants read a story about one person responding to another's distress. In some versions of the story, the person responds in a way that is "unambiguously" supportive or rejecting. Lakey, Moineau, and Drew (1992) alter this procedure slightly by having participants read messages in which it is unclear whether they are meant to be supportive or rejecting. Pierce, Sarason, and Sarason (1992) had research participants with different levels of perceived available support rate a message the researchers intended as supportive. In all of these studies, the research questions and findings focus on how individual differences (e.g., persons who are high or low in perceived available support) explain variability in the evaluations of messages. However, implicit in the design of the experiment is the assumption that it is possible for researchers to create hypothetical messages that *are* unambiguously supportive (or rejecting) or ambiguous with regard to intent. This suggests that although there is some degree of individual variability in the evaluation of a message, there are also shared bases for classifying a message as supportive, rejecting, or ambiguous.

shared are frequently the ground against which the figure of individual difference attracts researchers' attention.

To say that there are social bases for shared meaning is not to say that arriving at similar interpretations or evaluations of some supportive action is unproblematic or that participants in conversation have identical meanings. Indeed, there are a number of studies that suggest providers of support, recipients of support, and outside observers may reach interpretations and evaluations of support that are partially overlapping but not necessarily identical. For example, several studies have compared support provider and recipient reports of the social support that is enacted in their relationship (Abbey et al., 1995; Antonucci & Israel, 1986; Bolger, Zuckerman, & Kessler, 2000; Collins & Feeney, 2000; Coriell & Cohen, 1995; Davis & Brickman, 1996; Emmons & Colby, 1995; Frazier, Tix, & Barnett, 2003; Lakey et al., 2002; McCaskill & Lakey, 2000; Ptacek, Pierce, Ptacek, & Nogel, 1999; Vinokur, Schul, & Caplan, 1987). These studies have found modest levels of agreement between one partner's report of support provided and the other partner's report of support received (e.g., correlation coefficients ranging from .35 to .60). Other studies have solicited from relational partners their ratings of a troubles talk conversation and compared these ratings to observer codings of the support enacted in the same conversation (Belsher & Costello, 1991; Collins & Feeney, 2000; Cutrona & Suhr, 1994; Cutrona, Suhr, & MacFarlane, 1990; Gurung, Sarason, & Sarason, 1997). The correlations between partners' ratings and observer ratings ranged from .16 to .79.

There are a number of factors that may contribute to the unshared variance in perceivers' reports of social support. Several have to do with design features of the studies themselves that might be expected to introduce discrepancies. For example, in some studies, the relational partners completed a slightly different scale or completed ratings with a different time frame in mind. Usually reports of support were aggregated across types of support, over time, and/or across providers. As a consequence, most studies have compared agreement on the general frequency or effectiveness of support rather than the shared meaning of a particular focal behavior or conversation. In most studies using outside observers, the relational partners provided an evaluation of the supportiveness of the conversation, whereas the observers were asked to tally the frequency of particular behaviors. Expecting a correlation between frequency of behavior and participant ratings of supportiveness presumes the quality of all support efforts is uniformly high and that more behaviors are necessarily better. Lower than expected correlations may say more about the problems with making this assumption than about the degree to which observers and participants share an understanding of what occurred in a conversation.

In addition to these methodological explanations for differences in reports of support, there are a number of substantive explanations for why we might expect providers, recipients, and observers to have some unshared variance in their reports of enacted support.

1. Indirect ways of providing support might result in differences in the interpretation of an act as support or as something else. For example, in a discussion of one partner's problem, the other might tell a story of her own experience with a similar situation as a way of indirectly giving advice or offering a perspective. The recipient of the story might choose to interpret it as a story rather than informational support and, in fact, this might serve to minimize the threats to autonomy and esteem that can accompany advice. These kinds of indirect support may be highly effective precisely because of the possibility for face-saving ambiguity in how they are interpreted (Bolger et al., 2000; Glidewell, Tucker, Todt, & Cox, 1983).

2. Perceivers might disagree as to whether support was useful. In the studies reported previously, many of the items used to measure support implied a positive evaluation. So, although both provider and recipient might agree that advice was given, they might disagree that it was "useful information." This suggests there may be a lack of shared meaning in the evaluation of support, but there might nonetheless be a high degree of shared meaning in the interpretation that a support attempt occurred.

3. What one perceiver remembers, another forgets. This source of discrepancy is most likely in studies that solicit reports over a longer time frame. For example, in rating the support provided in the past month, one spouse might focus on a particularly heroic instance of tangible support. If reminded, the forgetful partner might well agree that the support occurred and that it was useful but if she overlooks it in her independent ratings, she might report receiving a lower level of support than her partner reports providing.

4. Social desirability concerns may bias ratings. Concern for one's own positive image might lead to an inflated rating of support provided. Individuals who believe receiving support implies weakness may underreport support received. Partners may also be reluctant to give one another low support ratings. Concerns for social desirability or an unwillingness to admit that one's partner was not supportive might lead relational partners to inflate their ratings of support compared to the observations of outsiders with no investment in the relationship.

5. Individuals differ in memory, perception, and judgment. I have already mentioned studies that indicate that stable perceptions of available support may influence ratings of enacted support. Pierce and his colleagues (Pierce et al., 1997) summarized evidence that individuals also differ in their interpretation of and memory for

experimentally produced social support. To the extent that partners in a relationship are dissimilar in these traits, this could also
account for disagreement in their reports of support provided and
received.

6. Relational dynamics may shape perceptions of support. The gen-
    eral level of satisfaction or dissatisfaction in a relationship can color
    the interpretation of specific behaviors (e.g., Carels & Baucom, 1999;
    Collins & Feeney, 2000; Frazier et al., 2003; Pasch, Bradbury, & Sul-
    livan, 1997). Over time, partners may develop idiosyncratic ways of
    enacting, interpreting, and evaluating support. In some situations,
    support judgments may be inferred from other relational qualities
    such as liking or similarity (Lakey, Ross, Butler, & Bentley, 1996;
    Lakey et al., 2002).

Several authors who have reviewed studies comparing receiver,
provider, and observer ratings of enacted support have stressed how little
agreement there appears to be. Alternatively, we might express surprise
that there is as much agreement as there is! In light of the methodological
challenges involved in assessing agreement and the substantive reasons
why we might expect there to be some degree of disagreement, the consistent finding of some agreement on support provided and received emerges
as something to be accounted for. The shared components of meaning are
also important theoretically and practically. They enable relational partners to achieve a modicum of understanding and coordination and they
enable researchers to propose some baseline generalizations about what
ways of communicating support tend to work and how. They also provide
a basis for pedagogy and intervention to help individuals improve their
interactions with one another. A communication approach views shared
meaning as an accomplishment and is concerned with discovering the social resources that enable participants to act in ways that are commonly
recognized as *intended* to assist with coping as well as the common criteria
by which the *utility* of those actions is evaluated.

There are two kinds of social resources that can provide a basis for the
emergence of shared meanings. One set of resources are the *social practices* that participants in a conversation share. Social practices are recurrent
meaningful actions recognized and imbued with value by a social group
(see, for example, the discussion of practice in Miller & Goodnow, 1995). Social practices include patterns of language use that enable us to infer what
is happening in a given interaction. For example, we learn that the phrase
"If I were you, what I would do is..." is usually a precursor to advice and
we understand that advice is an action that the speaker presents as being in
our best interest and something we might not otherwise do without having
it pointed out to us. We learn to recognize that when someone says "I'm
sorry" in response to a description of a problem for which they bear no

responsibility, they are expressing sympathy with our distress rather than apologizing.

Social practices also include evaluative criteria associated with patterns of action. For example, in a study of advice-giving practices among some white, middle-class, college-educated North Americans, Kristine Fitch and I found that advice recipients responded more positively to advice that not only suggested a course of action but also showed caring, concern, and respect for the recipient's autonomy (Goldsmith & Fitch, 1997). Some of the ways of speaking that enable advice givers and recipients to show respect or caring include variations in how to word advice (Goldsmith, 1994b; Goldsmith & MacGeorge, 2000), in the content of messages that accompany advice (Goldsmith, 1999), and in how advice is introduced into a conversation (Goldsmith, 2000). Similarly, Bippus (2001) identified common criteria by which a sample of college students evaluated comforting messages and these were systematically related to various aspects of comforting behavior (see also Burleson & Samler, 1985).

A second category of social resources for achieving shared meaning are *social processes*: the kinds of framing and coordinating moves in which we engage as we are going along in a conversation. For example, sometimes we tell one another that we mean to be helpful ("I know you might not want to hear this right now but I really think the best thing to do is . . .") or that we find one another supportive ("I really appreciate your support"). We may explicitly comment on what we are doing ("Do you want my advice?" or "I just need a shoulder to cry on"). At other times our coordination moves may be more subtle (e.g., referring to a problem as "mine" or "yours" rather than "ours" serves to indicate whether one partner is providing help to another or whether both are engaged together in mutual problem solving).

Both of these bases for social meaning (social practices and processes) can be systematically inferred from observable features of talk, such as the content of what people say, the choice of particular words or styles of speaking, the sequence of responses, or the use of pauses or back-channel responses ("yeah," "right," "mm-hmm"). This is another sense in which shared meaning is social. Talk occurs between people and this is a different emphasis than that in research that explains meaning with reference to characteristics of either individual. To illustrate this type of focus, we can return to the conversation between Joel and Liza that appeared at the beginning of the chapter. We might propose that Liza's statements about the effects on an elderly parent of losing one's license may be taken as advising Joel to rethink having his mother's license revoked. This interpretation could be grounded in postconversation interviews with Joel and Liza designed to solicit their individual points of view. However, it can also be grounded in observations of this and other conversations. For example, one way of giving advice, particularly advice that disagrees with an action someone has proposed to take, is to do what Liza does in this conversation:

to state an undesirable outcome of the proposed course of action but without explicitly stating the implied advice, "don't do that" (Brown & Levinson, 1987). Close observation of this conversation also provides indications that Joel and Liza orient to this common advice-giving practice. For example, Liza's statement about the elderly losing licenses is prefaced by "though," which acknowledges that her information runs counter to Joel's proposal. The beginning of her turn is also marked by the filler "oh" and a brief pause. This is consistent with a pattern widely observed in other conversations: agreeing with another speaker's assessment typically occurs smoothly and without delay but disagreement is more often marked by hesitation and indications of awkwardness (Pomerantz, 1984). Attributing the disagreeable information to something "I read somewhere" is another feature of Liza's statement that is consistent with giving advice but giving it in a way that tries to compensate for any criticism it might entail (Brown & Levinson, 1987). The point of this example is not to fully develop claims about Joel and Liza's conversation but rather to illustrate how observable features of interaction can provide a basis for claims about meaning. The assumption that there are social bases for meaning revealed in observable patterns within and across conversations directs serious attention to the conversation itself.

The processes of communicating support are not so routinized that we can predict with certainty how a given utterance will be interpreted or evaluated or that two hearers will reach an identical interpretation or evaluation. However, it is equally inappropriate to suggest that each troubles talk conversation is novel or unique to each pair. There are some shared, taken for granted practices that undergird our recognition of what is meant when others speak, some commonalities in the features of talk that are meaningful and consequential, and some shared principles for evaluating how successfully an action accomplishes various goals such as providing support, presenting a particular identity, or conveying relational power or intimacy. At the same time, these social templates must be put to work in particular interactions, with the possibility of needed adjustments and coordination. As Luckmann (1995, p. 179) explains, most interaction is "characterized by a mixture of successful application of routine knowledge and situational exploration and negotiation." Or, as Levinson (1995, p. 238) puts it, we arrive at an interpretation of what is going on in a conversation "by relying on some simple heuristics about the 'normal way of putting things' on the one hand, and the feedback potential and sequential constraints of conversational exchange on the other."

This perspective is consistent with the findings of several innovative studies that have attempted to sort out how much of our interpretations of support are because of differences in the eye of the beholder, differences in the person providing the support, or to some combination of the two factors

(Lakey, McCabe, Fisicaro, & Drew, 1996; Lakey, Drew, & Sirl, 1999). These studies document that there is a consistent (and relatively small) portion of evaluations of supportiveness that is attributable to individual differences among perceivers. However, there are also consistent effects due to the supporters who are being rated – that is, there are shared evaluations that some individuals are better supporters than others.[9] In addition, there are substantial effects that are associated with the unique combination of provider and perceiver of support. Lakey and colleagues have focused on the cognitive processes that can account for this provider-by-perceiver statistical interaction, but they acknowledge that there must also be behavioral processes involved. These are the focus of my communication approach, in which the social bases for shared meaning are brought to life in the conversational actions of support providers and support recipients. There are some ways of communicating social support (social practices) that are often interpreted in similar ways by participants and these social practices are enacted and coordinated with particular individuals in particular conversations (social processes).

Enacted Support Is Situated

Knowing the situation or context in which a conversation takes place helps individuals coordinate actions and their meanings. For example, the ways that advice is given and interpreted, and the potential effects on the recipient, are likely to differ depending on the context in which it occurs. Advice might be offered in the context of a professional consultation in a place of business, troubles talk with a friend over coffee, a call to an abrasive radio talk show host, or a parting line from a weary bartender at last call. Each of these different configurations of source, setting, and sequence is likely to shape the purpose attributed to the advice giver: in professional consultation, an adviser is performing his or her job; a friend giving advice may be doing so as an expression of concern; a radio talk show host may be motivated by a bid for better ratings; and the weary bartender may give advice simply as an attempt to conclude interaction. In addition, different configurations of source, setting, and sequence also shape the significance of the advice for the relationship, the credibility of the advice, the persuasiveness of the advice, and so on. The context in which an action occurs is a powerful resource for narrowing down the plausible meanings of that action.

[9] These effects are greatest when the raters all observe a particular conversation (i.e., a videotape of a person giving support in a conversation) and there is less consensus when raters are asked to give global assessments of an ongoing relationship with a particular individual (perhaps because each rater has a different history of interactions with that supporter).

Context can be viewed with a wider or narrower lens (see, for example, Duranti & Goodwin, 1992; Tracy, 1998). In the wide-angle lens is the sociocultural community within which an interaction takes place. Ways of enacting support are recognizable within the expectations and practices of social groups and the ways of interpreting and evaluating enacted support may vary across different sociocultural contexts. My understanding of the significance of sociocultural context is shaped by Hymes's (1972) concept of *speech community* as a group that shares not only a language but also ideas about how language may be (and should be) used to accomplish various social purposes. Although Hymes's original definition focused on communities whose members interacted with one another, others have expanded his notion of speech community to encompass broader social groups. Of particular relevance to my work is Philipsen's (1992) research on ways of speaking that are recognizable to many white, middle-class, North Americans and prominently represented in media and public life as characteristic of that group (see also Carbaugh, 1988, p. 2; Fitch, 1998, pp. 23–24; Katriel, 1991, p. 6). In other words, what matters about the sociocultural context is not race or class or nationality per se; instead, "white, middle-class, North American" becomes a gloss for a group that employs some common ways of interpreting and evaluating speech that are distinctive from other groups. Not all North American residents of European American descent who consider themselves middle class would necessarily endorse or enact the social practices and processes I identify in my research and there are likely persons who are not white, middle class, or North American who nonetheless recognize and participate in the patterns I identify (e.g., members of racial/ethnic minorities within the United States who participate in multiple speech communities and members of western European industrialized nations who share some commonalities with North Americans). Nonetheless, this is the group to whom my research is most likely to apply and with whom the patterns I describe are most likely associated.

Most of the research that forms the core of this book (Chapters 3, 4, and 5) has been conducted in Urbana–Champaign, located in rural central Illinois (140 miles south of Chicago). The two contiguous cities are adjacent to the village of Savoy and surrounded by small rural communities in Champaign county; the total population of the county is approximately 180,000.[10] The community is predominantly white (78.8%) with some representation of African Americans (11.2%), Asians (6.5%), and Hispanics or Latino/as (2.9%). Although the University of Illinois is prominent symbolically and economically, the community is also a commercial and healthcare

[10] My information about the community is based on 2000 Census data for Champaign county. Because participants in my research came not only from Urbana–Champaign but also from surrounding communities in Champaign county, this is the most appropriate unit for description.

center for surrounding small rural communities and most residents are employed in education, health, social services, or retail. The median household income is $37,780; median family income is $52,591. Some studies reported in this book have been conducted among undergraduate students at the University of Illinois, approximately 70% of whom are white and 60% of whom come from Chicago and the suburban areas surrounding Chicago.[11] "White, middle-class, North Americans" is a rough descriptor of the predominant sociocultural group within which my work has been conducted and to which my work is likely to apply; however, members of other racial/ethnic groups and social classes are included in my samples, just as they are a part of the campus and community.[12]

One of the ways in which sociocultural context frames the enactment and meaning of social support is by providing resources for interpretation. Genres of *speech events* are one such resource. Within sociocultural groups, members recognize different types of episodes, such as "professional consultation," "troubles talk," the "call-in" portion of a radio show, or "last call" in a bar. The term *speech event* comes from the ethnography of speaking tradition (Hymes, 1972), but similar concepts are central in a variety of traditions, including *speech genre* (Bakhtin, 1986), *social episode* (Forgas, 1979; Harre & Secord, 1972), and *frame* (Tannen, 1993). As a synthesis of these various concepts, Leslie Baxter and I have defined a speech event as "a jointly enacted communication episode that is characterized by an internal coherence or unity and punctuated by clear beginning and ending boundaries" (Goldsmith & Baxter, 1996, p. 88).

Focusing on the social support that is enacted in the context of the *troubles talk* speech event shapes the types of actions I have studied and the types of generalizations I draw about effective support. For example, the statement "you'd better go talk to him" may be interpreted as caring advice in the context of a troubles talk conversation but might be taken as a task-oriented directive in the context of a reprimand from one's boss. Similarly, the ways in which features of a supportive action are evaluated is context-dependent. A hug may be a welcome expression of caring, an unexpected but touching gesture, or an unwelcome overture. Which interpretation we reach is likely shaped in part by contextual features such as our relationship to the other person, the setting, and other things that are said and done in the course of

---

[11] My information about the undergraduate student body comes from the university's Division of Information Management. In estimating the percentage of students from "Chicago and surrounding suburbs," I include students from Cook, DuPage, Lake, Will, and Kane counties.

[12] In particular, African Americans are included in most of the studies I report, making up 5.9 to 21.1% of respondents in various samples. The representation of African Americans relative to the total sample size has not been large enough to permit systematic examination of possible racial/ethnic variation and so I have treated participants of various races simply as part of the larger speech community in which the research has been conducted.

the conversation. We expect and tolerate different kinds of assistance from different participants in different settings and so on.

Enacted support also is situated in the unfolding conversation that becomes a context within which interpretation and evaluation occur. For example, the same piece of advice may come across as "butting in" when offered unsolicited but is likely to be received more willingly when given in response to a recipient's explicit request for advice (Goldsmith, 2000). When spouses talk with one another about work stresses, attempts to help solve the problem may be interpreted as a desire to shut down discussion if offered immediately following disclosure of a problem. In contrast, problem solving is more likely to be seen as an expression of caring if it occurs after having listened for a time (Pearlin & McCall, 1990). The relevance of informational support for a particular problem, the sincerity of an expression of concern, or the acceptability of alternative ways of seeing a problem might be expected to vary considerably, depending on what precedes and follows these actions.

The relationship between speaker and hearer is another important facet of context, particularly where troubles talk is concerned. In the introduction to this book, I reviewed research suggesting that for many white, middle-class North Americans, personal relationships are the first and most important place individuals turn for help with all kinds of problems, from daily stresses to major life crises. Although troubles talk can occur in other kinds of relationships,[13] the expectation that it occurs in personal relationships shapes its meaning and significance. For example, the costs of seeking help, the types of help sought, and the style of seeking help differ in close relationships compared to relationships between strangers (Clark, 1983) and the intimacy of spouse, friend, and family relationships contributes to satisfaction with the social support one has received (Hobfoll, Nadler, & Leiberman, 1986).[14] The reciprocity, intimacy, perceived similarity, and communal norms that characterize many close relationships

---

[13] The conceptualization of troubles talk in the conversation analysis tradition focused on structural parameters that were distinctive to troubles talk, and so the concept was not defined with reference to the type of relationship between participants.

[14] Indeed, studying enacted social support in the context of close relationships introduces the possibility for idiosyncratic meanings of support based on unique relational history. This does complicate any generalizations we might reach about optimal ways of enacting social support. However, relationships are a blend of social resources, relationally specific nuances, and moment-to-moment enactments of both (Goldsmith, 1993). Although members of a close relationship may develop a distinctive, relational "culture" (Baxter, 1987, 1993), they draw from broader cultural resources to do so (Fitch, 1998). My goal is to understand "close relationship" as a recognizable kind of context and to discover some of the patterns and expectations of close relationships that are shared and that differentiate close from other types of relationships.

shape the willingness to seek help and reactions to help that is provided (Wills, 1992). Likewise, the expectation that support will be forthcoming from some types of relational partners may be so strong that a failure to receive support in that relationship is devastating and not compensated for by support from other sources (Harris, 1992).

Recognizing the sociocultural, episodic, and relational context of enacted social support is both constraining and necessary. It does limit the generalizability of findings. Some of the patterns and findings I report in subsequent chapters may or may not provide a good representation of how enacted support works in other sociocultural groups. When we study the ways in which social support might be enacted in conversations other than troubles talk or in relationships that aren't close, we will likely find that some things change and some things stay the same. The degree to which we can generalize beyond a particular context is an empirical question but we shouldn't assume that findings derived within a contextualized approach such as this can be readily transplanted. At the same time, studying enacted support within a particular context is necessary if we are to ask and answer questions about meaningful, purposeful action. Meanings are derived and purposes recognized within a context.

Enacted Support Is Rhetorical

The term *rhetoric* may have negative connotations in its everyday usage (e.g., empty rhetoric: all talk and no action). In contrast, there is a long-standing tradition of rhetorical inquiry from which communication research has developed and it is this understanding of rhetoric that informs my work.[15] This rhetorical tradition studies features of a communicative performance that make it successful at achieving some purpose in a particular social context (Clark & Delia, 1979). Explanation proceeds in terms of close analysis of speech, as well as examination of its adaptation to the social circumstances of its delivery. The study of rhetoric also directs attention to the constitutive power of language (O'Keefe, 1988). That is, effective communication is not simply a matter of matching or adapting one's use of language to various features of a situation. Communication also has the power to shape our understanding of the situation.

By saying that enacted support is rhetorical, I draw on both these senses of the term *rhetoric*. Specifically, I mean to direct our attention to (a) the multiple purposes that become relevant when relational partners engage in enacted support, (b) the features of messages and conversations that are well-designed (or ill-designed) to achieve purposes and overcome

[15] Elsewhere, I have also characterized this set of assumptions as a normative approach (e.g., Goldsmith & Fitch, 1997; Goldsmith, 2001).

constraints, and (c) the reciprocal relationship between features of the situation that constrain what relational partners say and the features of what relational partners say that construct the situation.

Multiple Purposes[16]

When conversational partners seek, provide, or receive social support, they are enacting more than just social support. Each person is also enacting an image of himself or herself and his or her partner. Together the partners are also enacting their relationship. So, for example, in providing information, conversational partners are also enacting identities as knowledgeable or as one in need of knowledge, as experienced or inexperienced, as competent or incompetent, as caring or uncaring, and so on. The partners are also enacting a relationship that may be more or less symmetrical, more or less close, more or less involved and responsive.

One useful way of thinking about multiple purposes is to differentiate the task, identity, and relational implications of any message or conversation. Clark and Delia (1979) proposed that in any purposeful communication situation, it is possible to identify an instrumental issue (task) that is the focus of interaction, as well as features of messages that implicate characteristics of the interactants' relationship and features that define their identities in that situation. O'Keefe and her colleagues (O'Keefe, 1988, 1990; O'Keefe & Delia, 1988; O'Keefe & McCornack, 1987; O'Keefe & Shepherd, 1987) propose that effective communication is action that not only accomplishes the task in a situation but also creates or sustains desired identities and relational attributes. As applied to the particular case of support enacted in troubles talk, the _task_ component of the interaction has to do with facilitating coping and might be accomplished by any number of actions

---

[16] In previous work (Goldsmith, 1992, 1994b; Goldsmith & Fitch, 1997), I have referred to the multiple _goals_ involved in the successful provision of social support. Here, I have opted for the term _purposes_ instead. The term _goal_ may connote for many readers the notion of a speaker's private, internal motivation and/or cognition. My interest is not in the cognitive or motivational state that leads a speaker to produce a message. Instead, a determination of _purpose_ is located in social practice rather than in individual motives. _Purpose_ is the answer to questions such as What can you be recognized as doing? and What can you be held accountable for doing? So, for example, someone who gives advice to a friend in the course of troubles talk would typically be recognized as having enacted support because the socially recognized purpose of advice is to assist another in resolving some problem. It is always possible that the advice giver has a variety of motives that may be apparent to an observer, a recipient, or even to the advice giver him- or herself (e.g., making oneself look smart, managing one's own anxiety or emotional arousal, or exercising control over the other). In other words, it is not necessary to know why the person gave advice to say that advice has been given and to count it as one type of enacted support (which could then be analyzed further for those features that might make it more or less effective in the purpose of assisting the other, including, perhaps, the degree to which the advice appears sincere rather than self-interested and so on).

that seek to help another in solving a problem or managing his or her emotional reaction to it. The *identity* component includes features of an interaction that reflect on who individuals are as they engage in the task (both specific identities that are important, such as mother, friend, or expert, but also more general attributes such as one's autonomy, efficacy, and worth) and the *relational* component has to do with participants' roles relative to one another (which might be characterized as relational types such as good friend or supportive wife or by characteristics such as reciprocity, similarity, power, and solidarity).

In some cases, accomplishing the task of giving advice, comfort, or tangible aid is consistent with the identities and relationships partners wish to enact. However, as outlined in Chapter 1, seeking, providing, and receiving support are fraught with potential risks and costs to the individuals involved and to their relationship. Reconciling these potentially competing purposes (e.g., giving advice without coming across as pushy, showing concern in a way that is taken as sincere, or offering to help in a way that doesn't arouse concerns about obligation) can complicate the task of assisting another person with coping. Success at enacting social support involves adaptation to these multiple purposes (Goldsmith, 1992). A rhetorical approach to the study of support is characterized by a focus on how *different ways of carrying out the same task (i.e., coping assistance) may be better or worse at adapting to these multiple purposes as they arise in particular situations.*

Comparing "different ways of carrying out the same task" involves not only comparing the utility of different forms of support (e.g., in a given situation, is it better to give informational support or emotional support?) but also focusing on differences in quality among examples of the same type of support (e.g., in a given situation, why are some instances of informational support better than others?). Conceiving of multiple purposes of enacted support also challenges the presumption behind most schemes for measuring or coding enacted support, namely that a given utterance or action corresponds to a particular type of supportive function. So, for example, in most research advice is treated as problem-solving support and is presumed to facilitate the recipient's problem-solving coping, whereas an expression of concern or empathy is treated as emotion-focused support and is presumed to facilitate emotion-focused coping. Alternatively, we can view any enactment of support as potentially having multiple functions. Advice can shed light on solutions to a problem but can also communicate relational caring (or criticism) and self-efficacy (or threats to identity and efficacy). An offer of assistance might turn out to be irrelevant to the recipient's needs but nonetheless appreciated for the caring it conveys. Alternatively, tangible assistance might be recognized as necessary for coping with some problem but resented because of its implications for the recipient's autonomy.

To illustrate, we can return to our example conversation and examine the evaluations Joel and Liza gave to their conversation. It is clear that Joel responds to Liza's information about elders losing licenses not only in terms of its instrumental value but also in terms of how it makes him feel and what it reveals about their relationship. Likewise, his reaction to her attempts at expressing understanding and empathy have to do not only with the caring and emotional support they might convey but also with the factual basis for claimed similarity (i.e., whether the comparison between her father and his mother is reasonable).

Recognizing these distinctions moves us beyond counting the mere frequency of different types of support to consider more adequately the degree to which support is crafted so as to satisfy the complex task, identity, and relational purposes that inhere in attempts to help one another cope with stressful events. Failure to sustain acceptable identities and relationships can be costs of support that undermine the perceived usefulness of assistance and increase the level of distress. Conversely, bolstering a threatened identity or sustaining a valued relationship may be of greater value than the aid that is offered. Even when suggestions and information are facts the recipient already knows, an offer of tangible aid is politely declined, or the expression of caring is not particularly articulate, the implicit messages about who the interactants are, and who they are to one another, can be highly valued.

Adaptive Message Design

A second implication of conceptualizing enacted support as rhetorical is to focus attention on the features of messages or conversations that are well-suited (or poorly suited) to accomplishing multiple purposes. Any message or conversation has innumerable features that might be studied (O'Keefe, 1987), including various aspects of what people say, how they say it, when they say it, and so on. Conceptualizing the problem of enacting social support as responding to task, identity, and relational purposes provides a basis for formulating hypotheses about why messages with some features are more likely to receive a positive evaluation than messages without those features or with other features. We study those features of messages that can be expected to influence judgments about how well the enacted support facilitated coping (task purpose) while simultaneously enacting valued identities and relational qualities.

For example, imagine two support providers who each offer a $500 loan to a friend stressed by financial difficulties. One loan is offered spontaneously, in a warm tone, and with a reminder of a past relational history of give and take and pleasure in being able to assist. The other offer occurs only after a prolonged discussion in which the recipient has to explicitly ask for a loan, and the lender replies with a tone of resignation and expression of concern about when it will be repaid. The sequencing of the offer in the conversation, the nonverbal cues that accompany it, and the other topics discussed serve to define quite different relationships and identities. These, in turn, seem likely to affect the perceived usefulness of the loan in coping with stress. Although the substance of enacted support is the same and equally appropriate to the task of replacing a missing resource, the offerings differ in their adaptability to the multiple purposes of enacted support. A pattern of findings quite similar to this hypothetical example may be found in Kitson and Holmes's (1992) longitudinal study of adaptation following divorce. Divorcees who initially received services (e.g., babysitting, being driven places, or invitations to events) or financial support had lower levels of distress 2 to 3 years later, as did those who received information and guidance but not tangible support. However, those who reported receiving services or financial support *coupled with* information and guidance experienced higher levels of distress than those who received no help at all.[17] The combination of tangible aid with advice appeared to undermine the message of solidarity and care; help came with strings attached, so that recipients felt obligated to follow the advice as a condition of receiving aid. The authors concluded that to predict the usefulness of support, it is necessary to understand the relational meanings associated with various types and combinations of support.

Situation as Constraint and Construction

Rhetorical adaptation involves responsiveness not only to the task, identity, and relational purposes that inhere in any instance of enacted support but also to the situationally specific forms these take. The likelihood that risks and costs to identity and relationship are realized, and the particular form they take, vary from one conversation to the next. So, for example, the degree to which giving advice risks being perceived as "butting in" is likely to depend on the advice giver's expertise with a particular problem, the closeness of the parties involved, and the sociocultural background of the participants (Goldsmith & Fitch, 1997).

However, the notion of rhetorical adaptation to a situation is not simply a process of objectively lining up an optimal combination of variables. If a supportive message succeeds, it is not simply or only because of the proper alignment of source characteristics, recipient characteristics, relational status, and/or any other of a myriad of possible variables. Particular features of the person speaking, the recipient of the message, the type of problem, and so on may make some kinds of messages and some ways of saying a message more plausible or appropriate than others (e.g., a speaker with

---

[17] Kitson and Holmes also controlled for the level of distress at time 1 to attempt to rule out the alternative explanation that those with the highest levels of distress were more likely to receive a combination of types of support. Although this attenuated the effects, the basic pattern of results remained significant.

great expertise and a close relationship to the hearer might be in a better position to give advice than a stranger with little knowledge of a problem). However, there is also room for the message uttered to shape the way participants view the speaker, the hearer, the problem, and other relevant factors (e.g., giving advice in a passionate and concerned manner could suggest to the hearer that the speaker is more expert and feels closer to the hearer than the hearer might have expected).

Thus, a rhetorical approach to the study of enacted support emphasizes how the situation can shape and constrain what is likely to be effective but also recognizes the ways in which language shapes and constrains how we see a situation and what we see as relevant within a situation. Identifying the features of talk through which this occurs is part of understanding the resources skilled communicators may use to bring about effective social support. Support is not just paint-by-the numbers – it is a practical art with situational constraints, styles, and techniques but also with creativity and adaptation.

CONCLUSION

Enacted support is communication. Rather than viewing it as an objectively defined behavior to be counted or as a subjectively experienced perception lodged in individual cognition, I propose to view enacted support as meaningful social action, situated within particular contexts, and undertaken for purposes by which its success may be evaluated (by participants and researchers alike). It is possible, and useful, to focus on observable features of talk in a context and to provide systematic explanation for how these features may be related to participants' understandings and evaluations of the support they experience.

The approach I take is a hybrid developed from the cross-pollination of the experimental and survey-oriented research that has characterized the study of enacted social support and the discourse analytic, ethnographic, and conversation analytic work that has characterized the study of troubles talk. In contrast to a focus on the amount or frequency of support and its distal effect on individual outcomes, I examine what is said in the enactment of support and how it is said. Although the literature on troubles talk shares this focus on discourse, it has not typically focused on how discourse features and participants' evaluations of them might be linked to coping with stress or to relationship satisfaction. I am not only interested in exploring processes through which actions are constituted and coordination is achieved; I also believe that these are preconditions for the effects messages will have on participants. The program of research I report in this book provides descriptions and reconceptualizations of the features of talk in which social support is enacted. In addition, I begin to explore some of the most immediate effects that these features of talk have on participants: the evaluations participants give to enacted social support.

These assumptions about the nature of enacted support point to a different kind of research agenda that asks new questions, using different concepts and yielding conclusions that are different from but complementary to those common in the literature on social support or in the literature on troubles talk. Subsequent chapters show how application of these assumptions provides a new take on several puzzles in our understanding of enacted support. Under what circumstances is advice an effective form of support? Why haven't matching models been more successful? How do we account for the relational nature of social support as assisted coping?

3

Communicating Advice

When someone close to us discloses a stress or problem, it is quite common to respond with advice about how to resolve or improve the situation (Cutrona, 1986; Cutrona & Suhr, 1994; D'Augelli & Levy, 1978; Goldsmith & Dun, 1997; Horowitz et al., 2001; Laireiter, Baumann, Perkonigg, & Himmelbauer, 1997; Reisman & Shorr, 1980). However, advice receives quite mixed evaluations from recipients, even in situations when we might expect it to be helpful (Cutrona & Suhr, 1994; Dunkel-Schetter, 1984; Dunkel-Schetter et al., 1992; Laireiter et al., 1997; Lehman et al., 1986; Notarius & Herrick, 1988; Pearlin & McCall, 1990; Pistrang et al., 2001; Tripathi et al., 1986; Zich & Temoshok, 1987). Research on coping suggests when people experience a controllable problem, it is adaptive to engage in problem-solving efforts (for reviews, see Aldwin, 1994; Thoits, 1995). Yet when others attempt to assist with problem-solving efforts by offering suggestions about what to do, the effects are quite varied. Why is advice not more widely appreciated and why do people persist in offering a type of support with such dicey prospects for success?

In this chapter, I develop an explanation for these puzzling findings and describe some of the conditions under which advice may be a useful type of enacted support. Using the framework described in Chapter 2, I view advice as one way of pursuing the communicative task of assisted coping. The likelihood that advice is an appropriate response is shaped by the degree to which it is adapted to the problem about which it is given and by the way in which the actual formulation of advice, and its coordination within a conversation, are adapted to the identity and relational implications of seeking, giving, and receiving advice.

To understand why advice poses a puzzle, it is useful to provide a critical review of the empirical research on its reception and effects and the explanations for these findings offered by other researchers. Then I summarize findings from a series of studies I have conducted, which show

how a communication approach accounts for when and why advice can be helpful.

ADVICE IN THE TROUBLES TALK OF CLOSE RELATIONAL PARTNERS

Although many of the findings about advice reveal contradiction and ambiguity, one clear finding that emerges is the frequency with which close relational partners give advice to one another. For example, in tape-recorded conversations of spouses discussing problems, Cutrona and Suhr (1994) reported advice was the most common type of response: 97% of the participants offered advice or factual input at least once in a 10-minute interaction. Studies by Carels and Baucom (1999) and Barker and Lemle (1984) also show high frequencies of advice giving in the troubles talk conversations of spouses. Reisman and Shorr (1980) found that across the life span (participants ranging from Grade 2 to age 65), advice was a common response to a friend's disclosure of a problem, more common than expressions of empathy and accounting for 35% of all responses. In a study of divorced women, more than two-thirds reported that friends gave advice about their divorce and about personal matters and more than half reported advice given by close family members (Henderson & Argyle, 1985). Even adolescents, who may have concerns about establishing autonomy from parental oversight and suggestions, report seeking and receiving advice from their parents. In one study, early adolescents reported receiving more "directive guidance" than any other form of support (Hosley, 1999). In a diary study of everyday interactions with all significant others over a 14-day period, Cutrona (1986) found advice was the second most frequently occurring type of helping behavior ("listening to confidences" occurred just slightly more frequently, perhaps because disclosing a problem is prerequisite to engaging in any kind of helpful talk about it).

Although advice is a frequent response to a close other's disclosure of a problem, it is not always appreciated (Cramer, 1990; Cutrona & Suhr, 1994; Davidowitz & Myrick, 1984; Dunkel-Schetter, 1984; Dunkel-Schetter et al., 1992; Laireiter et al., 1997; Lehman et al., 1986; Pearlin & McCall, 1990; Picard, Lee, & Hunsley, 1997; Pistrang et al., 2001; Young et al., 1982; Zich & Temoshok, 1987). For example, Dunkel-Schetter and her colleagues (1992) summarize findings from a number of studies of the behaviors perceived as helpful or unhelpful by individuals coping with health problems and life crises (e.g., individuals who were bereaved and persons with cancer, AIDS, diabetes). Advice was occasionally identified as a helpful form of social support, especially when it was given by those with expertise or similar experience, but it was more often mentioned as an example of an unhelpful attempt at support. Cramer (1990) asked students to rate the helpfulness of thirty-two different support behaviors a close friend might say in response to a personal problem or upsetting experience. The mean ratings of help-fulness placed advice squarely in the middle of the thirty-two behaviors, neither *very helpful* nor *very unhelpful*. Young and colleagues (1982) report similar findings in a sample of adults in two rural communities. In interviews with recently divorced parents, Picard and colleagues (1997) found one-third of their sample desired advice from their own parents, whereas another one-third reported receiving unwanted advice. Pearlin and McCall (1990) interviewed twenty-five couples about the support they gave to and received from their spouse for problems experienced at work. Although partners were generally satisfied with the support they received from one another, Pearlin and McCall found that "in most instances where respondents report dissatisfaction with the support given by their spouses, they point to unwanted or untimely advice as the reason" (p. 55). A study of individuals who had lost a loved one in the last 5 years found advice was the most common response reported but it was nearly always recalled as unhelpful (Davidowitz & Myrick, 1984).

One account for the frequency of advice and for its problematic reception is that giving advice is an unskilled and inferior way of responding to another person's difficulties. In the late 1970s and early 1980s, several programs of research sought to make informal helpers more effective by training them to reduce advice giving and other directive responses and to increase nondirective responses such as reflective listening (for reviews, see D'Augelli, Vallance, Danish, Young, & Gerdes, 1981; D'Augelli & Vallance, 1982; Wiesenfeld & Weis, 1979). This strategy was grounded in techniques of nondirective counseling, in which therapeutic change is believed to be facilitated by providing an accepting environment (e.g., conveying genuineness, unconditional regard, and empathy) that enables clients to explore their feelings and find their own solutions (e.g., Carkhuff, 1969; Danish & D'Augelli, 1976; Rogers, 1957). Surprisingly, these interventions were undertaken with little empirical exploration of whether the techniques of professional counselors provide a valid basis for describing what *laypersons* should do in their *personal relationships* (Cramer, 1987).

Subsequent studies that have compared evaluations indicate laypersons and helping professionals hold differing views about what is helpful (Pistrang, Clare, & Barker, 1999). In studies of reactions to nondirective support offered by nonprofessionals, students preferred a friend or peer counselor who gave advice to one who adopted a style modeled on nondirective counseling techniques (Barnet & Harris, 1984; Reisman & Yamokoski, 1974). In addition, there is evidence that in close personal relationships, giving advice does not preclude communicating empathy, genuineness, and unconditional regard (Cramer, 1987; Pistrang et al., 2001). Reviews of research on the effectiveness of social support interventions (e.g., Gottlieb, 1974, 1985a; Rook & Dooley, 1985) caution against interventions that attempt to make laypersons into paraprofessionals without better understanding of how responses such as advice operate in their natural context, a reservation acknowledged by those involved in the advice-extinguishing interventions as well (D'Augelli et al., 1981; Wiesenfeld & Weis, 1979).

A contrasting explanation for the mixed evaluations of advice is that advice is not necessarily unskilled or undesirable; instead, the appropriateness of advice (compared to some other type of enacted social support) depends on the situation (e.g., Cohen & McKay, 1984; Cramer, 1990; Cutrona & Russell, 1990; Horowitz et al., 2001). For example, Cutrona and Russell (1990) propose that different types of stressful events call for different forms of coping and, consequently, different forms of social support will be an optimal match to the needs of the distressed person. One dimension along which stressful events vary is the controllability of the situation. They propose that advice (and other forms of information and guidance) will be most helpful in challenging or threatening situations in which negative consequences can be prevented or altered. In contrast, uncontrollable situations involving harm or loss to which the individual must simply accommodate create needs for emotional and instrumental support rather than advice. It is not only the advice *recipient's* control over his or her problem that influences the appropriateness of advice but also the degree to which the advice *giver* has control over the problem or expertise with similar problems (Cutrona & Suhr, 1992). Advice givers who have more control and expertise will be seen as better sources of advice than those without control or expertise. This is consistent with findings from other studies indicating, for example, that cancer patients found advice more helpful from physicians than from family or friends (Dakof & Taylor, 1990).

In a test of their optimal matching model, Cutrona and Suhr (1992) asked spouses to discuss stressful situations in their lives while observers coded the occurrence of action-facilitating support (including information, advice, factual input, feedback, and offers to provide goods or services) or nurturant support (including expressions of caring, concern, empathy, or sympathy as well as offers of inclusion in group activities) and rated the degree to which each spouse had expertise on the problem or the ability to influence the problem. Spouses were satisfied with information, advice, or offers of assistance they received if the *spouse providing* the support was rated by observers as having expertise or control over the problem. However, recipients of action-facilitating support were less satisfied when observers rated the *recipient* as having expertise or control over his or her own problem.

In a second study (Cutrona & Suhr, 1994), spouses rather than observers rated how much control they could exert over the problems they discussed. Advice recipients' ratings of own and spouse control over the problem were unrelated to their satisfaction with action-facilitating support. In post hoc analyses, Cutrona and Suhr reasoned that when discussing a problem with school or work, the spouse with the problem would have greater control than when discussing a problem with health or relationships. Consequently, they predicted advice from one's spouse would be less welcome in the context of work or school stressors and this hypothesis was supported. After disclosing a work or school stressor, individuals reported more depressed mood when a spouse gave frequent advice; however, when disclosing a problem that was not related to work or school, receiving advice from one's spouse was associated with less depressed mood.

Horowitz and colleagues (2001) found further support for the situational appropriateness of advice in a study of college students interacting in an experiment. One member of each stranger pair was asked to describe a current or recent problem; some students were told to focus on a problem that required action, whereas others were instructed to talk about a problem that produced negative feelings. The listeners in each pair were instructed either to "help your partner solve the problem" or "try to understand and empathize." Following a 4-minute interaction, both participants rated their performance and reported on positive and negative affect. Participants were most likely to desire future interaction with their partner in conditions when the type of problem matched the type of response provided (i.e., a problem requiring action met with problem-solving assistance, or a problem producing negative affect met with understanding and empathy). Participants also reported significantly lower levels of negative affect in the matched conditions compared to the unmatched conditions.

Taking into account the situational appropriateness of advice advances our understanding of when and how advice may be a helpful (or unhelpful) response. However, this approach still treats all instances of advice as equal, without respect to the quality of the advice. Cutrona and Suhr (1992, 1994) also focused on the sheer quantity of advice and its correlation with evaluations and outcomes. If we are to take into account the quality of advice, as well as its occurrence or quantity, it is useful to focus on what advice givers say and how they say it – issues of communication.

AN ALTERNATIVE MODEL: COMMUNICATING ADVICE

The communication approach developed in Chapter 2 suggests effective support is adapted to the situation and to the multiple purposes of assisted coping. Advice will be more likely to be perceived as helpful when it satisfies three conditions: (1) it is an appropriate type of support for the problem, (2) the content of the advice is useful, and (3) the way in which the advice is communicated is responsive not only to the task of assisting with problem solving but also to the identity and relational implications of directing another person's behavior. Condition (1) has been explored in studies such as those summarized previously. Conditions (2) and (3) require a kind of focused attention to the content and style of communication that has largely been missing in research on advice.

As previous studies have demonstrated, advice is more likely to be helpful if provider and recipient see the situation as one in which problem-solving coping is appropriate. (In Chapter 4, I elaborate further on how provider and recipient may come to view a situation as more or less controllable, but for now, I assume that some types of stressful situations are more controllable than others and this shapes the degree to which advice will be useful.) Advice can assist with problem-solving coping by pointing out actions the other has not considered, by validating actions one has begun to consider but about which one is still uncertain, or by simply encouraging a problem-solving discussion of various options, including those advised as well as alternatives. The willingness to engage in problem solving together can also signal caring.

Just as no one type of coping is effective in all situations, no one type of coping assistance will be uniformly helpful. Advice may not be the best choice for facilitating emotion-focused coping and many advisers are motivated by a desire to alleviate their own discomfort rather than by an assessment of what the other needs (Burleson & Goldsmith, 1998). The frequency of advice in close relationships suggests that many support providers likely rely on advice as their first and most common response. If we assume, as seems reasonable, that problems vary in their controllability, then some of the advice that is given in troubles talk in close relationships fails because it is not appropriate to the situation. This may explain some instances of unappreciated advice.

Even in situations in which advice is a potentially appropriate response, however, an advice giver might go wrong in the particular advice given or in the manner of communicating the advice. The second and third conditions for effective advice giving explore these possibilities. The content of advice can vary in quality so that the helpfulness of advice depends on *what*, specifically, is advised. Some pieces of advice are smarter, more practical, more attainable, than other pieces of advice. Although this is obvious to anyone who has ever received bad advice, it is seldom taken into account in studies of the helpfulness of advice. Typically, researchers code for the presence/absence or sheer frequency of advice. This implicitly assumes that bad advice would be better than none at all or that multiple ill-considered suggestions would necessarily be better than one especially wise recommendation. Finding a way to assess the quality of advice is quite challenging because such an assessment depends on particulars of the person and problem, but the failure to assess quality may explain why some studies find no systematic relationships between advice frequency and perceived helpfulness.[1]

---

[1] This can also explain why some studies (e.g., the studies by Cutrona & Suhr, 1992, 1994, summarized above) find that expressions of emotional support are helpful across a wide range of conditions, whereas the effects of advice are much more contingent on features of the problem and advice giver. Informational support and advice are defined in such a way

Finally, the perceived helpfulness of advice is influenced by *how* the advice is given and its symbolic implications for identity and relationship. Even when a problem is amenable to solutions and the advice given is a useful suggestion, the advice may be experienced as unhelpful if it is delivered in a critical or condescending manner. A number of previous studies of advice, including my own, have usefully conceptualized the identity and relational implications of advice giving in terms of the concept of face. *Face* refers to "the socially situated identities people claim or attribute to others" (Tracy, 1990, p. 210). Individuals are emotionally invested in successfully performing particular identities in an interaction and in having others' actions sustain those performances (Goffman, 1967). So, for example, in seeking advice from my spouse for a problem I am experiencing at work, I may wish to appear as someone who is competent in her job, though experiencing a legitimate difficulty for which some degree of stress is a reasonable response. I may also be projecting an image of a partner in a close and caring relationship, in which both parties share many aspects of their experience and interact as peers in solving problems together. These identities will be threatened if the advice I receive from my spouse challenges my image as a competent worker (e.g., by suggesting a solution I perceive as patently obvious or by giving a reasonable solution but in a condescending tone) or as a particular kind of spouse (e.g., by implying that it is inappropriate for me to bring a work problem up at home or by failing to devote adequate attention to the discussion).

An infinite variety of particular identities could be at stake in any troubles talk conversation in which advice occurs. Fleshing out the example of spouses discussing a work problem suggests additional identities that might come in to play. If the particular work problem involves dealing with sexist behavior by a coworker, we could imagine that identities as "woman," "person of principle," "feminist," "person with a sense of humor," and the like might be relevant and affirmed or undermined by the spouse's advice to "confront the jerk," or "maybe you should be less sensitive about these things." Considering the spouses' prior history of

that they include wise, useful, well-informed contributions as well as foolish, irrelevant, or impractical contributions. In contrast, emotional support is often operationalized so that it includes only a portion of the range of ways in which people attempt to assist with emotion-focused coping. For example, Cutrona and Suhr (1992) define nurturant support to include expressions of closeness and love, shows of physical affection, promises of confidentiality, expressions of sympathy, listening, understanding, empathy, encouragement, and prayer. In contrast, other researchers have included in emotional support those types of behaviors that may attempt to manage the emotions of others but are likely less effective in doing so (e.g., distraction, minimizing the problem, and denying the emotion; see, for example, Burleson, 1994; Barbee & Cunningham, 1995). When emotional support is defined to include a full range of ways in which one person might attempt to assist in managing another person's emotions, then it too receives varied ratings, with some attempts perceived as more helpful and supportive than others.

discussing the problem raises other identities that might be relevant. Whether prior advice about the same problem has been heeded might call into question whether the advice seeker is an active problem solver who is seeking alternative solutions versus a complainer who fails to take appropriate actions.

The myriad of identities that might be at stake in any given interaction resist generalization. One useful framework for examining these processes across particular conversations is that offered in Brown and Levinson's politeness theory (1987).[2] They identify two facets of identity that cut across the situation-specific images that are performed. *Positive face wants* are individuals' desires to receive approval and appreciation for the specific identities enacted in an interaction. *Negative face wants* refer to the desire that others display respect for the autonomy and deference that are appropriate to a particular identity (i.e., a desire *not* to be imposed on). Positive face wants move individuals to approach others, seeking connection and solidarity, whereas negative face wants move individuals to avoid infringing on one another, keeping a respectful distance. In this way, identity support is closely tied up with relational definitions. A failure to support identity performances can reflect on the closeness of relational partners, their degree of similarity and understanding, their power or expertise relative to one another, and their respect for one another's autonomy.

An understanding of positive and negative face wants helps to account for why advice is a potentially hazardous response to a close relational partner's trouble. Although we may recognize that advice is intended as help with problem solving, we may resent the way in which telling us what to do can undermine our self-presentation as competent, independent adults capable of managing our own lives. Whether an action is interpreted as face threatening, and the specific type of face threat that is implied, depend on inferences a hearer draws about what the speaker is attempting to do (Wilson, Aleman, & Leatham, 1998). In the context of troubles talk, the identity and relational issues may include questions about whether one who gives advice is truly concerned for the hearer or simply attempting to exercise control, whether one who seeks or receives advice is capable of solving his or her own problems, whether the recipient of advice is obligated to follow it, and whether the identification of a solution to the problem implies that further expression of distress is unreasonable or self-indulgent (Goldsmith, 1999).

In turn, the inferences partners draw are shaped by the *manner* in which the advice is communicated. For example, imagine a conversation over the fence with the next door neighbor (who happens to be a dietician) in which the neighbor responds to a comment about feeling tired by volunteering "you really ought to lose fifty pounds." The advice may be recognized as helpful in its intention but runs the risk of threat to positive and negative face. If, instead of "you really ought to lose fifty pounds," the neighbor said "I found I had a lot more energy after I lost weight" or "Have you thought about losing some weight?" the face threat may be muted (though the intent to give advice and the precision of the advice are muted as well). Similarly, that the neighbor offers advice unsolicited poses a greater risk than if the advice followed a request for guidance. Research on face work suggests subtle variations in how face threatening actions are communicated and can influence how they are interpreted and evaluated (see Goldsmith, in press, for a review).

Whether threats to identity are realized also depends on the relational and cultural *context*. A close relationship between the neighbors and the advice giver's perceived authority to give the advice (e.g., by virtue of expertise) would likely reduce the risk that the advice is heard as butting in. Conversely, it may well be that advice about losing weight is a particularly sensitive topic in the culture to which the neighbors belong, so that the relationship would have to be very close, or the advice giver's authority very high, to justify so bold an intrusion. In contrast, advice about brands of fertilizer for the lawn would likely be a less sensitive topic. Brown and Levinson (1987) usefully crystalize these types of situational considerations into three factors: the power between speaker and hearer, the closeness or similarity between speaker and hearer, and the "rank" or culturally understood sensitivity of the action in question.

Manner of communicating and context are reciprocally and dynamically related such that preexisting perceptions of particular relationships may shape choices about how to convey a face-threatening action such as advice. At the same time, the way in which one chooses to communicate advice enacts a particular kind of relationship. Neighbors who are not yet very close might be more reluctant to offer advice in a blunt and unsolicited way; however, doing so might be one way (albeit a risky way!) of demonstrating one's belief that they are (or desire to be) close. Similarly, by saying "you really ought to lose fifty pounds," to the neighbor may sound more like a dietician, whereas saying "I found I had a lot more energy after I lost weight" may sound more like a friend.

Rather than viewing advice as an intrinsically problematic response to another's disclosure of trouble, this alternative framework suggests that advice may be quite helpful when it is adapted to the situation in which it occurs and to potentially conflicting task, identity, and relational purposes. In contrast to other models of situational adaptation, this framework emphasizes not only the appropriateness of problem-solving assistance for controllable problems but also the actual quality of advice and how it is communicated. Advice is a challenging type of action because it can threaten face and this is especially true in troubles talk conversations. Even when it is recognized as well-intended, advice can raise potentially troubling inferences about each partner's motivation, obligation, competence, and autonomy. When these risks are juxtaposed against the possible benefits of advice, participants in troubles talk conversations may experience dilemmas as to how they can best accomplish the task of assisted coping while sustaining desirable identities and relational definitions.

EMPIRICAL SUPPORT FOR THE MODEL

This framework for understanding reactions to advice in troubles talk conversations has evolved through a program of empirical studies. Using a variety of methods and measures, I have accumulated substantial support for the following key tenants of this model:

1. Advice has implications for identities and relationships that result in challenges and dilemmas.
2. Advice is seen as more useful in some situations than others and, even in the same situation, some pieces of advice are seen as better than other pieces of advice.
3. Advice that is seen as honoring valued identities and relational qualities is seen as more effective than advice that undermines identities and relationships.
4. How advice is given contributes to its perceived helpfulness, sensitivity, and supportiveness.

In what follows, I summarize the empirical support for each of these tenants.

Challenges and Dilemmas of Advice

Previous research on reactions to advice given in close relationships made clear that advice was not uniformly appreciated by recipients. This led me to wonder: What does advice mean to those who give and receive it? Why do close relational partners seek or give advice and under what circumstances do they feel it is appropriate to do so? What factors shape advice recipients' reactions to the advice they receive? Theories of identity and face suggested that threats to face might be one reason why advice was a controversial type of social support but these general theories left unanswered many questions about the meanings and purposes attributed to advice in particular cultural, relational, and conversational contexts.

Kristine Fitch and I pursued these questions in an ethnographic study of seeking, giving, and receiving advice among some white, middle-class, college-educated adults (Goldsmith & Fitch, 1997). Our research team engaged in observation of advice in the naturally occurring settings of our everyday lives in a western university community, two different midwestern university communities, and a large eastern metropolitan area. We also conducted ethnographic interviews with friends, family, and coworkers and with others referred to us by these contacts. Through methods of qualitative analysis, we developed descriptions of three dilemmas of seeking, giving, and receiving advice as well as some of the contextual factors that shaped the experience of these dilemmas and the evaluation of advice (see the Community Advice Study in the Appendix for additional information about participants and procedures).

We found clear evidence that advice can be a valued form of assistance for coping with problems of everyday life. We saw and heard about instances when advice provided expert opinion on how to solve a problem or simply another point of view on a difficulty or decision. Advice could also be part of a conversation in which various options were presented and evaluated. The participants in our study would have readily concurred with researchers' categorizations of advice as a form of informational support. However, our participants also made clear that advice was seldom just about information. The identity and relational implications of seeking, giving, and receiving advice came through clearly, both in the accounts of participants and in our own observations. These multiple meanings and purposes of advice produced the potential for three dilemmas: (1) a dilemma between being helpful and caring versus butting in, (2) a dilemma between being honest versus supportive, and (3) a dilemma between appearing autonomous and competent versus disrespectful and ungrateful.

Being Helpful and Caring versus Butting in

In addition to the problem-solving utility of advice, our respondents discussed the relational caring it expressed. For example, when asked why he gives advice, one 22-year-old man explained, "My friends and I give advice because we are friends and we care about each other. . . . If I saw them having a problem with something, I would offer my advice." Conversely, we found instances in which a close relational partner's refusal to give advice about a problem when asked was taken as a lack of caring.

Juxtaposed against the task-related utility of advice and the relational message of caring were other, potentially problematic, meanings of advice for identities and relationship. Consistent with Cutrona and Suhr's (1994) findings about advice given by spouses, we found that advice given in a variety of close relationships can imply that the giver has greater expertise or influence relative to the recipient. Several young adults in our study objected to advice from their parents because they felt it continued a childish identity and undermined their attempts to be seen as adults. Several married interviewees said they were careful about giving advice to or receiving advice from their mates. One 40-year-old woman reflected that "Maybe if you're trying to have an egalitarian marriage, giving advice or asking for it seems to put one person on a higher level than the other and it disrupts it, so we're careful not to do that." Another 35-year-old woman explained her reluctance to advise her siblings because "we're so close in age and everything, to offer suggestions would sound like 'See, I have my life so together I know just what you ought to do about yours.'" These threats to individual identity and to relational symmetry were captured with the negative judgment that an advice giver was "butting in."

In some relationships and for some problems, the power asymmetry and relational implications of giving advice do not detract from its helpfulness. However, the risk of asserting a claim to greater expertise (and the corresponding implication of lesser expertise and competence for the recipient) can undermine otherwise positive reactions to advice. Across a variety of episodes and participants, we identified contextual features that were salient in reaching an evaluation of advice. Acknowledged expertise or experience legitimated the giving of advice, so that differences in knowledge were an acceptable part of the identities and relational definition of the parties in a particular episode. In some situations, advice seekers intentionally sought out advice givers whom they perceived as different in some key way (e.g., women seeking advice from men or vice versa) because they believed the different point of view entailed by contrasting identities provided a valuable basis for information to which they would not otherwise have access. Relational closeness was also salient in interpreting advice giving as an expression of caring rather than butting in. Finally, respondents complained that unsolicited advice ran a risk of butting in where it was not desired. When one party asks the other for advice, it not only makes clear that informational assistance is desired, but it also suggests a willingness to accept the asymmetry of identities and relational power that advice implies.

Being Supportive versus Being Honest

When an advice giver's frank assessment of a situation is at odds with what an advice seeker is doing or is leaning toward doing, advice runs the risk of being critical rather than comforting and of being judged as "unsupportive." In some instances, an advice giver may not be sure whether to simply give advice that agrees with what the recipient appears to want to hear or whether to state what he or she believes is the best course of action, even though that may be at odds with the advice seeker's preferences. A young adult framed this dilemma as an opposition between support and honesty. She described an interaction with her mother, who was talking about the stressful decision to move in the aftermath of a divorce. The daughter said her mother did not really want to move but had also engaged in repeated conversations about the difficulties of remaining in their old house. At one point in the conversation, the mother asked the daughter for her advice, and the daughter reported that the relationally appropriate (but potentially challenging) response was to "support the other but be honest."

As this example illustrates, this dilemma arises in part from potential ambiguity in the intentions of relational partners who disclose problems and ask for advice. Honesty was frequently mentioned as a valuable char- acteristic of advice and advice givers. However, we encountered in our observation and interviews instances in which advice seekers asked for advice after having already reached (or nearly reached) a decision about what to do. In these instances, advice givers may feel as if the request for advice is disingenuous: The seeker wanted to appear to be engaging in problem solving but was, in fact, fishing for approval. To withhold what one feels is the best information is to risk one's identity as honest and to fail in the expectation that close relational partners want what is best for one another. However, to advocate for a course of action the other disprefers may call into question the other's competence, the partners' similarity, or the advice giver's loyalty. This dilemma resembles a larger set of issues Rawlins (1983) has characterized as intrinsic to friendship. Friends are ob- ligated to honestly express to one another their beliefs – and doubly so when a concern for the other's well-being is at issue. However, friends are also expected to show restraint and discretion when their candid opinion might cause hurt or anger.

This dilemma is not intractable, of course, but it calls for skill and tact in communicating the disagreeable advice. For example, we observed oc- casions when an advice seeker solicited permission to be honest or used the preface "honestly" before giving advice. Though simple and subtle, observed uses of this strategy served to forewarn the advice recipient that the advice might be disagreeable but that it was offered in the spirit of a valued attribute of individual identity and of close relationships.

Showing Gratitude and Respect versus Making One's Own Decisions
A third dilemma concerns the recipient's orientation toward acting on ad- vice. Because advice can express the giver's desire to be helpful and car- ing, recipients may feel pressure to follow the advice given so as not to disrespect the giver or appear ungrateful for his or her concern. However, following others' advice may threaten one's own image as competent and autonomous.

When asked why they sought advice, many respondents mentioned the respect they had for the giver. This respect not only flows from expertise on a particular problem but also implies a more global affirmation of the other's good judgment, competence, and concern. For example, a 32-year- old man in our study discussed how he felt that his relationship to his parents was becoming more symmetrical as they aged. To him, their will- ingness to seek and take his advice was a potent expression of their respect for him as an adult. Our respondents also spoke about giving advice as a positive relational move for which one could feel grateful. A 32-year-old woman explained, "If you offer help [by giving advice], you're offering friendship." To fail to take advice seriously or to reject advice risks showing a lack of gratitude for the giver's concern and a lack of interest in the relational bond that is implied. However, taking advice may involve swallowing pride, admitting dependence, or accepting control. Even advice that is acknowledged to be instrumentally sound may threaten a recipient's self-image as an autonomous adult, capable of conducting his or her own affairs with competence.

How far advice recipients were expected to go in taking advice was variable. In many instances, participants reported that all that was required was to listen to the advice and to "take it seriously." We noted that nearly one-third of all of the episodes of advice we observed ended with formulaic expressions of gratitude and respect, such as "all right," "you're right," "sounds good," "I'll do that," and/or "thanks." In some relationships and episodes, this interactional stance may be sufficient, even if the advice is not taken. There were other instances in our data in which failing to act on advice implied rejection of the giver's competence and caring, with corresponding negative implications for the relationship.

Observing and listening to respondents' advice experiences made clear the ways in which assistance with problem-solving coping is intertwined with partners' understandings of their identities and relationships. In turn, our respondents' evaluations of the usefulness of advice were based not only on the value of the advice for solving a problem or making a decision but also on the way advice made them feel about themselves and their relationship. Sometimes, giving advice was a rewarding way of helping a loved one cope more effectively while reaffirming a caring relationship and enacting valued individual identities. In other situations, the advice that might be most useful was challenging to give because of the ways in which it could undermine one or both partner's images of self and relationship. Relational partners took into account features of the situation as well as nuances of the conversation as they navigated these task, identity, and relational cross-currents.

Adaptation to the Situation

A second assumption of my model that I have examined in several studies is that advice is seen as more useful in some situations than others and, even in the same situation, some pieces of advice are seen as better than other pieces of advice. As we have seen, other researchers have also pointed to the importance of adapting advice to the situation if the advice is to be well-received. Previous research has frequently emphasized the controllability of a problem as a key dimension to which advice must be adapted and has characterized the adaptation required as "do/do not give advice." The ethnographic study I have just summarized makes it clear that a variety of other situational features figure into evaluations of advice and that the nature of adaptation goes beyond a simple decision to give or not to give advice. For example, participants mentioned relational qualities such as closeness, similarity, experience, expertise, and power as relevant to their judgments of advice. The temporal unfolding of the advice recipient's decision-making process (e.g., still weighing options, leaning toward a particular solution, or already committed to a course of action) figures into the interpretation of advice seeking and the evaluation of advice received. Features of the conversation itself shaped interpretations of advice and served as resources for making advice more palatable. Participants mentioned whether the advice was solicited as an important feature of talk and we also observed recurring patterns that may be meaningful (e.g., prefacing disagreeable advice with a disclaimer about "honesty," concluding a segment in which advice is offered with a ritual show of gratitude).

Another facet of situational adaptation is the substance of the advice that is given and its utility for a particular problem. Even in a situation in which advice is a potentially appropriate type of social support, some pieces of advice are perceived as better than others. Evidence for this assumption comes from two studies I have conducted (Goldsmith & MacGeorge, 2000; Goldsmith, McDermott, & Alexander, 2000) in which respondents read about a hypothetical situation and then rated the effectiveness of one or more pieces of advice.[3] In each study, we examined multiple examples of advice, making it possible to estimate the amount of variability in ratings that may be attributed to different advice messages. In the same hypothetical situation (e.g., a failed exam), messages that had different substantive pieces of advice (e.g., go talk to the professor versus study harder) received significantly different ratings. These differences accounted for 12 to 24% of the variability in respondent ratings. Although we do not know for certain what particular features account for message-to-message variability, it is clear that not all instances of advice are equivalent.

Taking into account the quality of advice given is a challenging task because each problem situation presents a range of possible advised actions, some of them distinctive to the person and his or her problem. Although some of these person-specific and situation-specific determinants

---

[3] The studies used similar scales to measure the perceived usefulness of advice. Goldsmith and MacGeorge (2000) used semantic differential-type scales anchored by effective/ ineffective, helpful/unhelpful, appropriate/inappropriate, and sensitive/insensitive. In a subsequent study (Goldsmith, et al., 2000) we developed separate measures of problem-solving utility (e.g., helpful/unhelpful), relational assurance (supportive/unsupportive), and emotional awareness (e.g., sensitive/insensitive). The effect sizes reported here are based on the sum for each set of items.

of quality defy generalization, for common life events or problems there are common themes in the advice given (Goldsmith, 1999). Many college students perform poorly on an exam and hear from their friends that they should "study harder" or "forget it and go have a beer." Many new parents struggling with sleep deprivation encounter common themes in the advice of friends and family to "let the baby cry it out" or to "bring your baby to bed with you."

Once we identify some of the common themes in advice for a particular problem, there are a variety of ways to go about tapping differences in the quality of advice. Quality might be established by patterns of preference within a group. For example, MacGeorge, Lichtman, and Pressey (2002) studied students' responses to a hypothetical scenario in which a friend failed an exam. Students rated "talk to the professor" as significantly more effective than "study harder" and "study harder" received significantly better ratings than "drop the class." For some kinds of stressors and for some kinds of research purposes, it may be useful to differentiate advice quality on the basis of expert recommendations. For example, medical practitioners make normative recommendations about the types and levels of activity that are advisable at various stages in a heart patient's recovery and about dietary choices that might reduce the likelihood of recurring problems. These could provide a yardstick against which to compare advice received from laypersons about resuming activities or consuming food. O'Reilly and Thomas (1989) studied men who had participated in a cardiac risk reduction program to see how social support might contribute to maintaining an improved physical risk status (i.e., blood pressure, serum cholesterol, smoking, use of health services). General measures of social support did not consistently predict whether the men maintained an improved risk status 3 years after the conclusion of the risk reduction program. In contrast, the degree to which participants reported support that was specific to risk reduction was a significant predictor. Men who received information and advice that was specific to their risk reduction efforts were more likely to sustain physical gains than men who received less of this kind of support.

Alternatively, measures of an advice-recipient's assessment of the wisdom, utility, feasibility, and effectiveness of an advised action could capture the contribution of advice quality to a recipient's overall evaluation of the effectiveness of a supportive conversation. When we have used distinct scales to differentiate the problem-solving utility of an advice message from its relational and emotional implications, we found that these are interrelated but potentially distinct dimensions of evaluation (Goldsmith et al., 2000). Sometimes the advice we receive is perceived to be of high quality as well as expressing a caring relationship and sensitivity to our emotions. However, on other occasions, we acknowledge that the advice is useful but it hurts our feelings and makes us question our partner's concern or loyalty. Or we may perceive that the advice stems from concern for us and from a close relational bond even though it is not very practical or helpful.

Whether based on normative or idiographic judgments, assessing the quality of advice is a needed addition if we are to understand why advice is well- or ill-received. The quality of advice is an important facet of an advice giver's adaptation to the situation and an essential component of a recipient's evaluation of the support rendered.

Identity and Relational Implications

The third component of my model that has received substantial empirical support is the prediction that advice that is seen as honoring valued identities and relational qualities will be seen as more effective than advice that undermines identities and relationships. In several studies (Goldsmith, 1999, 2000; Goldsmith & MacGeorge, 2000), we have asked respondents to read advice messages and indicate how it reflects on positive and negative face.[4] Messages that show high regard for face are consistently rated as more effective than messages that fail to show regard for face (with correlations ranging from .30 to .65).

Additional insight into these message ratings came from a study in which respondents were asked to give a brief open-ended rationale for their ratings of message helpfulness (Goldsmith, 1994b). Of 28 respondents, 20 mentioned face-related reasons for selecting the message they rated as most helpful. Positive face rationales mentioned how the message conveyed liking, caring, solidarity, or acceptance, whereas negative face rationales mentioned respecting privacy, giving options, and not telling the friend what to do.

MacGeorge and colleagues (2002) found dramatic effects of face work and face threat on evaluations of enacted social support. They contrasted advice with face work to blunt advice and to advice that was face-threatening (i.e., messages that insulted or blamed the other person). Messages with face work were consistently seen as more effective than blunt or face-threatening messages. Similarly, Caplan and Samter (1999) found that social support messages (including advice) that honored positive face were seen as more helpful than messages that threatened positive face.

Although advice is conceptualized as assistance for problem-solving coping, the identity and relational implications of this form of support are

---

[4] For example, items assessing regard for positive face solicited perceptions that the recipient would feel good about his or her own abilities, accepted, criticized (reverse scored), and disapproved of rather than liked (reverse scored). The negative face regard items assessed perceptions of the advice giver as pushy (reverse scored), butting in (reverse scored) not imposing, and respecting the other's right to make his or her own decisions.

quite salient in respondents' evaluations. Across several different studies, the identity and relational meanings of advice giving (as those are captured in the concept of face) are strong predictors of how respondents react to the effectiveness of the advice given.

How Advice Is Communicated

Finally, my model focuses on variations in *how* advice is given and what specific features of messages or conversational sequences contribute to the perceived helpfulness, sensitivity, and supportiveness of advice. In fact, my interest in advice was initially sparked by a pilot study comparing various kinds of social support (including advice, offers of help, and expressions of concern) in which advice messages were rated as the most helpful and least helpful of all messages, depending on how they were communicated (Goldsmith, 1994b). In a series of studies, I have explored how reactions to advice are influenced by the language style a speaker uses, by what other ideas a speaker expresses in the course of giving advice, and by the way in which advice comes up in a sequence of turns in a conversation. Each of these features of a message or conversation (style, substantive context, sequence) has implications for the hearer's face. Theories of face work provide a framework for identifying communication features for study and for explaining how and why these features affect a hearer's evaluation.

Differences in Style
The same advice can be communicated in a variety of ways that imply different relationships between speaker and hearer and different identities for each partner. To illustrate, we can return to our example of neighborly advice about weight loss. Following are just a few of the many alternative wordings we might imagine:

1. "You should lose fifty pounds."
2. "Ever thought of knocking off a few pounds?"
3. "I hope you won't mind me saying this but you might try just trimming off a bit of weight."
4. "I know I felt much more energetic after I lost some weight."
5. "I read the other day that carrying even a few extra pounds can really tire you out."

Although the advice given is substantially the same, the alternative wordings suggest different sorts of advice giver, advice recipient, and relationship. Some of these wordings make the speaker sound more authoritative, whereas other examples sound more tentative. Some of these statements make clear that the speaker is adopting a position of expertise and assuming a right to direct the other's behavior; others sound more like a peer sharing information about which the recipient can make up his or her own mind. Brown and Levinson's (1987)[5] distinctions among different forms of face work provide a useful framework for capturing some of the features of language that shape these identity and relational meanings.

One dimension along which these example messages differ is *directness*: Does the speaker actually state the advice in so many words or is the advice implied between the lines? For example, statements 1, 2, and 3 mention an advised action, whereas statements 4 and 5 are descriptions of the speaker's own experience that need not necessarily be taken as advice. Expressing advice directly has the advantage of communicating clearly what action the speaker feels the hearer should take but it also makes clear that the speaker *is* suggesting the hearer do something differently than he or she is currently doing with the attendant risks to the hearer's desires for autonomy and approval. In contrast, indirect ways of conveying advice may mute the risks to autonomy and approval. For example, statement 4 implies advice by sharing one's own parallel experience with fatigue and statement 5 offers a fact (attributed to an outside source rather than one's own authority). It is possible to treat these indirect statements as something other than advice. Rather than taking offence at advice, the recipient of statement 4 could think, "my neighbor doesn't think I'm overweight – he/she was just sharing a similar experience." Likewise, if accused of giving advice inappropriately, the speaker of statement 5 could plausibly say, "I wasn't telling you what to do! What you said just reminded me of something I'd read on the topic." This is simultaneously a source of protection against undesired identity and relational implications as well as a detractor from the clarity and force of the recommendation to change behavior.

Even when the advice is stated explicitly, as it is in statements 1 through 3, various features of the language used to state the advice may communicate a different sort of relationship between speaker and hearer. Language features that are associated with *solidarity* between speaker and hearer (e.g., use of in-group language, humor, informal language, and reason giving) may offset threats to face by making clear the speaker likes and approves of the hearer. Alternatively, language features that are associated with distance or *deference* between speaker and hearer (e.g., hedging, use of formal language, and apologizing for imposing) may offset threats to face by showing respect for the other's autonomy. Statement 2 uses an informal style of speaking appropriate to those who are similar and close to one another – the type of relationship in which giving advice is not butting in

---

[5] Brown and Levinson (1987) are the source for the distinctions in language style that follow. In the interests of making the categories more readily understood, I have used slightly different terminology to label the styles (e.g., "blunt direct" rather than "bald on record" and "deferential style" rather than "negative face redress"), but readers familiar with Brown and Levinson will find that the categories are the same and that my alternative labels are consistent with Brown and Levinson's conceptualizations of these categories.

and it is assumed that partners accept and care for one another. Statement 3 uses a deferential style of speaking to acknowledge the potential for offense and to downplay both the forcefulness of advice ("you might try" versus "you should") and the magnitude of the advised action ("trimming off a bit" versus "fifty pounds").

I first explored the potential impact of directness, indirectness, solidary language, and deferential language in a small study of social support in a college student population (Goldsmith, 1994b; for details of sample and method, see the Advice Pilot Study in the Appendix). I asked students to read one of two scenarios, describing problems that were common for this population: a friend who failed an exam and a friend who was dumped by a romantic partner. Students then read twelve different statements that one might say in response to the friend's disclosure of the problem. The twelve statements were developed by crossing three types of social support (advice, offer of assistance, and expression of concern) with four different ways of expressing support (direct and blunt, direct and solidary, direct and deferential, indirect). For example, the blunt advice in the relational break-up situation said, "You should just forget him and date other people." In contrast, the same advice given in a deferential style said, "Maybe it would be best to just try to think about it less. It might help to date other people – you know what they say, 'there are a lot of fish in the sea.'"

The effects of different ways of communicating advice were striking. Advice given in a solidary language style was rated not only as the most helpful of the four styles of advice giving but as the most helpful of all twelve support messages (i.e., including offers and expressions of concern given in the various styles). In contrast, advice given in a blunt style was rated as the least helpful of all twelve support messages. Advice given indirectly or in a deferential language style was seen as significantly less helpful than solidary advice but significantly more helpful than blunt advice. This preference for solidary language was consistent with the details of the hypothetical situation: the advice-recipient was portrayed as soliciting help from a close friend. A deferential or indirect style might have been preferred had respondents been asked to imagine a different type of relationship (Brown & Levinson, 1987) or a situation in which the advice recipient had not admitted a problem and requested some form of help (Goldsmith, 2000).

Erina MacGeorge and I sought to replicate and extend the findings from the pilot study by examining a larger number of advice messages, situations, and relationship types (Goldsmith & MacGeorge, 2000; for details of sample and method, see the Advice Follow-up Study in the Appendix). We asked each student respondent to read one of sixteen hypothetical situations (created by crossing four problem types with four configurations of high and low power and closeness between speaker and hearer) and one of forty-eight advice messages (created by crossing three different pieces of advice in each of the four problem situations with the four different styles of advice giving). The differences in styles of advice giving were not associated with respondents' ratings of the usefulness of the advice.

There are several possible explanations for why the follow-up study failed to replicate the findings of the pilot study (see Goldsmith & Mac-George, 2000, for a detailed discussion). Of particular interest here are differences in the way in which the advice-giving styles were operationalized. In the pilot study, the advice messages were slightly longer and the different styles of advice were created by using a combination of linguistic cues and substantive content. Following is one of the two solidary style advice messages that received such high marks from respondents in the pilot study (this particular message was a response to a scenario in which the hearer has just been dumped by his or her romantic partner):

Instead of focusing on him/her, think about all you have to offer someone. You're fun to be with and you're good-looking. There are lots of other people who would like to go out with you and who would appreciate you.

This message uses the straightforward style that a friend might use but it also creates solidarity through its content – for example, it compliments the other. In contrast, the follow-up study used very brief messages that focused narrowly on operationalizing differences in linguistic style (a choice motivated by a desire to test categories from Brown and Levinson's politeness theory). For example, solidary style advice in a relational break-up scenario said simply, "I know it hurts right now, but your best bet is to go on with your life." One interpretation of the difference in findings between the two studies is that linguistic forms alone do not have strong effects on respondents' perceptions, particularly when the advice stands starkly and abruptly on its own rather than being embedded in other content such as compliments, reasons, or reassurances. This led me to explore the statements surrounding advice as another message feature that shapes recipient reactions.

Substantive Context
Consider the following advice messages that might be offered to a coworker who is worried about company furloughs:

1. Man, you gotta go talk to Jim about this. Otherwise, you're just gonna keep worrying. Hey, I saw your car in the lot this morning. You were right – the body work and paint job really made a difference.
2. Man, you gotta go talk to Jim about this. People like us with families to support need to be able to plan ahead and Jim knows that.
3. Man, you gotta go talk to Jim about this. I'd be worried too but this is probably a rumor and Jim is the only one who can tell ya for sure. You've done a lot for this company and you have a right to get a straight answer.

All three messages give the same advice ("talk to Jim") and each message uses language forms such as informal style, compliments, and reason giving that are associated with solidary language. Yet the identities that are being supported are quite different and these identities derive from the content that accompanies the advice. The first message honors an identity distinct from the problem under discussion. Although the identity as auto afficionado is represented positively, in the context of troubles talk about losing one's job, it could imply a negative evaluation of one's identity as someone who is worried and the topical shift constrains the hearer's ability to pursue further discussion of the trouble. The second message honors the shared identity of concerned family man but also projects an identity as vulnerable. The third message honors the hearer's identity as valued employee and simultaneously presents an image of one who has assets and an ability to control some aspects of the problem.

As this example illustrates, the content that accompanies advice has important implications for the identity and relational implications of the particular action advised. Although all three messages give the same advice, and each employs language designed to mitigate threat to positive face, the messages differ in their identity implications in ways that we might expect to shape the recipient's reaction. In the Advice Content Study (Goldsmith, 1999; see Appendix for details), I explored how content can address identity concerns associated with giving advice.

A significant difficulty in taking into account the content that accompanies advice is that so much of it is situation-specific. Specific and idiosyncratic knowledge of another person and of a situation will undoubtedly be useful in showing sensitivity to identity concerns. However, it is also possible to identify some more general *types of topics* that are relevant to identity and potentially useful for advice givers to consider. Using previous research on enacted social support and content analysis of messages produced in the Naturalistic Experiment study (described in the Appendix), I identified seven types of topics that might be addressed in a message that includes advice. Speakers might focus attention on the other's emotions (e.g., don't have the emotion, I share your emotion, and your emotion is temporary), facets of the problem (e.g., problem cause, controllability, commonality, duration, and severity), problem-solving actions (e.g., actions you can take and joint actions we can take), attributes of the speaker (e.g., knowledge and similar experience), attributes of the hearer (e.g., abilities and positive attributes), attributes of the relationship (e.g., caring and companionship), or attributes of the conversation itself (e.g., commentary on how to interpret a statement or on the importance of a statement).

I designed a study to test whether the topics that accompanied a piece of advice shaped a hearer's perceptions of the identity implications of the advice. In a previous study (the Naturalistic Experiment, see the Appendix), I asked college students to speak into a tape recorder what they would say in response to hypothetical others experiencing various problems. I selected messages from this corpus and asked a second group of college students to read and react to them. Using messages produced by other students, rather than constructing carefully manipulated messages myself, provided insight into the effects of naturally occurring variability in the type and amount of content that accompanies advice.

The messages students read were responses to a scenario in which a friend was nervous about giving a speech in class the next day. Eighty-five percent of the responses to this scenario contained at least one piece of advice, so these messages included many different examples of advice as well as variability in the other comments that accompanied advice. For example, the following two messages both include similar advice (indicated in bold); however, the other contents that accompany this advice differ as follows:

1. Don't make such a big deal out of it! It's only a speech in front of the class. It's not against people you don't know – it's people in your class . . . they will understand if you mess up . . . **practice by saying it in the mirror**. And just it shouldn't be that big of an ordeal.
2. You can do it! . . . . You're prepared for the speech and you've done your research and you know what you're talking about so you shouldn't have any problem. . . . **Just look in a mirror, talk to yourself**. . . . I think if you're prepared it makes it a lot easier. So good luck!

Both messages include the same advice – to practice in front of a mirror – but the content in which that advice is embedded portrays a different image of the nervous friend. The first message talks about the friend's emotions in a way that suggests he or she is inappropriately upset and talks about the situation as one that does not merit concern. At the same time, the message mentions that the friend may mess up. In contrast, the second message includes content about the friend's abilities and preparation as well as encouraging words to accompany the advice.

As these examples show, the messages in this study included not only advice but also other content that provides a context for interpreting the advice and its implications for face. I coded these contents into the seven types of topics (listed above) so that each message could be represented as a combination of different frequencies of different types of topics (emotion, problem, action, speaker, hearer, relationship, or conversation) accompanying different types of advice. I then asked another, independent sample of students to evaluate how well these messages showed respect for positive and negative face. The topic codings were entered as independent variables in regression equations predicting respondent's ratings of regard for face (Goldsmith, 1999; see the Advice Content Study in the Appendix for additional information about participants and procedures).

The content that accompanied advice had little impact on the *negative* face implications of giving advice (that is, the degree to which the message honored or threatened the hearer's autonomy), accounting for only 2% of the variability in negative face regard ratings. However, accompanying content predicted 25% of the variability in perceived regard for *positive* face (that is, the degree to which the message honored or threatened the hearer's desires for approval and liking). When advisers commented that the advice recipient's problem was not so serious, that he or she was inappropriately upset, or that the problem was uncontrollable, these contents created a context in which advice was seen as threatening to the hearer's positive face. In contrast, when advisers emphasized how the hearer's anxiety was temporary, made reassuring comments about not feeling anxious, or pointed out that the audience was like a group of your friends, these combinations of advice plus content were seen as honoring positive face.

Sequential Context
Most of the studies I have described thus far have focused on the advice message; however, with the exception of voice mail recordings or e-mail correspondence, most advice we receive in daily life is likely to occur in the give-and-take of conversations. Other authors have speculated that the sequential placement of advice may shape its identity and relational implications. Pearlin and McCall (1990) hypothesized that advice between spouses is more likely to be accepted and effective if it is offered last in a sequence of acts rather than first. Based on interviews with spouses about their discussions of work stress, they proposed that an ideal sequence of supportive acts would "begin with listening, followed by an expression of affection, after which there would be an exchange organized around questions that were in the service of gathering relevant information, and last, the offering of advice" (p. 57). Such a sequence makes it more likely that advice will be seen as a caring expression of a desire to help rather than a disrespectful dismissal of the other's distress or a desire to take control, fix the problem, and move on (Jefferson & Lee, 1992). The same advice can have different relational implications, depending on what precedes and follows the it.

Although there are a variety of sequential patterns in which advice may be embedded, one facet of sequence that is particularly salient to recipients' reactions is whether the advice was solicited (Goldsmith & Fitch, 1997; Smith & Goodnow, 1999). Through inductive analysis of the field note data from the Community Advice Study, I identified several patterns through which advice was introduced (Goldsmith, 2000, Study 1).

One way in which advice may come about in a conversation is through the recipient's direct solicitation. Recipients may explicitly ask for advice (e.g., prefacing a description of a problem with "I need your advice" or concluding a description of a problem with "what should I do?") or for opinions or information about a proposed action or solution to a problem (e.g., "should I do *x*?" or "what do you think of *x*?"). In this pattern, the advice recipient introduces the problem topic into the conversation, acknowledges that it is a problem, and explicitly asks for advice.

In clear contrast, advice may come about in a conversation through the advice giver's initiative in a way that is unambiguously unsolicited. The adviser may introduce some problem topic into the conversation and then immediately give advice about it. In close relationships, partners may know of one another's problems, observe one another's behaviors, or hear about one another's actions. This can provide a basis for introducing the problem topic into the conversation, identifying it as a problem, and then volunteering advice. In many instances, the recipient of advice has already undertaken or is in the process of completing some act and the fact that the recipient is doing so suggests he or she does not see it as problematic.

Although solicited/unsolicited may seem like a straightforward dichotomy, there are other ways in which advice is introduced into troubles talk that are ambiguous with respect to whether the recipient asked for advice. A third sequential pattern I observed in our data was one in which the advice recipient simply disclosed a problem or announced a plan of action. In these instances, the advice recipient introduces into the conversation the topic about which advice is eventually given; however, it is not clear that the advice recipient was seeking advice.

Field notes were particularly useful for providing information about advice giver's interpretations of these patterns. Not all disclosures of problems are assumed to be requests for advice, but a disclosure of a problem can be heard in this way. For example, our field notes included a discussion between Lola and Judy about a prior conversation Lola had with Karen regarding the misbehavior of Karen's 2-year-old child. Lola wondered aloud with Judy whether Karen had been seeking child-rearing advice: "Well I almost wonder if it was a cry for help. You know, she [Karen] was on the phone and she was just listing everything he had done. 'He just tipped over the hamper, now he's standing on it and getting into the medicine chest and pulling everything out, now he's got my lipstick and he's putting it all over himself.'" Similarly, a participant observer who reported on a conversation with a friend said that her friend's disclosure of problems with her boyfriend indicated her desire "to be told she can call him." The way in which a problem is announced may influence its "hearability" as solicitation of advice. For example, some problem announcements included a confession of ignorance or uncertainty (e.g., "My teaching evaluations were terrible again. I really don't know what to do; this is so depressing," "I do not know what to do! My credit card bills are due on Tuesday, and I spent the money my Dad sent me to pay for them with," and "I'm not feeling very well. I think I might go home. I'm not sick enough to be sure I should but not well enough to want to stay").

A final sequential pattern in which advice may be embedded is one in which the advice giver introduces the problem topic into the conversation but obtains assent from the recipient that the situation is problematic before going on to give advice. For example, our field notes included the following advice about a medical condition:

DORI: You look allergic.
KATY: Yes, it's been awful. I've never had allergies before.
DORI: I'm taking Seldane and that really helps.

Like sequences in which advice is clearly unsolicited, it is the advice giver who introduces the problem topic into the conversation and the advice recipient does not say anything to clearly indicate that he or she desires advice. However, gaining the recipient's agreement that a problem exists may make this type of sequence less clearly unsolicited.

After identifying these patterns, I designed a test to see whether these different sequences made a difference in perceptions that advice had been solicited, with corresponding effects on evaluations of advice. I asked a sample of college students to read a conversation in which one of ten different pieces of advice was embedded in one of the different sequences (Goldsmith, 2000; see the Advice Sequence Study in the Appendix). The students responded to questions about the degree to which the advice had been solicited as well as questions about the degree to which the adviser showed regard for the recipient's positive and negative face wants. The results confirmed that the four different sequential patterns ranged from clearly solicited to clearly unsolicited. I also found advice was seen as more or less face-threatening, depending on how it was introduced into a conversation. Differences in the degree to which advice was perceived as solicited or unsolicited made a difference in respondents' perceptions of the identity and relational implications of giving advice. The scale measuring perceived solicitation was significantly correlated with regard for the recipient's positive face ($r = .35$) and negative face ($r = .16$).[6]

These findings indicate conversational sequencing is another feature of how advice is communicated that shapes reactions to advice. Different patterns by which advice is introduced into a conversation imply different kinds of roles and relationships between participants. Whether the advice is solicited by the recipient is one particularly important attribution that people draw from the placement of advice in a series of turns at talk. This, in

---

[6] The items measuring positive face asked if the advice giver thought highly of the recipient's abilities, could identify with the recipient, and liked and accepted the recipient. The negative face items asked if the advice giver respected the recipient's right to make his or her own decisions, didn't impose too much, left the recipient free to do what she or he wanted, and made sure the other felt he or she could choose whether to take the advice.

turn, is related to their judgments about relational qualities such as liking, acceptance, respect, understanding, obligation, and so on.

CONCLUSIONS

Advice can be tremendously meaningful – for ill or for good! For example, in a study of memorable messages (messages from one's past that had a significant impact on one's life), advice occurred in 72% of the messages respondents reported (Knapp, Stohl, & Reardon, 1981).[7] The meanings of advice have ramifications not only for how the advice recipient copes with the particular problem for which advice is offered but also for the advice recipient's personal identity and relationship with the advice giver. Successful advice giving is adapted, both to the situation and to these multiple purposes.

The approach to the study of advice I have presented in this chapter moves us beyond simpler models that examine only the frequency, amount, or presence/absence of advice. Instead, the appropriateness of offering problem-solving assistance in a particular situation, the wisdom of the advised action, the style of conveying advice, the other types of statements that accompany advice, and the sequencing of advice in the course of a conversation were all shown to play a role in whether advice recipients felt advice was an effective response to a problem. This model not only helps to account for the variability in responses to advice found in earlier studies, but it also demonstrates the usefulness of attending to the communication processes described in Chapter 2. Advice is a meaningful, socially situated, multipurpose activity.

In contrast to other approaches that might have us adopt the nondirective counselor's proscription against advice giving, the findings presented here suggest an alternative set of prescriptions. First, do not make advice the first or only response to a close relational partner's distress and recognize that sometimes people talk about problems for reasons other than seeking advice. Second, recognize that there is more to advice than just solving the problem. Effective advice givers appear to consider how the advice makes them look, how it makes the other person look, and what it says about the relationship. Third, recognize the negotiated character of these sequences: Is the other person seeking advice? Is the other person at a point, emotionally, to receive it?

One caveat is in order as I close this chapter, with its emphasis on situational adaptation. Thus far, I have characterized situational adaptation as a problem of determining what kind of response is most appropriate to the type of problem that is presented by a distressed other. If the problem

---

[7] I have interpreted the authors' category of "prescriptions about what one should or should not do" as consistent with advice.

is one that is amenable to solution, then advice may be an appropriate response. Although this is an important step toward understanding the circumstances under which different forms of support are likely to be seen as helpful, this way of framing the issues unproblematically assumes that we can differentiate situations according to the type of coping that is needed. In the next chapter, we see that this simplification is in need of challenge, posing yet another puzzle to our understanding of how we assist one another in coping.

4

Reexamining Matching Models of Social Support

In Chapter 1, we saw that although there is great intuitive appeal to the idea that we can say and do things to help family and friends when they are experiencing stress, studies of enacted support have seldom found convincing or consistent evidence for a stress-buffering effect. One explanation for this apparent anomaly is that many early tests of the buffering effect overlooked the fit between the type of support offered and needs elicited by a particular stressor. The bereaved, the ill, the unemployed – all were treated as similarly stressed and the various types of support that might be given (e.g., information, tangible aid, comfort, and assurance of worth) were aggregated into single measures of the frequency of support. This way of measuring stress and support assumed that any form of support from anybody at any time could be equally effective for any problem.

Many researchers now agree that the effectiveness of supportive behaviors depends on how adequately they are matched to the particular needs created by a stressor (e.g., Barrera & Ainlay, 1983; Eckenrode & Wethington, 1990; Heller et al., 1986; Hobfoll & Stokes, 1988; Pearlin, 1985; Schaefer, Coyne, & Lazarus, 1981; Shinn, Lehmann, & Wong, 1984; Shumaker & Brownell, 1984; Thoits, 1986; Vachon & Stylianos, 1988; Wilcox & Vernberg, 1985). A similar logic is evident in research on how different forms of support are helpful from different providers (e.g., Cutrona et al., 1994; Dakof & Taylor, 1990; Dunkel-Schetter, 1984; Dunkel-Schetter & Wortman, 1982; Gore & Aseltine, 1995; Gottlieb, 1978; Lanza et al., 1995; LaRocco, House, & French, 1980; Martin et al., 1994; Okun et al., 1988; Wan, Jaccard, & Ramey, 1996; Yates, 1995) or in different phases of coping with a crisis (e.g., Folkman & Lazarus, 1985; Helgeson, 1993; Jacobson, 1986; Pearlin, 1985; Ugolini, 1998). This reasoning has been explicitly articulated in several matching models of support, most notably Cohen and McKay's (1984) stressor-specificity model of support and Cutrona and Russell's (1990) optimal matching model (see also Cutrona & Suhr, 1992, 1994).

In this chapter, I review matching models and the evidence for their utility. Although they represent a conceptual improvement over approaches to the study of support that fail to consider the match between support and stressor, these models have not succeeded in producing clear evidence for a buffering effect of enacted support. In this chapter I suggest this could be due in part to the limited model of communication processes implied by the matching metaphor. This restricts its utility for explaining how particular supportive conversations are evaluated and it may attenuate the effects of enacted support that are observed in studies that measure support received across multiple conversations.

As an alternative, I propose that skillfully enacted social support does more than simply match support to a situation; it rhetorically and collaboratively constructs situations within normative constraints. A study of social support in the daily lives of college students provides examples of how supportive messages can define situations and lays the foundation for an alternative model of the relationship between stressful life events and optimal support. A study of troubles talk conversations between adults from a midwestern community further elaborates this model by showing how relational partners may coordinate (or fail to coordinate) representations of problem situations and coping options.

MATCHING MODELS OF SUPPORT

Cohen and McKay's (1984) stressor-support specificity model differentiated three kinds of support and conceived of these as different mechanisms through which personal relationships could buffer the harmful effects of stress. Relationships may be a source of tangible support (provision of material resources), appraisal support (assistance in defining a situation as less threatening or in deciding how to cope), or emotional support (bolstering self-esteem and a sense of belonging). They suggest "stressors and stress experiences can be categorized in terms of those that elicit coping requirements for tangible support, appraisal support, self-esteem support, and belonging support (or some combination of these), and only those interpersonal relationships that provide the appropriate forms of support will operate as effective buffers" (p. 261).

Cutrona's optimal matching model (Cutrona, 1990; Cutrona & Russell, 1990) utilizes previous theory and research to distinguish five types of support and four dimensions of life stresses to which support must be matched to be optimally effective. The five types of support are as follows: *emotional support* ("the ability to turn to others for comfort and security during times of stress, leading the person to feel that he or she is cared for by others"), *network support* ("a person's feeling part of a group whose members have common interests and concerns"), *esteem support* ("the bolstering of a person's sense of competence or self-esteem by other people"), *tangible aid* ("concrete instrumental assistance"), and *informational support* ("advice or guidance concerning possible solutions to a problem") (Cutrona & Russell, 1990, p. 322). In subsequent work (Cutrona & Suhr, 1992, 1994), these types have been grouped into the broader categories of *action-facilitating* or problem-solving support (including informational support and tangible aid), *nurturant support* (including emotional support and network support), and *esteem support.*

Following Thoits (1986), Cutrona and colleagues view social support as assisted individual coping and their model is based on the assumption "that interpersonal interactions that maximize appropriate coping behaviors are most beneficial" (Cutrona & Russell, 1990, p. 328). For example, if a particular kind of life stress creates a need to regulate emotions, then the optimal support by others is that which facilitates emotion-focused coping behavior. The relationship between types of coping and types of support is assumed to be straightforward: Emotion-focused coping is facilitated by emotional and network support, whereas problem-focused coping is facilitated by tangible aid and informational support. Esteem support enhances both types of coping.

Life stresses differ in *desirability* ("the nature and intensity of the negative emotions they engender," Cutrona & Russell, 1990, p. 329), *controllability* (the degree to which an individual can prevent the occurrence or consequences of an event, Cutrona, 1990, p. 8), *duration of consequences* of an event, and *life domain* in which a stress occurs (loss or threat to assets, relationships, achievements, or social roles). These dimensions influence the types of coping demands individuals experience. For example, desirability of stress influences whether support is directed toward reducing uncertainty (for positive events) or toward preventing depression (for negative events), and negative events may require more support overall. The controllability dimension has received the most attention in Cutrona's subsequent work. For uncontrollable life stresses, there is little the person can do about the stress except regulate his or her emotions, so emotional support and network support are predicted to be optimal. In contrast, a person with a controllable stress can cope by doing something to prevent or alleviate his or her problems and this will be facilitated by information and tangible support. Cutrona and Suhr (1992, 1994) have suggested that in interdependent relationships the controllability dimension should take into account not only the extent to which the individual with a problem can take action to alleviate or remove the stress but should also consider whether the support provider can control the problem. Thus, action-facilitating support will be more helpful if the *provider* has expertise or influence over the stressor.

A number of studies have tested matching models of buffering effects of enacted social support. Some find mixed evidence of buffering effects (Cutrona & Russell, 1990; Cutrona & Suhr, 1992, 1994; Grant, 1990;

Kaniasty & Norris, 1992; Krause, 1986; Peirce et al., 1996; Swanson-Hyland, 1996; Wenz-Gross, Siperstein, Untch, & Widaman, 1997). Others find little or no evidence of buffering effects (Baker, 1997; Krause, 1987; Rosenberg, 1985; Tijhuis, Flap, Foets, Groenewegen, 1995; Ugolini, 1998; Wade & Kendler, 2000). In summarizing their own attempts at testing the optimal matching model, Cutrona and Suhr (1994, pp. 131–132) conclude the original model needs "a significant overhaul" and that "considerable work remains before we will uncover consistent patterns of optimal matches between stress and support type."

Although not entirely unsuccessful, matching models have not yielded a clear solution to the problem of finding buffering effects of enacted support. In any given study, we might point to limitations that could detract from a clear pattern of support for the matching model (e.g., problems with sample size or analytic strategy). However, I wish to propose several conceptual problems with matching models that limit their utility for explaining and predicting the effective enactment of social support.

FROM MATCHING TO CONSTRUCTING

Matching models presume that problems have readily identifiable and fixed parameters that exist independent of any supportive interaction that might occur, so that once a support provider has correctly identified the relevant situational parameters, the communicative task is simply to formulate any message that conveys the matching type of support. Similarly, it is presumed that once a provider has selected and produced the right type of support, the recipient will find his or her coping abilities enhanced. This view of the communication of support is limited in at least three ways. First, it fails to consider whether the substance of the support that is offered would, in fact, facilitate adaptive coping. So, for example, if a problem is controllable, then any piece of information or offering of tangible aid is an optimal match. Providing a recovering alcoholic a ride to an AA meeting would not be differentiated from providing a ride to the liquor store. A closely related problem is the tendency for tests of matching models to focus on the sheer frequency of support that is received, so that ten pieces of bad advice would be treated as better meeting one's needs than a single piece of expert advice. Coding or obtaining reports of functional types of support allow researchers to generalize across many types of situations (and to utilize off-the-shelf self-report measures or coding systems) but they fail to adequately capture the spirit of matching models, which is to examine whether the support that is offered is well-suited to the coping needs of the recipient.

Second, matching models assume that social support brings about change in the recipient's thinking, feeling, or behaving. If a provider utters advice, the recipient will engage in problem-solving coping; any utterance of emotional support will result in alleviation of emotional distress; and any expression of esteem support will improve one's self-evaluation. This assumption ignores the important processes of social influence that make some messages more persuasive and compelling than others. A curt recommendation to an ill friend to "go to your doctor" would be treated as equivalent to messages that include reasons for seeing the doctor, reassurances about the feasibility of doing so, or personal testimony about one's own similar experience. Sharing with the bereaved a touching memory of a lost loved one would be treated no differently than a perfunctory statement of sympathy.

Finally, the matching metaphor fails to adequately acknowledge the ways in which situations may be represented and constructed in communication. In tests of the matching model, the researcher defines a situation (e.g., as controllable) or identifies the demands of the situation to which support should be matched. Cutrona (1990) suggests that situations might also be defined normatively through a survey of individuals who have experienced a problem. Either way, the focus is on features of situations that exist prior to and outside of individual appraisal or communicative construction.

Appreciating how life stresses may be communicatively defined begins by recognizing there are multiple facets of stressful situations. The life events to which matching models have been applied (e.g., bereavement, divorce, unemployment, and illness) affect more than one life domain and have both controllable and uncontrollable aspects (Folkman, 1984, p. 843). Even daily hassles such as an argument with one's spouse or an unusually stressful commute to work can have more than one impact and will have some features that are controllable and others that are not. Consequently, there are multiple aspects of a situation to which support might be matched and there is room for different interpretations of most situations. Communication is not only a conduit for the delivery of support, it also entails selecting what aspects of a problem to discuss and then presenting a way of viewing the problem and the support offered.

The features of a situation that most influence adaptation to stress may be those that are constructed. An individual's appraisal of a situation as harmful, threatening, or challenging plays a pivotal role in how individuals experience and cope with stressful events (Lazarus & Folkman, 1984; Lazarus, 1991). Normative beliefs and real-world impacts constrain how we define situations and wildly unrealistic assessments of situations will probably not be adaptive. Yet there is usually room for more than one constructive appraisal of a stressful situation (Lazarus & Folkman, 1984) and support providers may aid (or harm) individuals under stress by implicitly and explicitly proffering their own assessments of the situation.

Advocates of matching models and their measures of enacted support have not overlooked the possibility that support can provide a new perspective or assist in reappraisal of a situation. However, recognizing appraisal support as a distinct type of act or function has not led researchers to question the assumption that effective support is matched to features of situations that are defined independently of the support that is provided. When others assist us in defining or redefining a situation, this is labeled appraisal support and is categorized as a subset of information support. Once coded in this way, the utility of appraisal support would be predicted based on predefined features of situations! Alternatively, we should view situational definition as a potential feature of *any* supportive message and we should examine the interrelationship (rather than the one-way match) between situational features relevant to adaptation and message features relevant to situation appraisal.

Although I have thus far focused on how stressful events are defined, communication can also serve to define relationships and phases of coping. Models that attempt to match support to particular relationship types or coping phases may also be altered to consider communicative definition of the closeness of a relationship, the expertise of a provider, the denial phase of bereavement, and so on. Some relevant statuses such as doctor or fellow cancer patient exist independently of communication; yet the relevance of these statuses or the definition of more complex identities (e.g., doctor and family friend, or cancer patient who had the same fears you do) may be accomplished communicatively. Similarly, we can propose normative stages of coping with life crises but marking stages and transitions between stages occurs in part through communication.

I first began to explore the potential for messages to define situations in the Naturalistic Experiment study (Goldsmith, 1994a). In that study, I asked undergraduates to speak into a tape recorder what they would say in various situations in which another person disclosed a problem and appeared to be upset (cf. Tracy, 1989). The problems portrayed were daily hassles (e.g., a classmate feeling overwhelmed by schoolwork, a friend breaking up with a boyfriend or girlfriend, and a friend feeling nervous about giving a speech) and the situations were selected from a larger set that had been pretested realism, variation in the power and closeness of the relationships portrayed, and the relevance of support as a response to the distressed character (see the Appendix for additional information about sample and procedures).

Responding to hypothetical situations such as these and producing a monologue rather than a dialogue may seem removed from our understanding of what occurs in natural conversations. However, this technique was quite useful for showing how even when "the situation" is held fairly constant, there is still wide variability in ways of representing it. For example, excerpts from this data set show some students assumed that a failed exam was a temporary setback from which the student could recover, whereas others felt it was necessary to drop the class; some imagined

a scenario in which the end of a romantic relationship was good rid-
dance, whereas others were surprised that a good relationship had abruptly
ended. When comparing naturally occurring conversations (as I do later in
this chapter), we attribute some of the variability in supportive messages
to differences in the problems that are being discussed (e.g., the things
one says to support a friend who experiences job stress are different from
the things one says to support a friend who is facing a serious illness). In
contrast, the data solicited in response to a common hypothetical situation
help to highlight the possibilities for variation in messages even for a single
problem. In other words, I don't expect that the monologues participants
produced would occur in exactly this form in an actual conversation. However, these data are a useful representation of the various thoughts that are
possible for expression in common situations and are well-suited for examining the range of possible ways of defining the situation and some of
the features of messages that contribute to situation definition.

My analysis of these messages challenged matching models in two ways.
First, comparison of multiple messages in response to the same situation
showed speakers can and do say things that actively construct the controllability of the problem and the speaker's expertise. Second, comparing
messages showed how the common research practice of attending only
to functional types of support (ignoring their content, form, and style)
severely limits our ability to understand how effective enacted support
is fitted to the problem for which it is offered. A conversation in which
effective enacted support occurs is likely to be one in which participants
develop a normatively adaptive *and* rhetorically compelling view of the
situation and coping options – factors that are ignored by simply coding
support for a functional type and matching it to a predefined notion of the
situation.

Features of Talk That Construct the Situation

One of the first differences that was apparent in these messages was the
variability in the degree to which speakers said things to define the situation. Some speakers took for granted the parameters of the situation and
simply said things that could readily be coded as one or another type of
social support. These students offered advice or comfort and said very little about the type of problem the other person was experiencing or about
what the situation was like. In contrast, other students implicitly or explicitly discussed the situation in addition to offering some form of support.
Several examples from the failed exam scenario illustrate this variability
in situation definition as well as some of the features of messages that
accomplish situation definition.

One of the more common offerings of social support in the failed exam
scenario was the advice to "talk to the professor" (present in 42.2% of the

messages). Following is an example of one of these messages that does little to define the situation: "Go ask the teacher for help. Maybe he'll let you take a makeup. Don't worry about it. Just go talk to the teacher." In contrast, other messages contained the same advice but added detail about what it would be like to talk to the professor. One message suggested the content of the talk with the teacher: "Explain, you know, your situation or something that you didn't understand." Another described what the general tenor of the talk would be like: "Tell him that you really had trouble with the first exam. Most professors are really nice about it and I'm sure he'll take that into consideration." Some messages went into even greater detail, including a description of what to say, as in the following message:

Tell them that you've studied really hard. And, you know, and you thought that you really understood the material but you didn't seem to understand it as well as you thought, and that, you know, you know that you could do better and you wanna be given a fair representation of what you can really do.

Embroidering the advice "talk to your professor" with the details of what to actually say could increase the apparent feasibility of the advice, making it more likely that the recipient would engage in problem-solving coping. In addition, in describing what to say to the professor, the speaker also offered the friend a way of viewing his or her situation (e.g., you thought you knew the material and you know you could do better), with implications for the degree to which the problem was seen as controllable.

Another type of situation-defining elaboration was content that placed the current problem in a broader temporal context. In the failed exam responses, many messages pointed out that there would be other exams in the course and so this one exam would not end up damaging the student's cumulative GPA. Other messages suggested the failure provided insight into how to study better for future exams. These situation definitions reinforced the notion that this stress was controllable.

A combination of features sometimes contributed to the persuasiveness with which a situation was defined. For example, one message combined a description of what the advised action would look like with a justification and a personal testimony that supported going and talking to the teacher in the following way:

Go to the teacher and talk to your teacher and explain to them how you tried and you studied really hard. And that way, you can get a little bit of extra credit, some brownie points while you're with the teacher. And that way they know that you're making a conscious effort. I failed an exam before one time, it was the first one and I went and talked to the teacher, and they gave me some little private time, and you can't get extra credit or anything but just the fact that you were there, they know you're making a conscious effort. And that makes all the difference in the world.

This message did not just presume the situation was controllable – the speaker made an effort to describe the situation in such a way that action sounded feasible and effective.

Those messages that contained situation-definition material also varied in the way in which the situation was defined. Similar offerings of support were accompanied by different views of what the problem was like and how the support offered was related to the problem context. Because controllability has been emphasized in the optimal matching model, I paid particular attention to features of messages relevant to this facet of the situation.

Once again, useful illustrations come from comparing those messages that advised talking to the professor in the failed exam scenario. All of these messages suggested one controllable action in the aftermath of the exam and some suggested other actions as well. However, the messages varied in their portrayal of the professor's action and the friend's role in improving his or her grade in the course. Some messages placed more emphasis on the professor's actions in alleviating the source of distress (the professor may curve the grade or change your grade). Other messages suggested joint actions by the professor and student to alleviate the problem (the professor might allow you to retake the exam or do extra credit). At the other end of the continuum was a view in which most of the control lay with the student: The professor could tell the student what he or she did wrong so the student could study harder and more effectively for the next exam.

The different attributions speakers offered for the exam failure also implied different views of controllability. Some messages suggested the friend may have failed because of other problems occurring in his or her life at that time or because the exam was too hard, whereas other messages focused attention on how much time the student spent studying for the exam. Finally, some of the messages included explicit statements about control: "If you're gonna be upset then do something about it," "There's a lot you can do," "Make a conscious effort with your teacher that you are trying and I think that makes a lot of difference in your grade," and "There's nothing else you can do now except keep trying and studying and do the best you can with the rest of the course."

The messages from the Naturalistic Experiment study also illustrate how speakers construct their own control or credibility with respect to the problem. Cutrona and Suhr (1992, 1994) suggested that it is not only the support recipient's control over the problem but also the support provider's degree of control over a stressor, including his or her expertise, that determines the effectiveness of action-facilitating support. In my own data, attempts at constructing speaker control and expertise were especially evident in responses to the public-speaking scenario, in which students responded to "a close friend who is quite upset about giving a speech in class the next day." In all of the examples that follow, the speaker gave advice about what the friend should do to feel calmer and to perform well. In addition, each of these messages included some content that spoke to the support provider's credibility to give advice.

The most common expertise appeal was "I get nervous too," followed by advice about how the speaker had successfully dealt with the situation. A contrasting and less frequently occurring appeal was that "I don't get nervous," followed by an explanation of what the speaker did to avoid feeling this way. In addition, many speakers mentioned experience or knowledge as a speech major. Others referred to specific public-speaking courses they had taken or the great number of speeches they had given. One speaker mentioned how successful his speeches were – he not only gave speeches, he gave "awesome" speeches:

I'm a speech major. It's funny. I'm a speech major and every time I get up, I've never had a problem giving them . . . and every time I get finished giving a speech it's "A," you know, and "you did it awesome" and this and that. (Pause) I could never, ever, ever wear shorts to a speech 'cause when I stand up my knees, like, my kneecaps, shake up and down! . . . So you're not alone. What your best thing to do is. . . .

This message has a conspiratorial, "I'll let you in on my secret" tone. The speaker began by establishing that he was a successful speaker. Then, after a dramatic pause, he confessed that he too gets nervous, including a vivid and humorous reference to his shaking kneecaps. He then explained how he does so well despite feeling nervous.

Some speakers indicated that they had given advice before in a similar situation and it had worked for others. Other speakers simply asserted that they were well-qualified without elaboration or support (e.g., "Well I'm the perfect person to call if you're nervous for a speech!"). Several speakers grounded the advice they gave in some other authoritative source, such as an unspecified survey that indicates fear of public speaking is the "number one fear or number two fear in all people" or a claim that "actors and actresses say they get nervous all the time . . . you just get up there and you try to do the best job." One speaker referred to an episode of the classic TV series *The Brady Bunch* as support for his advice to "imagine the audience in their underwear" and one speaker quoted the Bible in support of advice to pray about the situation.

In addition to emphasizing their knowledge of public speaking, a few speakers emphasized their knowledge of their friend (the support recipient), as in the following example:

'Cause I know you understand this material. I've heard you talk about it a number of times. And you know I just get a feeling, I don't know, that you're gonna do really well on this. I mean, like I said, you talk about it a lot and your outline is well-prepared. It looks like you're organized. All ya gotta do is practice it.

In effect, the speaker claimed "I am an expert on *you* and have a basis for my confidence that you can take this advice and succeed."

In addition to explicitly claiming expertise, speakers also implied it in various ways. For example, some speakers gave detailed descriptions of their physical symptoms in a way that gave credibility to the statement that "I know how you feel" or "I know what it's like to be nervous," as in the following example:

> I've given speeches before. My hands get all sweaty, I get nervous, I get all choked up. My throat always gets dry right before I'm about to start talking [laugh] and it's the funniest thing . . . your heart will be pitter pattering and all that. . . .

In other messages, detailed instructions about how to breathe, how to organize note cards, where to look while speaking, and the like gave the advice giver an air of authority. Some speakers made mention of particular details of the public-speaking class at their university (e.g., the length of the assigned speeches, the process by which speaker order is established) and this kind of intimate knowledge of the assignment conveyed expertise as well. Finally, a number of speakers used words and phrases that contributed to an authoritative tone: "That's really important . . . what you need to do . . . Just remember," "Buh-*lieve* me! . . . I guarantee it," "Take my word for it," and "I'm tellin' ya, look, just practice. Trust me."

Judging the Adaptiveness of Different Constructions

The Naturalistic Experiment study provided ample evidence that speakers can and do attempt to construct a view of how much control speaker and hearer have over some problem. Yet I did not conclude that any representation of the situation would be equally adaptive or that situation-defining material was necessarily a beneficial feature of enacted social support messages. Instead, I found that support messages varied along two dimensions: normative adaptiveness and rhetorical appeal. The definition of these dimensions and their significance can be illustrated with messages from the relational break-up scenario, in which students responded to a female friend who had just been dumped by her boyfriend. Following are four contrasting responses to this communicative task:

1. I know, I wish I knew what to say to you. I wish I had really wise words to say to you. I know it hurts, the only thing I can say, and you probably don't want to hear it right now, is that it heals. The wounds heal, it doesn't hurt forever. I know you might not be able to see that right now. When I broke up with my boyfriend two years ago, it seemed like outta nowhere he broke up with me, and I was devastated, devastated beyond belief. I sat on my bed and I cried and my roommate just sat there with me. And that's all really, acknowledge

just to get rid of the feelings, get rid of them, I mean not ignore them but you need to express them and get them outta the way.
2. God, I know you must be so upset. I'm sorry to hear that, I hope you feel you can talk to me, or you know you can.
3. Would you wanna come with me and my friends tonight? We're gonna be going out, you might wanna do that. If not, I can come over there. If you wanna be alone though, I would understand that too. The best thing to do would be to get right back into the swing of things. Right back out there. Show him it hasn't affected you at all. It's his fault if he can't see you're such a wonderful person.
4. If honestly you guys weren't right for each other, then maybe this is the best thing, and maybe we'll go out tonight, we'll go to the Santa Fe [a local bar] and check out who's there and we'll see if there are any cute men for you because you're not going to sit home and mourn over this person, especially if he is the one who broke up with you. I mean let him mourn, let him be upset. Totally don't be upset. I mean I know it's going to take a while for you to get over it but you're a good person and you totally deserve to be happy, and if he's not going to make you happy, then maybe you should go out and look for someone who can make you happy.

A matching model analysis of these messages would proceed as follows. We would likely consider a relational break-up (particularly one in which the focal person was the rejected party) as an uncontrollable life stress. Each of the four messages would be coded as nurturant support: messages 1 and 2 include expressions of empathy and messages 3 and 4 include invitations to get together or go out to bars together (an example of meeting needs for belonging) and statements of esteem for the other (e.g., "you're a good person"). Therefore, we would conclude that these four messages are equally optimal. Alternatively, we might attend to *what* the messages say, and *how* they say it, to further discriminate the likely usefulness of these messages for helping the recipient cope.

One dimension of contrast among these messages concerns whether the kind of coping assistance that is offered is *normatively adaptive* to external circumstances. In the immediate aftermath of a relational break-up, we might question whether going out to look for a new partner (messages 3 and 4) is as adaptive as expressing feelings of grief and loss (messages 1 and 2). We might derive this evaluative judgment from theories of emotional appraisal or coping with loss (e.g., Burleson & Goldsmith, 1998) or from a survey of what this particular population believes is the best way to cope.

Notice that this analysis of normative adaptation is consistent with the original intent of the matching model. It simply recognizes a need to look more closely at the specific types of coping assistance that are commonly offered for a particular type of problem or life event. Rather than coding responses into general functional categories such as "emotional" or "informational" support, we would need to recognize variability within these categories based on the content. For example, are the needs experienced in the immediate wake of relational loss better served by staying in and talking or by going out and looking for a new partner?

Another dimension of contrast concerns differences in *rhetorical appeal* between messages that advocate the same coping response. Messages 1 and 4 include material designed to represent the situation in a particular way. In message 1, the problem is portrayed as uncontrollable: The relationship is over, and all that can be done is to acknowledge the feelings of loss and wait for time to heal the sense of hurt. In contrast, in message 4, the problem is portrayed as much more controllable. The recipient may not be able to change the lost relationship but she is encouraged instead to focus attention on those facets of the situation she can change (specifically, initiating a search for a new partner who will make her happy). In addition, the style of presentation in messages 1 and 4 may suggest greater concern and effort on the part of the support provider. In interviews with students who viewed these messages, many commented that messages 2 and 3 seemed to be lacking in sincerity, whereas messages 1 and 4 were more convincing. For example, students commented that the speaker in message 3 made a half-hearted offer to be with her sad friend but sounded like she did not really want to change her plans to go out.

Recognizing that the coping demands in a situation can be defined both normatively and rhetorically suggests a more complex hierarchy of optimal matching. An effective supportive message is probably characterized both by coherence with external constraints and coherence within the message. Optimally effective support provides a type of support consistent with adaptive coping and offers that support in such a way that the recipient is likely to engage in the adaptive action (e.g., message 1). Less effective (but not harmful) is support that is consistent with adaptive coping but rhetorically unconvincing. The support is directed toward adaptive coping but its chances of producing that form of coping are reduced by ineffective communication (e.g., message 2). Next are messages that suggest a maladaptive coping strategy coupled with a weak communicative strategy. If adopted, the way of coping would be ineffective or harmful but ineffectual communication reduces the chances this will occur (e.g., message 3). Least helpful (and potentially harmful) are messages that are rhetorically skilled at recommending a maladaptive coping strategy (e.g., message 4).

Conclusions from the Naturalistic Experiment Study

Had I applied a conventional matching model analysis to the messages from this study, I would have concluded that nearly all the messages students produced were "optimal" matches. In response to the controllable problems of a failed exam or an upcoming public speech, a majority of students produced messages that contained action-facilitating support and in response to the uncontrollable problem of a failed relationship, a majority of students produced messages that contained some variety of nurturant support. Yet having looked closely at the variety of ways in which social support was enacted, it seems likely that variation in the style and substance of these messages further differentiates more and less effective ways of communicating the support. Some of these messages do more than simply match support to the situation – they also engage in attempts to persuade the receiver that the situation *is* controllable or uncontrollable or that the provider *is* an expert. Some of these speakers provide evidence that the support they are offering fits the situation as they see it. If we assume that action-facilitating support is effective because it facilitates action (and not simply because it is a token of caring) or that nurturant support is effective because it alleviates distress, then messages that are more persuasive should be more effective than those that simply deliver the social support without the rhetorical support.

FROM CONSTRUCTING TO COCONSTRUCTING

Up to this point, I have focused on definition of the situation as something accomplished by a support provider in his or her messages to a support recipient. However, in the everyday interactions of friends and family, support is more likely to be delivered in a conversation between partners. This opens up the possibility for both partners to contribute to the representation of a problem and coping options and to do so over a series of alternating turns. It also opens up the potential for partners to differ in their assessments and to change their representation of the situation as a conversation progresses.

These processes are evident in several conversations from the Community Conversation Study, in which we asked adult residents of Urbana–Champaign, Illinois, to talk for 20 to 30 minutes with a friend, spouse, or family member about a problem one partner was experiencing. Prior to the conversation, participants completed a brief questionnaire that solicited demographic information, and we also asked one of the partners to list several problems, stresses, or hassles he or she was experiencing. For each topic listed, we asked for a rating of the importance of the problem, and we asked whether the partners had previously discussed the problem. After their conversation, partners completed scales designed to solicit perceptions of self and other, evaluations of the conversation, and appraisals of stresses and coping options. In the Appendix, I provide further information about the Community Conversation Study, including an explanation of measures and a key to the conventions used in transcripts of the conversations.

An analysis of examples from these conversations provides additional evidence that social support can construct a definition of the situation and one's coping options. These conversations also illustrate some of the features of talk through which this occurs and provide a basis for suggesting how these features may be related to a support recipient feeling supported and intending to enact changes in thinking, feeling, or acting with respect to a problem.

Talking about Cancer

Mary[1] and Jean were two white women in their fifties who had been friends for over 12 years. Mary was a cancer survivor who rated "health" as an important stressor in her life[2] and one she had previously discussed with Jean. Their talk about various friends and family members who have cancer illustrates how a problem can have both controllable and uncontrollable aspects. The conversation also shows how speakers may choose to focus on some aspects of a problem rather than others, with corresponding variability in the types of support offered.

The conversation began with an inquiry as to how Gena (a mutual friend) was doing following her chemotherapy treatment. Mary explained her reason for inquiring: "... because my friend Connie, her mom has lung cancer right now, just gettin' ready to start the chemo, and isn't that what Gena had? ... I can remember like really how bad she was and how nobody thought she was gonna make it." To this, Jean responded:

> JEAN: Well, it was funny about how all the girls worked with her too. Because, you know what we did, I don't know if we told you this, Mary, but we kind of told her when she went over there to have chemo and radiation, we told her, just to pretend like you had soapsuds on a brush, and when you're getting this chemo and radiation it's cleaning all that cancer out of you, and to think that this is what it's doin'. And it's cleanin' it away.
> MARY: Damn near killed her [*though*].
> JEAN: [*And so*] when she went over there, she tried to think like this. Because you can be real negative about the chemo, what's it gonna do to me, is it gonna burn me up, is it gonna

---

[1] I have used pseudonyms in this and subsequent examples.

[2] The stressor importance scale asked respondents to rank "how big a deal you consider each topic to be" with 1 corresponding to *very little* and 7 corresponding to *very much*. Participants in the study tended to rate stresses, hassles, and problems in their lives as fairly important: The mean rating for troubles topics was 4.86 ($SD = 1.16$). Mary rated this problem a 7.00 on a 7-point scale of importance, a rating in the 100th percentile ($z = 1.24$).

do this and that. And so, she was trying to put in her head that this was a cleansing type thing, and I think that a lot of that helped. . . .

In subsequent turns, Mary continued to ask questions about Gena's prognosis and treatments, confirming that Gena's tumor was initially inoperable but was shrunk as a result of therapy and that she was in a lot of pain even though she eventually recovered. Jean went on to describe how difficult it was for Gena's friends when the family limited access to her during the time she was feeling especially sick from side effects of treatment. Mary then raised another concern she was experiencing about Joyce (her friend Connie's mother):

MARY: And so did you ever feel guilty because you weren't going over to see her?
JEAN: Yeah.
MARY: [*Yeah*]
JEAN: [*But you know*] you couldn't, you know.
MARY: That's the way I am with Joyce right now. She's bad, and I'm really worried, and I don't know what to do.
JEAN: But you know what [*happens*]
MARY: [*Oooo*]
JEAN: sometimes Mary, I think you need to go by your gut feeling, because I tell you what, sometimes you get misinformation. Because this – well, Joanie. She's very protective of Gena and she's always – she's very protective of every one of us girls. And like, she was saying, you know she really didn't think we should go, and we felt like, you know. So, and I'm not so sure that that's the way it really was. 'Cause I think Gena then later on, you know, really expected us to come over there, and we're thinking we're not supposed to.

The conversation then turned to a discussion of Joyce. Mary told how Joyce had a goal of surviving until her grandchild was born and Mary and Jean agreed this was a useful coping strategy. Mary reported that she feared Joyce had given up because the child had been born but Joyce hadn't set another goal. Mary and Jean agreed this was dangerous and Mary confessed she was feeling guilty that she hadn't been over to visit for several weeks. This prompted Jean to ask, "How does she react when you come?" and "How do you talk when you talk to her – do you talk up, like keep her up?" Mary replied:

MARY: Yeah, she's the one though, she's like, she's she's so, just a lot of faith. You know, she says things so matter-of-factly, just like, you know, she knows=
JEAN: =Well, see, I think what happens sometimes too – like Gena kinda talk – you wanna say things, and everybody is always trying to keep

you upbeat you know and everything, but there's things you need to say, and people need to understand what you're going through you know.

Mary and Jean continued to discuss Gena's miraculous recovery and Joyce's poor prognosis and final wish to visit her home state before she died. In the course of telling stories about Gena, Mary observed the following:

> MARY: She's never done one thing wrong in her life, and of course, you know, she's with this group and, [*so, uh, she's and*]
> JEAN: [*She's ran around*] with you guys, she's had to do a few things wrong.=
> MARY: =And she's never eaten anything wrong, she's never drank, she never smoked, she never did anything wrong, I mean, she didn't=
> JEAN: =And so she's wondering why [*she, how she got this situation*]
> MARY: [*She's never did well I'm wondering too*], you know it's like, "Oh, my god, how could I be so lucky."

As the conversation continued, Mary mentioned having seen her oncologist (the only clear reference in the entire conversation to Mary's own battle with cancer) and this led to a brief mention of her brother-in-law with prostate cancer who "supposedly is doing well, but, according to Larry, 'He's not going to make it.'"

One theme that emerged out of this talk about various cancer-related issues is that contracting cancer is uncontrollable. For example, Gena was characterized as having avoided many actions that are considered risk factors for cancer and yet she got cancer, whereas others in her circle of friends who were less cautious did not contract cancer. Similarly, the discussion of Joyce and Mary's brother-in-law implied that for some with a negative prognosis, dying seems inevitable. However, throughout their discussion of how others were coping with cancer, Mary and Jean described controllable actions one could take to deal with cancer and with treatments (e.g., setting goals, thinking about difficult treatments with positive imagery, and being matter of fact about difficulties). They also discussed controllable actions one could take in response to friends and family who have cancer (making sure to visit them if you feel you should, even if overprotective family lead you to believe otherwise; not trying to keep talk upbeat if the patient has things he or she needs to say).

If, in the spirit of matching models, we were to categorize the problem Mary introduced into this conversation, we would likely presume that cancer is an uncontrollable stress. If we were to code the supportive responses Jean provided her friend, we would find a variety of types of support represented but much of what she said fell in the category of information about how she and others coped with their own or friends' cancer (i.e., problem-solving support). At this level of analysis, we might deem Jean's offerings a poor match to the problem Mary raised. Furthermore, we might question Jean's ready provision of advice and information to Mary, who was a cancer survivor herself. However, this level of analysis would miss the way in which Mary and Jean collaborated in constructing a finer grained recognition of the controllable and uncontrollable aspects of cancer. It also misses the ways in which Jean's informational support encouraged Mary to undertake problem-solving coping for those aspects of this stressor that were under her control. As a result of focusing on these controllable aspects and problem-solving actions (how to visit and talk to a friend, the success of Gena's treatments), Mary reported that she felt better able to cope with her own health problems and with the dilemmas of how to respond to friends who are in ill health. In her postconversation questionnaire, Mary gave Jean the highest possible ratings for helpfulness, supportiveness, and effectiveness and a high overall rating of support quality.[3] She also indicated the conversation resulted in a high degree of change in her own attitudes, behavior, thinking, and feeling and in her positive feelings about her relationship with Jean.[4] Specifically, she said she would go visit Joyce, she felt more confident about cancer treatments and about Jean's feelings toward ill health, and she felt even closer to Jean than before.

This conversation shows how these relational partners made choices about which aspects of cancer to make the focus of their talk and about how to portray controllability in their treatment of these topics. Consequently, there was variability in the kind of support that was appropriate and effective. It also shows how friends who had discussed these issues before, in the context of a close relationship, were able to move rapidly and smoothly through the terrain of topics about a complex stressor. Their trading

[3] We measured evaluations of social support with several 7-point semantic-differential-type scales: helpful/unhelpful, supportive/unsupportive, effective/ineffective, sensitive/insensitive, liked/disliked, accepted/criticized, and more calm/less calm ($\alpha = .80$). The scores on the scale were skewed, perhaps because participants elected to bring to the study a relational partner who tends to respond in positive ways: The scale mean was 5.45 ($SD = .99$) with a range of 3 to 7. Mary evaluated Jean's support a 6.14 on the 7-point scale (73rd percentile, $z = .70$).

[4] The change items were taken from the Iowa Communication Record (Duck, Rutt, Hurst, & Strejc, 1991). In the context of the full ICR, Duck and colleagues included all change items on a single factor. However, in the case of enacted support we found it useful to differentiate individual change from relational change, as these are two salient outcomes theorized to flow from social support. The four individual change items were change in attitude, feelings, behavior, and ideas ($\alpha = .73$). Attitude, feeling, and behavior change items were scaled from -3 to $+3$ to reflect positive or negative change in attitude or feelings and increasing or decreasing a behavior. The idea item ranged from 1 to 7. For ease of interpretation, we recoded items so that all were scaled from 1 to 7. The scale mean was 4.30 ($SD = .90$, range = 2.5 to 6.5). The two dyadic change items were change in relationship and change in attraction to partner ($\alpha = .89$). Both items were scaled -3 to $+3$ and the resulting scale mean was .75 ($SD = .96$, range = $-.5$ to 3.0). Mary's score on the individual change scale was 5.75 (94th percentile, $z = 1.61$) and her score on the dyadic change scale was 2 (91st percentile, $z = 1.31$).

of turns in the conversation was marked by features often associated with closeness and solidarity, including brief interjections of support during one another's turns at talk, overlapping expressions of similar ideas, and a smooth exchange of the floor.

To Have (or Not Have) Children

Lisa and Ralph's discussion about having children provides another illustration of a stressor that has both controllable and uncontrollable aspects. The couple had been married for nine years and both were in their early thirties. Prior to the conversation, Ralph listed "children" as a stressor of moderately high importance[5] that he had not previously discussed with Lisa. The topic came up fairly late in their conversation, when Ralph joked with Lisa that being pregnant might account for her craving for sweets. Although this topic was important to Ralph, the tenor of their conversation was joking and light-hearted as the following excerpt shows:

RALPH: We gonna have the baby this year?

LISA: I don't know.

RALPH: Well, if you decide we are, let me know ahead of time, okay?

LISA: Why?

RALPH: That way I can make sure I'm extra juicy.

LISA: Oh.

RALPH: Make sure all my tadpoles are in order.

LISA: I'm debating whether to have 'em or not. I mean, I see all the brats running around, and I don't want anything like that. I mean like Rob's kids. I don't think I could handle that.=

RALPH: =That's what I'm saying. We could have one. If it turns out good, great. If it doesn't, (*laughter*)

LISA: Sell it.=

RALPH: ="It's not ours. It's not ours, honest. It's not. We don't know where it came from. It was a stray. Yeah, we got our cats."

LISA: "It followed him home. We found it in the rain."

Their treatment of this topic suggested that having children was something not entirely under their control. When Ralph joked about making sure his "tadpoles are in order" the humor turned on the understanding that this was something he couldn't really control. In Lisa's comment about Rob's kids and in Ralph's response, whether kids turn out bratty was portrayed as an outcome about which you just have to wait and see rather than something that results from conscious choices about parenting. Their shared joke about selling a child who turns out bratty, just as one might get rid of

---

[5] See footnote 2 for information regarding the scale and distribution. Ralph rated this topic 5 (58th percentile, $z = .08$).

a problematic stray cat, served only to underscore the irrevocability of a decision to have children. The humor derived from the unstated premise that once you have children, you can't change your mind (a limitation on control).

After this passage, Ralph turned serious and asked, "How many kids do you want?" to which Lisa replied as follows:

> LISA: We don't always have control of the one at a time. I could pop out two or three.
> RALPH: Yeah, well then we're blessed. Odds are you won't pop out two.
> LISA: No because there's none.
> RALPH: On either side of our families.
> LISA: At least not for many many generations=
> RALPH: =mmm-hmm.=
> LISA: =to my knowledge.
> RALPH: We can't wait forever.
> LISA: I know.
> RALPH: You're getting old.

How many children a couple has is an issue that is neither completely controllable nor uncontrollable. Contraception or fertility treatments are choices couples control, but their effects are not 100% guaranteed. Objectively speaking, the couple could have chosen to frame a conversation about having children in many directions. In response to Ralph's question, Lisa didn't focus on how many children she would like to have (and the family planning choices that might entail) but instead spoke about a relatively uncontrollable aspect of this issue, namely, the chances of having twins or triplets. The reference to family history as a determinant of the chances of twins further underscored an uncontrollable issue, as did Ralph's reference to the aging process.

The couple engaged in a brief tangent about a bell that rang in the building and then Lisa returned to the topic of children as follows:

> LISA: I mean, I don't have the mothering instincts that I can't wait to have a baby either. That worries me. I mean, if I have one, fine, and if I don't, oh well. But then I worry, five, ten years down the road, will I be sorry we never had one, and it'll be "damn too late" then.
> RALPH: Mmm-hmm. Well your mothering instincts increase with pregnancy because you're releasing hormones to stimulate certain areas of your brain.
> LISA: (*Laughter*)
> RALPH: I learned this at Parkland.[6]

---

[6] Parkland is the local community college.

LISA: So when you're pregnant, your brain will be stimulating?

RALPH: Your brain will be stimulated to think mothering-, cuddling-, holding babies-, suckling-, type thoughts.

Lisa's ambivalence was associated with a course of action in which she did not suggest taking any proactive steps to produce or prevent a pregnancy. Like Ralph, she also saw the aging process as resulting in less control over the ability to have children. Ralph's reference to mothering hormones was another example of an uncontrollable process associated with this issue.

Throughout this conversation, both partners made statements that portrayed or transparently implied that the issue of having children was one over which they had relatively little control. However, other comments (e.g., let me know when you decide, I'm debating, we can't wait forever, and worry about regretting not having children once it's too late) stated or implied that there was a decision to be made. In addition, the form of their talk resembled that of other couples in the sample who were making a decision on some matter over which they had control: they exchanged opinions, asked questions about one another's preferences, and gave reasons for a particular course of action. Thus, this conversation illustrates not only that *life stresses* may have multiple dimensions, some controllable and others uncontrollable, but also that *conversations about life stresses* may have multiple features working simultaneously – some which work toward constructing a view of a situation as controllable, whereas others work toward constructing a view of a situation as not controllable.

Furthermore, this kind of ambiguity might have served a useful purpose for this couple. Because Ralph was raising for the first time a topic that was of some importance to him, we might expect that he felt some uncertainty about how his wife would respond. Lisa stated in the conversation that she had mixed feelings about this issue. The good-natured joking about the topic and the simultaneous construction of control and lack of control could be seen as providing a safe and noncommital space in which this couple could begin to explore their feelings and options. Ralph's evaluation of Lisa's support was fairly positive[7] and he anticipated some individual change as a result. In particular, he reported a high degree of change in thinking ("I see her plans better") and some degree of change in feelings ("I am reassured about our future").[8]

---

[7] See footnote 3 for information about the scale and its distribution. Although Ralph's score of 5.14 is above the midpoint of the scale, in comparison to other study participants, this is in the 40th percentile ($z = -.31$).

[8] See footnote 4 for information about the scales and their distributions. Ralph's individual change score was 5.25 (86th percentile, $z = 1.06$) and his dyadic change score was .5 (63rd percentile, $z = -.26$).

Coping with an Inconsiderate Sister

Georgia and Pauline were two African American women who were nearly 40 years of age and had been friends for a year and a half. Georgia opened the conversation with a narrative about the stresses involved in having her sister, Rhonda, visit her, a stressor of moderate importance to her.[9] In contrast to the previous two conversations, in which problems were portrayed as having both controllable and uncontrollable aspects, Georgia and Pauline collaborated in constructing a view of Georgia's family stress as quite uncontrollable. The entire conversation concerned Rhonda's inconsiderate behavior: She didn't clean up after preparing food, she inconvenienced Georgia by locking herself out of the house or expecting to be provided with transportation, She didn't control her children, she wasted water, and she disregarded the feelings of others to pursue a relationship with a married man.

Throughout the litany of problems, Pauline provided supportive backchannel responses (e.g., "uh-hmmm," "yeah," and "right"), completed Georgia's sentences, said "I understand," and expressed outrage or laughter at appropriate points in the story. The following passage is typical of the style of their conversation:

GEORGIA: I said, let's make, we was going to make a chicken.
PAULINE: Okay=
GEORGIA: =And then I said, no let's make some spaghetti.
PAULINE: Right, [*cause*]
GEORGIA: [*so*]
PAULINE: it is faster.
GEORGIA: Yeah, [*and by*]
PAULINE: [*yeah*]
GEORGIA: the time the kids get in there and take a bath and get out it would be ready to eat.
PAULINE: Right.
GEORGIA: So I made spaghetti, I [*mean,*]
PAULINE: [*uh-huh.*]
GEORGIA: I cut, you know did all the coo[*king*]
PAULINE: [*right*]
GEORGIA: and fed the kids and everything, made garlic bread, I had garlic bread in the freezer.
PAULINE: uh-huh.=
GEORGIA: =So I fed them and so then my cappuccino machine=
PAULINE: =uh-huh

[9] See footnote 2 for information regarding this scale and its distribution. She rated this topic a 5 on a 7-point scale (39th percentile, $z = .08$).

GEORGIA: had on it from where she had been frying like=
PAULINE: =Didn't even wipe it off?=
GEORGIA: =Yeah (*narrative continues*)

In those turns in which Pauline gave a longer, more substantive response, it was nearly always to provide emotional support to Georgia, either in the form of understanding for her feelings or summary statements that articulated the point of Georgia's stories. For example, at the conclusion of the kitchen story excerpted above, Pauline said, "If you're doing the kitchen duty, you put all the stuff up and do the dishes, I'll tell you." At the conclusion of a tale about a lost house key, Pauline asked, "Now how old is she?" in a way that underscored Georgia's point that her sister ought to have known better. Another story concerned Rhonda's refusal to ride the bus and her expectation that Georgia would drive her around town. Pauline responded, "And that reminds me of my sister. She's the same way" and gave a brief two-turn account of a similar story, concluding with a statement that expressed the exasperation common to all of the various stories in the conversation: "You know, I don't know, I just don't understand my family. I don't think I try to understand them anymore."

We might view Pauline's nurturant support responses as an optimal *match* to a problem that *was* uncontrollable. Alternatively, we could view Pauline's responses as a way of collaborating with Georgia to *define* the problem as uncontrollable. When Georgia first introduced an example of Rhonda's bad behavior, the conversation had the potential to take a variety of directions. For example, we might imagine an alternative course for this conversation in which Georgia and Pauline brainstormed possible actions Georgia could take and discussed their potential utility (e.g., having a talk with her sister, setting down rules for her sister, sending her sister back home, or arranging entertainment or work to get her sister out of the house). As shown in Chapter 3, giving advice about how to solve a problem is a likely way of responding to a disclosure of stress or frustration. At one point in the conversation, it appeared that the friends might move in this direction. Pauline had just concluded a brief description of inconsiderate behavior by one of her own family members and Georgia responded:

GEORGIA: Hmmm. Well I tell you this is the year that I have c[*ome in*]to
PAULINE: [*yes*]
GEORGIA: my own, [*sister.*]
PAULINE: [*Reme*]mber when we [*talked*]
GEORGIA: [*M-hmmm*]
PAULINE: about that. I said I
    wasn't going to take no crap this year and I haven't. [*You know.*]
GEORGIA: [*And even*]
    Tonya she told me, she said, "I told you over and [*over again,*"]

PAULINE: [*uh-huh*]
GEORGIA: and I
   didn't see it. (*she continues*)

At this point, the conversation turned from a description of infractions by family members to an exploration of the causes for their behavior (all of which, as shown in the next section of dialogue, were relatively stable and uncontrollable causes). Having mentioned confrontation as a possible strategy for coping with errant family members (i.e., "take no crap"), both Georgia and Pauline let this idea drop and continued on in ways that foreclosed a view of the situation as one that might be improved through problem-solving coping strategies. By allowing Georgia to simply narrate her frustrations, Pauline made it possible to view the situation as one in which Georgia had little control. By expressing understanding of Georgia's point of view, Pauline also supported an account of the situation in which Georgia was the wronged party who could do little more than simply endure the remainder of her sister's visit. Sometimes the type of support provided can imply and sustain a corresponding view of a situation.

The conversation also illustrates other features of talk that are more proactive in articulating a view of the situation as uncontrollable. Describing infraction after infraction was a feature of topical sequence that contributed to a feeling that little ever changed and nothing Georgia did or said had much effect on her sister. At another point in the conversation, Georgia and Pauline engaged in explicit identification of stable causes for problems. Georgia noted that her sister's behavior was just like "that side of the family" and suggested that environmental factors shape a person's attitudes in ways that are unlikely to change. She offered living in housing projects as an account for several of her sister's irresponsible behaviors and attitudes and credited Georgia and Pauline's own experience in the armed forces with shaping an alternative set of views and habits. Pauline not only responded to these causal attributions with support and agreement but also implied that people may be fundamentally different in their attitudes even before environmental influences (e.g., "just, I've always been that way" and "that was just me though"). Georgia and Pauline also called on broader shared premises about family life and individual behavior to make sense of the conflicting motivations in Georgia's household. For example, in the following passage, Georgia invoked the common notion that older family members want a better life for younger ones, Pauline referred to the belief that individuals have to want to change to do so, and they concurred in the analogy between the behaviors of their family members and those of an alcoholic:

GEORGIA: With Rhonda, I tried to think "Okay, this is the
   youngest [*one.*]
PAULINE: [*uh-huh.*]

GEORGIA: I want her to have the same type of things that I [*had,*]
PAULINE: [*yeah*]
GEORGIA: but
she don't want the same th[*ings*]
PAULINE: [*No.*]
GEORGIA: that I do.
PAULINE: See and if she don't want it it's not going to happen 'cause
she has to want it. That's like with anything.=
GEORGIA: =Y[*eah.*]
PAULINE: [*That*]'s like an alcoholic. Until they admit they are an al-
coholic or that they have a problem it's not going to get solved.
GEORGIA: But see they'll come over to your house.
PAULINE: Um-hmmm.
GEORGIA: and they'll sit up,
PAULINE: m-[*hmm*]
GEORGIA: [*use up*],
PAULINE: [*Yes,*]
GEORGIA: [*lay up*],=
PAULINE: =Uh-huh. [*Because it's plen*]tiful. [*Look at*]
GEORGIA: [(*unintelligible*)]   [*Yeah!*]
PAULINE: all this [*they got.*]

At the conclusion of this conversation, Georgia reported satisfaction
with the support Pauline provided and a slight positive change in her relationship with Pauline.[10] However, she also indicated that she expected
little or no change in her attitudes or thinking, a slightly negative change in
feelings, and only a slight change in behavior (commenting that she "will
place less emphasis on family situations and more on myself as an individual").[11] It is quite possible to interpret this conversation as entirely consistent with a matching model: The problem is uncontrollable and Pauline
provided nurturant support with the result that Georgia was satisfied with
the support received and determined to engage in forms of coping appropriate to uncontrollable problems (e.g., a change in her own focus so that
the uncontrollable problem is less salient). However, examination of the

[10] See footnotes 3 and 4 for information about the scales and their distributions. Georgia
evaluated Pauline's support as 5.14, a score above the midpoint of the scale, but below the
mean for the sample (40th percentile, $z = -.31$). This may reflect an error in her reading of
the questionnaire items: she gave Pauline the lowest possible ratings for effectiveness and
sensitivity. Although a low rating on effectiveness might be consistent with the theme of
the conversation as one without a solution, there is nothing in Georgia's ratings or written
comments to explain an extremely low rating for Pauline's sensitivity. It seems more likely
that the placement of the sensitivity item among other reverse-scored items may have led
Georgia to mistakenly give Pauline a very low rating on this item. Georgia's score on the
dyadic change scale was 1.5 (81st percentile, $z = .79$).
[11] See footnote 4 for an explanation of the scale and its distribution. Georgia's individual
change score was 2.75 (3rd percentile, $z = -1.72$).

communicative features and processes that occurred in this conversation suggest that its success might be attributed to more than a simple matching of support to problem. Instead, we might see the conversation as an iterative and collaborative process through which views of the problem, support, and coping are simultaneously constructed in a way that is coherent to both participants.

Changing Jobs (Take One)

Vicky was a 47-year-old African American woman who worked as a library technical assistant. She spoke with 34-year-old Susan, a fellow library technical assistant who had been her friend for 13 years.[12] Vicky listed her job as a fairly important stressor[13] that they had discussed previously. Vicky and Susan worked in the same stressful job and yet in this conversation they presented different constructions of the situation and different ways of coping. Their conversation further illustrates features of talk through which partners portray a situation as controllable or not, including explicit statements about control and descriptions of situational features that imply beliefs about control. However, in this conversation, these statements seemed to have an effect that was the opposite of the literal meaning of their statements.

Susan's first reactions to Vicky's introduction of the topic convey a kind of joking resignation to their stressful job as the following excerpts shows:

> VICKY: Well, I guess I've just been thinking about what it would take, I mean how much of a person's energy, you know, how much energy we actually spend trying to adjust to being in a job situation that we don't like?
>
> SUSAN: All of it Vicky.
>
> VICKY: I mean, I mean like, you think that all of your energy, well obviously all of your energy can't be spent just worrying about coming to work every day.
>
> SUSAN: Most of it. Okay, ninety-nine-point-nine percent. (*Laughs*).
>
> VICKY: (*Laughs*).
>
> SUSAN: Oh, I love it.
>
> VICKY: But no, really. I mean you're so much younger, so you can, you can, afford to to think about the fact that, you know, you can do something else. But honestly, I really am having a hard time, trying to get out of it. Out of that job because it's not like I, I mean not just can't afford, materially, to get another job. I mean, to lose money, starting all over again.=
>
> SUSAN: =I can't either. Who can? (*jokingly pretends to cry*)

---

[12] Susan declined to indicate her racial/ethnic identity.

[13] See footnote 2 for an explanation of the scale and its distribution. Susan rated the importance of this stressor a 6 (58th percentile, $z = .66$).

When Vicky persisted in trying to introduce a more serious discussion of the problem, asking point-blank about the prospects for coping, Susan responded with several statements that recommended problem-solving coping:

> VICKY: What do you think though? I mean are we just going to be stuck? Or are we just going bite the bullet and just quit and hope that something will come along, [*or*]
>
> SUSAN: [*I am*] going to be a realtor. And you can be my partner.
>
> VICKY: I don't know if I want to. See that's you, you can sell real estate. I mean that's who you are. I mean, excuse me, but let's face it you love to talk to people. And you have a sales mentality. People like you. You like [*them.*]
>
> SUSAN: [*People*] like you.
>
> VICKY: Uh.
>
> SUSAN: They do girl, please. Everyone likes you. People call you from all over the world.
>
> VICKY: Yeah, but I'm just saying I'm not somebody who just, you know. It's a different kind of thing.
>
> SUSAN: [*well*]
>
> VICKY: [*I'm*] just saying, you know, that's something that is good for you. That's excellent for you. That's not excellent for me.
>
> SUSAN: Well that's what I'm going to do. And. after that, uh, I want to become uh an interior decorator. I think I'll like that too. That would be nice. A realtor, an interior decorator, just think of the possibilities.
>
> VICKY: Yeah, that's exciting.
>
> SUSAN: That's what I want to do. I'm going to enjoy that.
>
> VICKY: Um-hmmm. [*So that means*]
>
> SUSAN: [*So that's my out*]

The content of several of Susan's turns encouraged a can-do, problem-solving response to their stressful job situation. However, Susan's playful tone seemed to undermine a view of the situation as a controllable problem that could be improved through one's actions.

In the opening turns of their talk on this subject (see previous excerpts), Susan joked and made glib assertions about solutions to the problem, whereas Vicky was in problem-solving mode, countering Susan's remarks with requests for information and serious objections to Susan's various suggestions. After several minutes of this pattern, Susan got serious about describing a take-control-of-your-life philosophy. In the following excerpt, Vicky continued to argue about whether this way of viewing things applied to her own situation:

VICKY: It's almost like you know, you know everybody says you shouldn't leave a [*job*]
SUSAN: [*OK*]
VICKY: unless you have a job.
SUSAN: That's not [*true.*]
VICKY: [*But then,*] well I mean, [*most people*]
SUSAN: [*In some cases.*]
VICKY: can't [*because*]
SUSAN: [*Well . . .*]
VICKY: they can't afford it.
SUSAN: Well, even people that can afford it, it's not always the right thing to do. But you have to just take that chance.
VICKY: Well, I mean, if you were the sole person paying for all of your bills that would be different.
SUSAN: Well that's true. (*Laughs*) Okay, good point.
VICKY: Yeah. So I'm just saying, but for most people that's just what they have to do. But of course you could, you know, there's always, you know, I never thought about it but, you know, there is a possibility that you could take a chance and just bring, just get your retirement and use that until you found something else. It's just hard for me, because I'm so security-minded. It's hard for me to think of taking my retirement and using that in case I didn't find anything else. I mean that's a real big chance I think.
SUSAN: Well look how many people have done that though. You could do it if you wanted to.
VICKY: I mean yeah you could do it. I'm just saying how difficult it is.
SUSAN: It's always difficult whether you use your retirement or other means. But it's just a matter of taking a chance. You know, taking a chance and doing something different.
VICKY: Um-hmmm.
SUSAN: That's what my friends said. You don't take chances, you know, you never know what the outcome may be. That's why people when they turn sixty and seventy and they look back and then they say, "Oh well I wish I had did this ten years ago and blah blah blah." And it's too late. I'm not, I'm not, going to be that person any longer. I am just going to start doing things and I will deal with the consequences.
VICKY: Yeah.
SUSAN: And that's my new philosophy on life.=

In contrast to the beginning of the conversation, in this passage both speakers were engaged in a problem-solving discussion of the possibilities for seeking a different job and the reappraisal of the situation that would enable that action. The form or genre of talk in which they were engaged was in sync, even though they disagreed or admitted defeat on the content of specific points.

Eventually, the speakers moved away from the topic of their jobs to discuss several other unrelated topics. Vicky returned to the subject of a job change:

> VICKY: I mean it's so honest and you know getting back to the honestly, I mean you're you're serious about in the next month or so you're just going to quit.
> SUSAN: Yes. I'm leaving you.
> VICKY: Well I'm happy for you I wish I was leaving you.
> SUSAN: And I'll fix you lunch maybe once a week, we'll have fruits and crackers and cheeses, tuna occasionally, nice soup.
> VICKY: [*That sounds good.*]
> SUSAN: [*Ice tea with lemon.*]
> VICKY: Yeah ice tea would be great.
> SUSAN: And if it's for breakfast I'll get your bagels=
> VICKY: =Wouldn't it be great if we could both quit at the [*same time?*]
> SUSAN: [*Let's just do it.*]
> VICKY: So how am I going to pay for my house?
> SUSAN: Come live with me.
> VICKY: Ah If I had to move, if somebody said you could move into the palace tonight, I would say "forget you I'm not moving anywhere anytime soon. I'm not packing another box, I'm not unpacking." I haven't unpacked those other boxes. I don't even know what's in them. I still haven't found my waffle [*iron*]
> SUSAN: [*We*] could redo the whole attic.
> VICKY: With what you're not even going to be working?
> SUSAN: I can do it with my retirement money.

Susan returned to her joking, fantasy-theme style of responding to the topic and although Vicky put up some protest (how am I going to pay for my house? How could you afford to redo the attic if you quit your job?), she seemed less intent on pressing a problem-solving discussion and more willing to be caught up in the fantasy (e.g., the food sounds good and wouldn't it be great if we both quit at the same time).

This conversation also suggests how coordination (or lack of coordination) of conversational style between partners may shape participants' reactions. At the very beginning of the conversation, Susan's tone of joking resignation contrasted with Vicky's attempts to discuss the feasibility of changing jobs. In the midsection of their talk, Susan and Vicky were both engaged in a serious discussion about changing jobs, though they had substantive disagreements about the feasibility of this coping option. In their concluding comments on this topic, Vicky was still objecting to Susan's problem-solving solutions but she appeared more willing to engage in a light-hearted exchange on the topic.

The ways that Vicky and Susan moved in and out of synch with respect to the style of conversation find a parallel in Vicky's mixed reactions in her postconversation survey. She reported that she felt some support for taking risks and she rated Susan's reactions as slightly effective. However, she also rated Susan's reactions as slightly insensitive and neutral with respect to support and helpfulness.[14] The conversation produced little intended individual change.[15] In describing her feelings about the conversation, Vicky said, "I realized that my friend doesn't really know who I am in relationship to who I appear to be," but she also indicated that the conversation had no effect on how close she felt to her friend.[16]

Once again, we can consider how this conversation might be viewed from the perspective of a matching model. Neither Vicky nor Susan ever contemplated the possibility that they could change conditions on their jobs to make them less stressful, but Susan felt she could control the stress by changing jobs and Vicky began to contemplate this possibility. Susan's problem-solving support for leaving the job might appear to have been a good match to Vicky's stressful situation and there was some evidence that Vicky felt support for taking this coping action at the conclusion of their talk. However, Vicky did not give positive ratings to the support her friend provided and her statement that she felt misunderstood might be taken to mean that she felt Susan's support was not matched to her needs. In other words, a mismatch between the support offered and features of the problem *external* to the conversation might account for Vicky's dissatisfaction with support. In addition, a close examination of the talk suggests ways in which content and style were not consistently matched within Susan's turns or between Susan and Vicky. This suggests a mismatch between the support offered and features *internal* to the conversation. We might speculate that these aspects of matching are also important in the optimal provision of support and may have contributed to Vicky's mixed reactions.

Changing Jobs (Take Two)

Renee and Bob also discussed changing jobs. In contrast to the mixed reactions Vicky reported in the conversation just examined, Bob went away from his conversation feeling reassured, encouraged, and resolved to act on a plan. This conversation is interesting for the way in which nurturant

---

[14] See footnote 3 for an explanation of the scale and its distribution. Susan's rating of Vicky's support was 4.43 (24th percentile, $z = -1.04$).

[15] See footnote 4 for information about the scale and its distribution. Susan's score was 4.25 (58th percentile, $z = -.05$).

[16] See footnote 4 for information about the scale and its distribution. Susan's score was 0 (47th percentile, $z = -.79$).

support is offered in the service of portraying a problem as controllable and in support of taking action to alleviate stress.

Bob was a 38-year-old white broadcast engineer and Renee was 42 years old, white, and a therapist working on a graduate degree. He described their relationship as "lovers," whereas she circled the descriptor "best friend." Prior to the conversation, Bob listed "current and future job situation" as a problem of some importance[17] that he had discussed with Renee before.

Both Bob and Renee presumed that Bob's unreasonable hours and work load were an uncontrollable feature of his current job. The early parts of their conversation were devoted to describing and agreeing that the job was stressful, with the implication that the stress was unbearable and inevitable. However, rather than simply matching emotional support that would help Bob to manage his feelings toward a bad situation, Renee used emotional and esteem support to encourage Bob to see a controllable course of action (quitting and seeking other employment). The following passage is characteristic of the way that Renee helped to articulate and validate Bob's feelings:

> BOB: So, it's that, you know, "what am I going to do next?" Well, in relation to this job thing. I mean I can only continue so long [*on this*].
> RENEE: [*Sixty hours*] a week could burn out anybody.
> BOB: And my goal, as I told you before, was to, ah, to be done by the end of this year, and have something else, hopefully have something else, but.
> RENEE: Yeah.
> BOB: That's my goal.
> RENEE: Well, like, likely you will. Just, sort of hard to know what it'll be.
> BOB: That's the scary part [*for me.*]
> RENEE: [*Yeah.*]
> BOB: I mean it, well, it is but it isn't. I mean, I'm excited that I can see, you know, maybe something else, but on the other hand, of course it is scary, because it's like we've said many times, is that, changing things, I mean it's very easy to become very comfortable in a situation.
> RENEE: It's scary, but it's exciting....

Renee also provided encouragement to Bob in a variety of ways. One recurring type of response was to describe to Bob her own experiences in quitting a job with a steady paycheck to go into her own business. This kind of experience-swapping response can be taken in a variety of ways:

---

[17] See footnote 2 for information about the scale and its distribution. Bob rated the job situation topic as a 6 (58th percentile, $z = .66$).

for example, as an indirect way of advising the hearer how to respond to problems (Glidewell et al., 1983) or as an expression of understanding and solidarity (Tannen, 1990). Renee combined these short narratives of her experience with explicit statements of her confidence in Bob's ability to do likewise, producing a style of support that had both advising and esteem-building qualities as in the following excerpt:

> RENEE: And you're a hard worker, and you know, the thing that really made an impression on me about myself is, if you're a hard worker and plan your time well and stuff, why should somebody be making a whole lot of money per hour for every hour you put in? I mean, it was certainly true of me.
>
> BOB: Right.
>
> RENEE: So, you know, and even some of the business ideas we've played around with, you know, knowing that there's a potential to do real well, and because of your own, you know, the fruits of your own work, [*is*]
>
> BOB: [*Right.*]
>
> RENEE: just kind of, you know, for those of us that are hard workers, it just makes good sense.

In this passage, Renee explicitly described a desirable attribute she saw in Bob (he's hard working) as well as including him in the "us" who are hard workers. Although she frequently compared her experiences with his to encourage him to take similar actions, she also was careful to acknowledge his feelings and the ways in which his situation might differ from her own as in the following excerpt:

> RENEE: ='Cause I know I gotta try and be as supportive, sometimes I feel supportive, sometimes I know I'm impatient, just because, well, I move quicker than you do, I think, and just, I don't know, well, the field I'm in also, there's more opportunity so it's easier for me [*to jump on*]
>
> BOB: [*Make a*]
>
> RENEE: the bandwagon. So I, [*I have to re*]mind
>
> BOB: [*Changes, yeah.*]
>
> RENEE: myself that, that it's been easy for me, but in part that's because of what I do,
>
> BOB: Right.
>
> RENEE: And a little just that, you know, I'm a different kind of person than you are.

Like Vicky and Susan, Bob and Renee assumed that it wasn't feasible to try to change Bob's working conditions. However, both Bob and Renee saw Bob as having the ability to control stress by seeking alternative employment. For a controllable stress, matching models would not necessarily predict that nurturant support would be the most effective type of response. Alternatively, Renee's ways of combining emotional, esteem, and informational support served to direct Bob's attention to the controllable aspects of his situation and encouraged him to undertake problem-solving coping.

Although matching models might not have predicted it, there are many indications that Bob found Renee's support to be highly effective and appropriate. At one point in the conversation he said, "you've shown me that it can be done and I appreciate that, I really do." Bob evaluated Renee's support very positively.[18] He indicated the conversation brought about a positive change in his attitudes and feelings, saying it "made me feel I was doing the right thing." He also said the conversation would result in changes in behavior ("will be more active in job search") and in thinking ("will put a plan discussed into action").[19] Finally, he felt the conversation increased his attraction to Renee and his feelings of closeness in their relationship.[20]

Conclusions from the Community Study

Analysis of these conversations indicated that most problems have controllable and uncontrollable features and one potentially consequential thing that occurs in troubles talk is selection of what aspects of a problem to discuss and then how to portray them. Various features of the talk itself may contribute to more or less compelling portrayals. The content of talk may contribute to an appraisal of a situation and coping options, including explicit statements about control as well as other features of content that may implicitly portray control (e.g., what aspects of a situation become the focus of talk and what causes of a problem are discussed). Other features of content have also figured in the preceding analysis, including appeals to common beliefs, the use of experience swapping, and participation in constructing fantasy themes. Stylistic features may play a role in constructing a view of the situation, including the use of humor, analogy, or solidary language such as back-channels, overlapping speech, pronominal usage, and collaborative completion of one another's sentences. The form and sequence of talk can contribute to situation definition, including repetition of similar narratives or discussion in a decision-making mode. Finally, this analysis has shown how partners coordinate (or fail to coordinate) their efforts

---

[18] See footnote 3 for information about the scale and its distribution. Bob's score was 6.57 (91st percentile, $z = 1.13$).

[19] See footnote 4 for information about the scale and its distribution. Bob's score was 6.5 (100th percentile, $z = 2.44$), a score significantly higher than the sample mean.

[20] See footnote 4 for information about the dyadic change scale and its distribution. Bob's score was 2 (91st percentile, $z = 1.31$).

as they weave together problem portrayals, coping possibilities, and support provisions.

CONCLUSIONS

Participants in talk about a trouble may represent the same situation in a wide variety of ways and can articulate similar information or support in different words, styles, forms, and sequences. Participants may cooperate in constructing a shared vision and that shared vision may be one that others would judge as adaptive or maladaptive. Participants may disagree over the parameters of the situation and this may lead to a variety of results: one partner may successfully persuade the other to adopt a more functional view of the situation and engage in better coping, one partner may lead the other astray, or the conversation may end with each person holding a different perspective and feeling misunderstood as a result.

The proponents of matching models are correct in pointing out that enacted support will buffer stress only insofar as it is responsive to the needs of the recipient and facilitates his or her coping. However, we would be well-served to discard "matching" as a metaphor for effective support provision. Instead, we must recognize the power of troubles talk to construct a view of the situation and coping options as well as the collaboration between provider and recipient that is required if new views of the situation and the support offered are to influence the support recipient's intention to change behavior, attitude, or feelings. Effective support must be rhetorically appealing and the success of a speaker's attempts are also contingent on coconstruction with the conversational partner. In addition, the utility of whatever vision of the situation and coping emerge must also be evaluated by external, normative standards of adaptation.

Perhaps *coherence* is a more useful notion than matching. Although matching suggests a simple selection of the correct option, coherence connotes a relationship that is plausible, intelligible, and meaningful. In this view, support is most likely to facilitate adaptive coping when there is coherence between the support a provider offers and the view of the situation he or she states or implies, coherence between the support provider's and recipient's views of the situation and its coping potential, and coherence between what is coconstructed in troubles talk and demands external to the conversation. Communicating stress-buffering support is less often a process of selecting the right answer to a multiple choice item ("For a controllable problem, provide: A. emotional support, B. tangible support," etc.) than it is a process of shaping a useful and meaningful response to a question or issue.

Several implications emerge from this analysis. First, understanding how enacted social support is appropriately fitted to the needs of a recipient requires content- and context-specific examination of stressors and support. To take into account the normative adaptiveness of enacted support, we cannot simply code or solicit self-reports of informational support or nurturant support. We need to know more about what was advised or how the person was nurtured.[21] We also need to know what kinds of tasks and challenges the person faces and what particular coping appraisals or actions we seek to encourage through the provision of social support. The importance of context-sensitive analysis was also discussed in the previous chapter on advice and I return to this theme in a more global way in Chapter 6.

Second, a useful set of questions involves not only whether appropriately matched support occurs but also *how*. When a support provider succeeds in offering a type of support that is well-suited to the recipient's needs and facilitates his or her coping, what are the features of talk through which this occurs? The descriptive analyses in this chapter provide a preliminary identification of some of these features of talk. This represents a different kind of research question but one that is particularly well-suited to demonstrating how the study of social support is related to broader theories of communication.

Understanding how social support is adapted to coping needs is also important if we wish to assist would-be support providers in offering support more successfully. Simply advising someone to offer informational support or nurturant support gives little guidance as to the form, content, style, or sequence that might be most effective. Similarly, pointing out to would-be providers that bereavement is an uncontrollable stress or that work stress is often controllable does not prepare them for the possibility that they might need to cajole a bereaved mother into accepting that her loss was not her fault or persuade a demoralized employee that problem-solving actions really are possible and effective.[22]

Third, recognizing the potential for social support to construct a view of the situation and coping options suggests fruitful links between social support and other important lines of research on how individuals cope with stress. For example, Snyder and Higgins (1988) reviewed research on the potential benefits to individuals of making excuses and they acknowledged the role others play in collaborating to construct causal attributions for personal failures. These processes bear some resemblance to the situation definition processes I observed in social support messages

---

[21] Coyne and Gottlieb (1996) make a similar argument with respect to our understanding of coping, discouraging the use of generic checklists and encouraging the development of measures that are attuned to the challenges and options experienced by individuals in particular kinds of stressful situations.

[22] Buttny (1996) has made a similar case with respect to the practices of professional therapists. He claims that helping clients to reframe, redefine, or reconfigure their problem is one of "the most artful practices of therapy" (p. 126) and proceeds to describe the conversational practices through which this art is accomplished in a session of marital therapy.

and troubles talk conversations. Perhaps one way close others support us is by validating or providing excuses (and this may also suggest a way in which well-meaning support could ultimately prove harmful as well). Similarly, there is a substantial and somewhat controversial body of research on the adaptive consequences of positive illusions (e.g., Colvin & Block, 1994; Colvin, Block, & Funder, 1995; Taylor & Armor, 1996; Taylor, Kemeny, Reed, Bower, & Gruenewald, 2000). This research has focused primarily on the cognitive processes of individuals; however, recognizing the ways that social support may construct a view of situations as more or less serious, manageable, blameworthy, and so on points to a role for close relational partners in coconstructing illusions. Finally, recent research suggests potentially complex relationships between an individual's predisposition to view situations as controllable or uncontrollable and responses to another's encouragement to become more self-reliant. Reich, Zautra, and Manne (1993) studied women with rheumatoid arthritis and found those who felt little control experienced greater distress overall. They then examined whether having a spouse who encouraged greater self-reliance improved a woman's state of mind. They found spouses encouraging a view of the situation as controllable did not uniformly produce beneficial results. It would be useful to examine variability in *how* a spouse encouraged self-reliance and whether, for example, a spouse's especially persuasive rendering of the situation as controllable might offset individual predispositions. In addition, it would be useful to examine how partners in ongoing relationships who have incongruent individual orientations to control can manage nonetheless to provide satisfying support to one another.

This chapter has challenged our view of the problem or situation as a static feature to which support providers must adapt as they attempt to help support recipients. However, I have presumed that we at least know who is the provider and who is the recipient of support and that the task at hand is for one person to give support to the other. In the next chapter, I challenge these notions as well.

5

Problematizing Provider/Recipient Roles in Troubles Talk

The terms *support provider* and *support recipient* are widely used in the literature on social support with little consideration of the model of communication they imply: that support is a resource or service given by a provider to a recipient to bring about assistance with a problem experienced by the recipient. Studies usually presume that over the course of a given troubles talk conversation (or even over the course of coping with some life stress), one person is the support provider and the other is the support recipient. These interactive roles are defined with reference to a problem external to the conversation: Once a problem or trouble has been identified, the recipient is the person who has the problem and the provider is the other person. It is assumed to be relatively clear who has the problem and, therefore, who is the provider and who is the recipient. Finally, the terms connote an economic exchange (many researchers even refer to troubles talk conversations as *support transactions*). Providers and recipients deal in goods, services, or resources rather than in symbols, routines, or relationships.

The provider/receiver transaction model is consistent with the historical impetus for the study of social support. One prominent area of social support research evolved out of interests in individual coping resources that protected a person from stress as well as with the possibility that social support might serve as an alternative to professional health services. The provider/recipient transaction conception that emerged from this early history is more sensible for some kinds of questions (e.g., Why do some people under stress fare better than others? What does a social network do for people that reduces the need for social services?) than for other kinds of questions (e.g., What are the communicative processes that lead participants to derive a sense of support from a conversation? Why are some conversations experienced as more satisfying and meaningful than others?). When we study how social support is communicated in the context of close personal relationships, a provider/recipient conceptualization begins to break down.

One problem with the provider/recipient conceptualization is that in close relationships, it may not be entirely clear who is the provider and who is the recipient of support. Because close relational partners are interdependent, they experience shared stresses (e.g., financial difficulties) and stresses originating in one partner's experience affect the other, either directly (e.g., one partner's illness creates caregiving stress for the other) or indirectly (e.g., empathy for one's partner leads to the experience of distress at seeing him or her upset) (O'Brien & DeLongis, 1997; Westman & Vinokur, 1998). This has led a number of researchers to call for a reconceptualization of coping and social support as relational phenomena (e.g., Bodenmann, 1997a, 1997b; Coyne & Fiske, 1992; Cutrona, 1996a; Lyons, Mickelson, Sullivan, & Coyne, 1998; O'Brien & DeLongis, 1997).

When both partners are experiencing stress in response to daily hassles or major life events, it may be difficult to determine what behaviors are providing support to the other and what behaviors are part of an individual's own coping (Coyne et al., 1988; Coyne, Ellard, & Smith, 1990; Lydon & Zanna, 1992). This is not simply a researcher's problem of categorization – the intertwining of partners' coping processes may lead to very real and potentially negative consequences for them. Some partners who believe they are trying to support one another find their efforts working at cross-purposes, with negative consequences for their individual well-being and for their relationship. For example, Coyne and his colleagues (Coyne et al., 1988) described how family members of a chronically ill patient became overprotective as a way of managing their own stress. Doing things for the patient or engaging in excessive monitoring could be motivated as much by a desire to feel control over one's own stress and anxiety as it was by a concern for the patient and, in fact, was detrimental to the patient's recovery. Gottlieb and Wagner (1991) described how some parents of chronically ill children had different preferred ways of coping and engaged in attempts to change one another's coping strategies. Is a wife who attempts to persuade her husband to express his distress more openly (or a husband who encourages his wife to become more stoic) altruistically trying to help the other person cope more effectively? Or is she (or he) selfishly trying to minimize conflicts or challenges to his or her own alternative way of coping? Likely there are elements of both motivations.

A second challenge to the provider/recipient conceptualization is that the most effective support may be that which goes unrecognized as support. For example, Bolger and colleagues (2000) studied sixty-eight couples in which one partner was preparing for the New York State Bar Examination. Partners reported daily on whether they had "listened to and comforted" the examinee and examinees reported whether they had been the recipient of this form of support. The analyses showed how an examinee's report of support received and his or her partner's report of support provided on one day influenced the examinee's anxiety and stress on the following day. Bolger and colleagues found that as the bar exam approached, examinees' levels of *anxiety* increased daily, independent of partners' reports of support provision. However, partner's reports of support provision were related to examinees feeling less *depressed* the next day and this effect was strongest in the final week before the exam. Perhaps more interesting, however, were the effects of examinees' reports of receiving support. When examinees reported receiving support, their levels of anxiety *and* depression tended to be greater the following day, and this effect became even stronger during the final week before the exam. Taken together, the findings on partner and examinee reports indicated that in the most stressful phase of preparation for the bar exam (the final week), the best situation was one in which partners said they provided support but examinees did not report receiving it.

Unfortunately, the measures in this study shed no further light on what these conversations looked like, why examinees' perceptions of being on the receiving end of listening and comforting might be related to feeling worse the following day, or why a partner's report of providing listening and comfort that went unreported by the examinee might be especially beneficial. However, Bolger and colleagues speculated that beneficial invisible support included two kinds of interactions. Sometimes, one partner may conceal the assistance he or she provides to the other, completing tasks without mentioning it or shielding the partner from concerns or problems to reduce his or her stress. Coyne and Smith (1994) have shown how this kind of *protective buffering* by spouses was associated with the recipient's improved self-efficacy. Bolger and his colleagues suggested that another type of invisible support is the provision of coping assistance with such skill that the recipient does not differentiate the episode from the ordinary level of caring and concern experienced in the relationship and, consequently, does not experience threats to self-esteem or feelings of obligation and dependence (see also Coyne & DeLongis, 1986; Lieberman, 1986). The support provider does not attempt to conceal anything but his or her freely offered assistance is delivered in indirect or tactful ways that obscure what might otherwise be costs or risks to the recipient's identity and to the relationship.

It may be when relational partners frame an interaction as social support (and take on the interactive roles of provider and recipient) that they are most vulnerable to the forms of unhelpful support and other difficulties that were discussed in Chapter 1. The roles of provider and recipient are asymmetrical: One person has and gives, the other lacks and gets. Having may imply greater knowledge, competence, and power. Giving may imply obligation, control, and evaluation. In contrast, social support that is provided in indirect, covert, and unobtrusive ways can avoid some of these threats to valued identities and relational definitions.

Further, instances when close relational partners define their interactions as explicitly seeking, giving, and receiving aid may be the exception to the more ordinary ways in which needs are met and support is assumed in the give and take of everyday communal life (Coyne et al., 1990; Gottlieb, 1985b). When a partner listens to an account of his wife's stressful day, is he providing support or is he merely participating in their daily ritual of recapping the day's events? When siblings work out an arrangement for getting their aging mother to a series of doctor's appointments, are they providing support to one another for the stresses of caregiving or are they simply having another session of problem-solving discussion? Of course, these events need not be one or the other: Social support can be, and often is, found in the mundane, flexible, and largely nonmemorable conversations about problems that make up daily life (Barnes & Duck, 1994; Leatham & Duck, 1990). However, the provider/recipient metaphor may not lead us to examine these conversations and may not prove useful for understanding how they work (or fail to work).

Provider/recipient roles are not the only ones that close relational partners may enact when they talk about a problem, nor are they the only roles from which coping assistance may flow. This chapter reviews several converging lines of evidence that point to limitations in the provider/recipient model of enacting social support. There certainly are conversations in which the identities and relationship enacted by participants can be aptly described as provider/recipient and there are circumstances in which the social support that occurs from within this frame is useful for coping and relationally satisfying. Indeed the analyses in Chapters 3 and 4 demonstrate there are effective ways of engaging in coping assistance that entail one person adopting a support provider role and the other playing the complementary role of recipient. However, to presume that this is the only, or even the primary, orientation close relational partners take is unduly limiting. Recognizing other roles partners may adopt as they talk about troubles and assist one another in coping is useful to theorists and close relational partners alike. As theorists, it helps us to identify a wider range of conversations as relevant to our understanding of enacted support, coping, and relational satisfaction. As relational partners, it alerts us to additional ways of talking about problems and coordinating coping.

This chapter reports findings from two studies of the interaction patterns of married couples who are coping with various kinds of stressors. I suspect the processes I describe are not unique to married couples, but the marital relationship is a useful place to begin (Coyne & Fiske, 1992). Although levels of interdependence in marriage vary, it is reasonable to expect that married couples will experience multiple forms of interdependence that set the stage for coordinated coping. By definition, the marital relationship entails legal interdependence and most marriages entail an intertwining of daily life, routine, space, and emotion as well. Married couples are likely to be exposed to some shared stressors and to be affected by one another's experience of stressors.

The first study examined conversations in which spouses talked about daily stresses and hassles, whereas the second study was based on interviews with couples coping with a major life stressor. Taken together, these studies form the basis for an expanded conceptualization of the interactional roles and conversational frames that are available to close relational partners as they talk about problems that affect both people and as they attempt to coordinate their coping.

COMMUNAL COPING WITH EVERYDAY STRESSES AND HASSLES

To understand some of the interactive roles available to close relational partners, Virginia McDermott and I (Goldsmith & McDermott, 2000) returned to the collection of conversations from the Community Study. We focused our attention on the seventeen married couples in our sample (a profile of the married subsample is provided in the Appendix) to better understand the range of interactive roles close relational partners might enact when they talked about daily stresses or hassles. Although the procedures we used to solicit troubles talk in our study identified one party as the "person who will introduce a problem topic into the conversation," we observed variability in the degree to which partners adopted clear provider and recipient roles.

Previous research has demonstrated that the interactive roles speakers adopt in troubles talk conversations are not simply given at the outset of a conversation but are enacted in the ways participants talk about a problem. For example, Jefferson (1980, 1984a, 1984b, 1988) showed that once a trouble had been introduced into a conversation, there was some pressure to speak seriously about that topic; laughter and topic changes could signal insensitivity to another person's hardship. However, persons with troubles sometimes wished to demonstrate that their troubles weren't getting the best of them, and this could explain why they initiated laughter and breaks in the talk about the trouble to discuss lighter topics. Being participants in a talk about a trouble involved turn-by-turn efforts to display an appropriate balance between taking the trouble seriously and resisting being consumed by the trouble. Jefferson's work described systematic patterns in the ways conversation partners managed the tension between attending to a trouble and attending to "business as usual" as well as simultaneously managing the transition from the interactional distance appropriate to routine conversation to the greater intimacy that occurred as a trouble was discussed.

Similarly, research by Coupland and colleagues (1991) focused on the ways that painful self-disclosures arose in intergenerational conversations between elderly and younger interactants. They showed that talking about one person's problems was not always the result of a simple decision by that person to introduce her trouble into the conversation. Instead, each person's contributions to the conversation could constrain or enable what the other person said next. Coupland and colleagues challenged the stereotype that elders want to talk about problems more often than younger interactants. Sometimes elderly speakers did volunteer information about their problems but there were also many instances in which statements and questions by younger conversational partners encouraged (or even demanded) elderly speakers to talk about their problems. Taking on the role of a problem discloser (and potential support recipient) was something accomplished through the actions of both participants in a conversation.

These studies demonstrate that it takes two to talk about one person's troubles. That provider/recipient roles are a conversational accomplishment, and not simply given, is also indicated by research suggesting there are alternative roles participants might adopt. Tannen (1990) suggested that participants in troubles talk may have different expectations about the roles and relationship they will enact.[1] Some participants may view the disclosure of a problem as an implicit request for problem-solving assistance, in response to which they are expected to adopt the interactional role of expert adviser or fixer. Within this set of expectations, the appropriate response is to give advice or offer aid so that the other person's problem might be resolved. This is a clear example of the provider/recipient frame that is prominent in the social support literature: One partner has a problem for which he or she seeks and receives support (in this case, informational or tangible support) and the relationship is asymmetrical.

Tannen pointed out that there is an alternative set of expectations for engaging in troubles talk that presumes that disclosure of a problem should be met with a gesture of solidarity, such as disclosing a similar experience or problem of one's own. Glidewell and colleagues (1983) called this second pattern *experience swapping* and described how it enacted egalitarian relationships and autonomous identities among teachers who sought support from one another for work stress. In this pattern, it was less clear that one partner was providing support to the other, because both individuals discussed problems and could have drawn various kinds of support from comparing situations and commiserating together. This alternative

---

[1] Tannen (1990) identified the two different orientations to troubles talk as corresponding to distinct male and female styles of speech. However, subsequent research has called into question whether men and women differ substantially in their adoption of these different orientations (Goldsmith & Dun, 1997; Goldsmith & Fulfs, 1999). Even if the two styles of engaging in troubles talk are not strongly differentiated by gender, they nonetheless represent two possible ways of engaging in troubles talk, suggesting that participants may pursue more than one frame and, therefore, enactment of one frame rather than the other is potentially negotiable between participants.

orientation to troubles talk shows social support need not always be enacted within the framework of clear-cut provider/recipient roles.

The conversations between spouses in the Community Study (Goldsmith & McDermott, 2000) demonstrated a common pattern that did not clearly resemble either provider/recipient or experience swapper patterns. Instead, many of the couples in our sample enacted a pattern in which *both* partners engaged in talk focused on coping with the same *shared* problem. These conversations appeared to be the enactment of what Lyons and colleagues (1998) call *communal coping*: a process in which one or more members of a dyad, group, or community define a problem as shared and engage in communication about the problem and cooperative action to reduce its negative impact.

Our data provide insight into what communal coping looks like in conversations of married couples. We identified the following four features of talk that could be involved in the enactment of communal coping with a stress, hassle, or problem: (1) explicit statements of one's orientation to the problem, (2) use of plural, possessive pronouns in referring to a problem or solution, (3) proposed participation in a solution that benefits both partners, and (4) alternation between partners in the enactment of problem disclosures and support behaviors. These features served not only to mark or enact communal coping but they also served as resources through which participants actively negotiated this role. In some conversations, both partners enacted communal coping, whereas in other conversations the roles were contested so that employing features of communal coping talk served to press for adoption of one partner's preferred frame for conducting the conversation. In what follows, I describe these four features and provide examples of their use in conversation.

Conversational Features of Communal Coping

Explicit Statements of Problem Orientation

One of the clearest ways participants signaled communal coping was through their explicit statements about whether a stress was shared by both partners or was primarily one person's problem. Because communal coping involves a shared problem, each partner needs to orient to a situation as problematic or stressful for him or her (i.e., it's not my problem or your problem alone, it's our problem). If both participants in a troubles talk conversation directly state that they are worried about the same problem, this is one way of constructing their roles as communal copers rather than as provider and recipient (roles in which the problem is primarily experienced by the recipient) or experience swappers (roles in which each person experiences a different but parallel or similar type of problem).

One example of explicit talk about problem orientation occurred in the conversation between Julie and Rob, a professional couple in their thirties who had known one another for over 9 years.[2] In the passage that follows, Julie and Rob discussed whether to begin trying to conceive a child in the near future and their worries and concerns about having a second child. They explicitly stated what was or was not a worry and for whom, collaborating in their construction of this as a shared decision with some accompanying stress as follows:

> JULIE: And if I got pregnant in September, we'd have a baby sometime in June. If I got pregnant in October, we'd have a baby sometime in July. I just don't want to be, huge pregnant in the middle of summer like I was with Becky. So I just figured,
> ROB: Hmmm.
> JULIE: and if, and if, I mean you could still go on your backpacking trip.
> ROB: 'Kay. I know, I know, I'm not worried about that.
> JULIE: What are you worried about?
> ROB: Having two children.
> JULIE: (*laughter*) That's what I was thinking about today, too. Just goin' to the doc, taking 'em to the doctor. You know,=
> ROB: =uh-hum.
>   {*6 lines omitted*}
> JULIE: And then I had this picture of me in the waiting room at the doctor's office, with a three-year-old and a newborn, "sit down Becky, don't [*Becky, don't*]
> ROB: [*It's frightening.*]
> JULIE: Becky," you know.
> ROB: It's [*frightening*]
> JULIE: [*And the bab*]y's over here cryin' and I'm "no no, get away,=
> ROB: =M-[*hmmm.*]
> JULIE: [*don*]'t do that, sit down, come here," y'know, it made me think.
> ROB: That's true,=
> JULIE: =two babies.
> ROB: But by [*then too she*]
> JULIE: [*it'll be crazy*]
> ROB: she'll be almost three or [*three or*]
> JULIE: [*I know.*]
> ROB: older   than three.
> JULIE: Plus I feel like,
> ROB: she'll be co[*mpletely different*]

---

[2] I have given study participants pseudonyms. All the married couples who appear in this chapter were white. Because participants in the community study came from a variety of relationship types, we asked simply how long partners had known each other. We have no data on how long the married couples had been married.

JULIE: [*I guess I feel,*] like, now that we have more friends with children, there can always be a trade-off,

ROB: Hm-hmmm.=

JULIE: =You know,

ROB: [*M-hmmm*]

JULIE: [*Like,*] can I take, can I drop Becky off because I have to take the baby for a doctor's appointment,

ROB: hum hum

JULIE: you know, and then tomorrow I'll take your, child, you know? So where as before when when I didn't have to do that she was the only [*child,*]

ROB: [*yeah,*]

In the opening lines of this excerpt, Julie anticipated one possible source of concern with the timing of getting pregnant (Rob's planned backpacking trip) and indicated this shouldn't be a problem. Rob explicitly stated he was not worried about that, which led to clarification of the worry they shared: how they would manage with having two young children. In addition to explicitly stating that this was a shared worry, they went on to collaborate in constructing a concrete example of the difficulties this could pose. Rob's agreement (e.g. "Mm-hmmm," "yeah") and summary statements of the gist of the story (e.g., "It's frightening") were interspersed throughout Julie's description of a hypothetical stressful situation. In their discussion of concerns about having another child, this couple clearly oriented to this as a shared concern with which they both were attempting to cope (in this case, coping prospectively). Their coping efforts were also shared: Both partners engaged in a cognitive reappraisal of their situation, with Rob pointing out that their older daughter would be at least 3 years old and Julie pointing out that they now have friends with children who could provide child care assistance.

In the previous example, communal coping roles were enacted through explicit statements about shared concerns. However, explicit statements about who is or is not worried could also serve to clarify that communal coping would not occur. Twenty-seven-year-old Rita and her 30-year-old husband Kevin were professionals who had known one another for 5 or 6 years (she says 5, he says 6). In the excerpt that follows, Rita viewed costs associated with a possible new job as a problem to which they should both orient, whereas Kevin saw this as a concern of hers about which he could provide reassurance:

RITA: Well, it seems like, yeah, but if we, if you got, if we got a new job, if we, when, we get our new jobs, then it could be very manageable because we could live the way we were used to after, well, that's not really realistic though because we're gonna move and things will cost more.

KEVIN: You think? I wonder about that. I wonder if they're really going to cost all that more?

RITA: When you move it costs a lot of money to move.

KEVIN: Yeah, up front it does. I agree with that.

RITA: But,

KEVIN: I mean, say, we're in Cincinnati, we're not going to move for any more or for any less than what at least five thousand increase a year, for somebody. You know in (*Kenmont*) [*the rents are the same,*]

RITA: [*The rents are the same.*] But, but if you remember when you moved here from Cincinnati that things cost less. Your insurance went down.

KEVIN: Right=

RITA: =um, we noticed some changes.

KEVIN: Gas was more expensive here than it was.

RITA: Umm, here?

KEVIN: I don't know, I just, I think that will work out. The problem is the up-front money to move and if you get the right job they'll move you.

RITA: We won't get that job.

KEVIN: Yeah, I don't know. It's possible.

In Kevin's first line in this excerpt, he questioned whether this issue was a concern ("You think? I wonder...?") and in the turns that followed he listed various costs that would be similar or less in a new location. At one point, he explicitly indicated that he thought "this will work out" and that this was not a concern for him. In subsequent lines, as Rita continued to introduce complications associated with a possible job relocation, Kevin continued in his role as provider of reassurance and information and also explicitly said, "No, I'm really not worried about that at all" and "Yeah, I don't, I don't see it as much of a problem." Some concession on their contrasting orientations to this problem finally occurred near the end of their discussion of this topic as follows:

KEVIN: But, it's gonna be hard when we start having to make decisions, I think.

RITA: Yeah, so far, we don't worry about anything yet.

Kevin's responses played the role of support provider, whereas Rita's expressions of concern enacted the role of support seeker/receiver. Kevin further clarified this orientation through his explicit declarations that he did not share her perception that this is a source of concern, much less of shared concern.

Use of Plural and Plural Possessive Pronouns

Pronoun choices are another way in which participants in troubles talk indicated their orientation to problems and to their respective interactive roles. In some conversations in our data set, participants enacted a provider/recipient relationship by referring to a problem as mine or yours. Ray, a 44-year-old laborer, and Brenda, a 50-year-old teacher, had known one another for 5 years. One of the troubles Brenda introduced in the conversation involved stress associated with achieving her goals for creative expression. As she introduced this topic in the following excerpt, she used *my, me,* and *I* in her description of the problem (I use italics to highlight these pronouns, but this doesn't indicate any kind of verbal emphasis):

Okay, that the Sundancers and everything, that has been a success in *my* creativity but when I wrote that thing down on the paper what I thought of is how many times, you know, just *me* personally, *I* have been so frustrated.

In contrast, communal coping was marked by referring to problems and solutions using *we* and *our*. Blaine and Karen were each 31 years old and had known one another for $5\frac{1}{2}$ years. They engaged in communal coping in their talk about fertility problems they had experienced and a decision about possible therapy. Karen began discussion of this topic by describing her listing and rating of this problem and Blaine immediately framed the problem as shared by saying "that's our goal" as follows:

KAREN: and like I put number six for getting, for having a baby
BLAINE: well that's our goal
KAREN: I know, but what if it doesn't happen though?
BLAINE: Well, there's always adoption, right?
KAREN: yeah, but that takes a lot of money
BLAINE: Mmm-hum. More than I have
KAREN: yeah [*I mean what if*]
BLAINE: [*more than*] we have.

Blaine self-corrected "more than *I* have" to "more than *we* have." That he made a point to do so, even though it meant talking over Karen, suggests he was actively orienting to the significance of pronominal choice.

Another example in which pronoun choices underscored role orientation occurred in the conversation between Jake and Mia, who were each 32 and employed by the university and who had been together for 4 years. They engaged in an extended discussion of "what bills *we* have coming up" but within this larger discussion of a shared problem, they marked one aspect of this stressor as his, both with an explicit statement of problem ownership and with corresponding changes in pronominal usage (to "*my* problem" and "*I* have to drop it in the mail"):

JAKE: Um, student loan.
MIA: That's not my problem.

JAKE: No, no that is my problem. OK.

MIA: When's that due?

JAKE: On the whatever, how many days this month – thirty, thirty-one?

MIA: It's on the last day of the=

JAKE: =last day of the month, yeah, so I have to drop it in the mail this week. I'm pretty close on all those 'cuz I'm gonna work.

It is conceivable that making his student loan payment could have been framed as a shared stressor insofar as the debt affects their joint total resources and they appear to share all other bills in common. Both Mia's explicit statement that his student loans are not her problem and the change in pronouns from we to I serve to set boundaries around the problem for which communal coping will occur.

Participation in Solution for Joint Benefit

It is possible for both members of a couple to participate in a solution to a stressor but to nonetheless adopt provider/recipient roles by defining the stress and the benefits of solving it as belonging more to one partner than the other. Ron and Kay were both educators in their late thirties who had known one another for $18\frac{1}{2}$ years. On his preconversation questionnaire, Ron listed as a stressor "schedule for summer vacation." In this passage, he and Kay discussed whether each person felt a need to take a summer vacation (i.e., Who was feeling the stress of needing to plan the vacation? Who needed, and would therefore benefit from, taking a vacation?) as follows:

RON: Ok, so full steam ahead on that. Ah, now let me ask you about um, summer vacation, if we're going to have one.

KAY: Haven't we had it already.

RON: Nah, I, yeah, but, what would you like to do once, I'd like to have some time to um, to do things, but [*I'm flexible,*]

KAY: [*What things?*]

RON: I don't know, we usually have a summer vacation after my work ends like the first week of August and I don't want to sit around, I don't want to sit around and I want a break somewhere in there and I, I suspect you do, but maybe I'm wrong,

KAY: I'm having a break.

RON: Well, ok, you're having one,

KAY: I'm having my break with the play.=

RON: =I'm not.=

KAY: =I understand,=

RON: =So, what, what do you, [*what are our possibilities?*]

KAY: [*Well, we have plans to be at*] we have plans to be at the ball game Friday, August Fourth

After Ron initiated talk about this topic, he indicated what he wanted and how that required a decision. Ron said he assumed that Kay would want a vacation and therefore felt some need to plan one (i.e., he presumed they would engage in communal coping) but he also acknowledged that he "may be wrong" in this assumption, likely in response to her statement that she thought they'd already had a vacation and her question about what kinds of things he wanted to do. Kay's responses consistently indicated that she experienced no pressure to plan a vacation because she had already taken a break by being in a play; however, they clarified that although she didn't experience this as a shared stress or feel a need for the benefit of a vacation, she understood that it was an issue for him. His "so" in his last turn in this excerpt seemed to imply that having clarified whose stress this was and who would benefit from its resolution, they could proceed to make a decision and, in fact, her overlapping speech (beginning with "well") showed that she, too, was ready to proceed to making plans.

The couple then talked for several lines about each person's ideas for a vacation. Before long, however, Kay again made clear that she didn't view this decision as a shared stressor. This time she did so by pointing out whose preferences were most relevant to resolving this stress and for whose benefit this vacation would be. In her first turn in the following excerpt, she made it clear she is playing support provider rather communal coper. She pointed out how the solution they are seeking should be one that benefited him and she provided problem-solving support (e.g., advice about how to proceed and questions that solicited relevant information) as follows:

> KAY: Well, I would like you to think about what kind of activities you would like to do. Do you want to, do you want to hang by the pool and go swimming, do you want to go to a lake where you can go swimming? Do you want to go boating? Do you want to go,
> RON: I, [*I don't know,*]
> KAY: [*You know,*] walking in the woods,=
> RON: =I'[*m not sure,*]
> KAY: [*What things*] do you want to do?
> RON: Yeah, I got to think about that,=
> KAY: =Once you know what things you want to do then we can figure out where we can go to do those things.=

Both partners indicated through their choices of pronouns that this was primarily Ron's decision ("*you* need to think about what activities *you* would like" and "yeah *I* got to think about that"), though in the concluding line, Kay indicated that once Ron knew his preferences, then "we" could go to do those things. The vacation plan that would conclude Ron's decision-making stress would be a shared experience, but the couple constructed a view of the problem (making a decision) and the benefits of solving the problem (taking the vacation) as primarily his.

Alternating Enactment of Disclosure/Support

Provider/recipient roles imply different kinds of contributions from the two participants in troubles talk: the support recipient discloses information about a problem he or she is experiencing and the support provider offers responses intended to assist in coping with that problem. In contrast, communal coping is marked by both partners participating in problem disclosure and discussion of coping responses. Ted and Cheryl were a professional couple in their early thirties who had known one another for nearly 14 years. In her preconversation questionnaire, Cheryl identified "problems with our house" as a stressor. She initiated talk about this topic but Ted was the first to identify a specific facet of the problem they would discuss. Similarly, in the ensuing lengthy discussion, they took turns proposing various coping options and either challenging or supporting one another's coping efforts as follows:

CHERYL: Oh well, so what about those projects?

TED: Um, the window outside our bedroom

CHERYL: Yeah, but we can't do that right, I mean, we have to get somebody to do that, and that's gonna cost money.

TED: You see I think it's gonna cost so much money and the guy that we got last time who would do it for a reasonable price was pretty much gonna do it pretty slap-dash, you know, just

CHERYL: Yeah but on that side of the house, why would it matter?

TED: Right, but that was still what, 250, 300 dollars?=

CHERYL: =No, he was gonna, it was un-, less than a hundred. It was like 90 something. But that's why he never showed up.

TED: Perhaps, um, but I figure I can probably do it.

CHERYL: Really? But that's why we went and, and got all the estimates in the first place, it was [*because*]

TED: [*because*] I didn't have the time either.

CHERYL: No, I thought it was because [*you*]

TED: [*it*] was both.

CHERYL: you had started it and

TED: Yeah and to do the job properly meant taking out the whole window and everything and I didn't want to do that, so we ended up going with this really cheap guy but he never came, so I think I can do as good a job as he would.

CHERYL: Uh hmm.

In response to Cheryl's question about "those projects," Ted identified the windows as needing repair. That he so readily came up with one of "those projects" implicitly endorsed Cheryl's assessment that there were problems around the house that required action. In the ensuing discussion (and continuing beyond this excerpt), both proposed and discussed the merits of various possible solutions and each provided problem-solving coping/support for this shared problem. They eventually reached agreement Ted could repair the window and Cheryl provided esteem support in the form of a compliment on his workmanship in making temporary repairs to the window. Ted then identified reinforcing the porch as another project, they discussed possible solutions until reaching a conclusion, and then Cheryl identified painting the doors and shutters as another facet of the larger "problems with the house" stressor.

The types of problem identification and support turns that are exchanged in communal coping did not always take the form of problem-solving coping. For an example, we return to the conversation between Ralph and Lisa (a couple introduced in Chapter 4). Ralph identified "children" as a stress for him and he initiated talk about whether to have a baby this year. The couple jointly constructed a humorous diversion from the topic in the following excerpt:

RALPH: We gonna have the baby this year?

LISA: I don't know.

RALPH: Well, if you decide we are, let me know ahead of time, okay?

LISA: Why?

RALPH: That way I can make sure I'm extra juicy.

LISA: Oh.

RALPH: Make sure all my tadpoles are in order.

LISA: I'm debating whether to have 'em or not. I mean, I see all the brats running around, and I don't want anything like that. I mean like Rob's kids. I don't think I could handle that.=

RALPH: =That's what I'm saying. We could have one. If it turns out good, great. If it doesn't, (*laughter*)

LISA: Sell it.=

RALPH: ="It's not ours. It's not ours, honest. It's not. We don't know where it came from. It was a stray. Yeah, we got our cats."

LISA: "It followed him home. We found it in the rain."

RALPH: "She brought him home. You know how she is. You know. She finds him, and she just brings 'em home. Remember that puppy you told me about. Man, she's the one. She knew. I had nothing."

LISA: I think she'd catch on.

RALPH: She'd know I was right though about you and bringing home puppies.

LISA: I just brought home one.

RALPH: We were just talking about one kid. How many kids do you want?

In this excerpt, communal coping was enacted as both partners alternated in identifying aspects of the problem and in contributing diversionary coping efforts and support for one another's diversionary coping efforts.

Ralph initiated both discussion of the topic and the first round of humorous diversion. Lisa returned to a serious comment about this problem ("I'm debating whether to have 'em or not . . .") and he responded with another humorous remark. Rather than continuing to press for a serious discussion (e.g., by pointing to another aspect of the problem or by offering some serious way of dealing with the prospect of bratty kids), Lisa joined in the humorous comparison of kids and pets. Then, it was Ralph who returned to a serious treatment of the topic ("We were just talking about one kid . . .").

In the two previous examples, and in other conversations displaying this pattern, partners not only alternated roles in identifying problems and proposing and supporting coping actions but also tended to do so in fairly brief and interlocking turns. In contrast, in conversations in which one partner was a support provider and the other was a recipient, there was less symmetry in length of turns. Paul and Tonia were both in their late forties and both employed in sales for the same company. They had known one another for 27 years. They discussed some of Tonia's dissatisfactions with her current job. Her extended narratives about the problem contrasted with his brief offerings of clarification, information, and suggestions as in the following excerpt:

> TONIA: When we were handing in paperwork into Raymond yesterday, we had to hand him in some forms, he wanted our, um, ahh, what do I want to call it, trip sheet, our stores, and he wanted ah, hand tabs of our new items and where they were. He said "I don't care how you turn this in to me or how it looks like," well, mine was the only one that was handwritten. I said, "I don't have a computer," see Betty and Sam have computers, even though they are RSR's[3] because they do ads.
>
> PAUL: Company?
>
> TONIA: Ye[*ah.*]
>
> PAUL: [*Sup*]ply?
>
> TONIA: Yeah, but they do ads, they need computers, I don't do ads, I know, according to the company, there's no reason to give me a computer and there's not, there really isn't. There's nothing that I do on it for the company, except the company and these little forms.
>
> PAUL: The sales reps don't even have them.
>
> TONIA: They don't have computers?
>
> PAUL: You know, just the little ones in the store.
>
> TONIA: Oh, I didn't know that. You know I can't say, I can't say for sure that they're company, I should check. I just assume because Sheila had one in Indianapolis and she was an RSR. {*This turn continues for some time with a lengthy narrative about Sheila.*}

---

[3] We think RSR probably refers to "Regional Sales Representative."

PAUL: Why don't you get the girl's who just left?

TONIA: Tami Sanders? Ah, I think she, I was going to say, she didn't have one.

PAUL: She should.=

TONIA: =She, she should have one. I don't know, see if that's, oh yeah, she's in, I don't know if she's an RSR. But, see there's no point in going through all that right now, I don't plan being there, I want to get out of there in like a month or two {*This turn continues with explanation about why she wishes to leave the job.*}

The clear adoption of support provider and recipient roles was especially interesting, given other background information that was revealed in the conversation. Tonia and Paul worked at the same company and at a later point in their conversation, it was clear that he was familiar with some of the problems with company policy she identified. Consequently, experience swapping about their respective frustrations with the same company shortcomings was a viable option for this couple, yet he opted to provide support in response to her troubles telling. At another point in the conversation, Tonia acknowledged that she brought her job stress home and that she knew it irritated him, opening up the possibility that her specific job stresses could also be treated as a shared problem for which communal coping could occur. Thus, it would appear that for this couple, discussing this particular problem, several possible role configurations could have emerged. One of the ways in which they jointly enacted the provider/recipient roles from among the available options was by her taking (and his allowing her to take) extended turns at problem description and by him offering (and her accepting) brief turns that gave support for her stress.

Conclusions From the Communal Coping Study

At the outset of this chapter, I described two limitations to the provider/recipient conceptualization of enacted support that dominates the social support literature. The analysis of married couples' conversations in the Community Study is particularly useful for demonstrating the first of these two limitations: the interdependence that characterizes close relationships may complicate our designation of one person as support provider and the other as support recipient. Our procedures instructed one partner to talk about a problem and so it would have been easy to presume that person was the support recipient and relatively straightforward to simply code the utterances of the other partner for the types of social support he or she provided. However, doing so would have obscured the degree to which some partners engaged in communal coping and the ways in which provider/recipient or communal coping were negotiated in subtle (and sometimes not so subtle) ways.

To this point, I have examined some of the different role orientations close relational partners may adopt when a stressor is the explicitly recognized topic of a conversation and when coping with that stress is a recognizable purpose of the conversation to which both partners orient. However, even expanding our conceptualization of partners' roles to include communal coping is too narrow. I turn now to data that address the second of the two limitations of the provider/recipient conceptualization of enacted support: the way in which it overlooks the enactment of support in the context of ordinary life and daily routines.

THE ROLE OF ROUTINE TALK IN CARDIAC RECOVERY

The Illinois Heart Care Project focused on how couples coping with one person's recovery from heart attack or heart surgery communicate and how this contributes to their individual well-being and relational satisfaction. In contrast to the Community Study, which focused on everyday hassles and stressors, the Illinois Heart Care Project focused on the ongoing challenges of rehabilitation and adjustment following a major life event. We use the term *cardiac event* to encompass the experiences of individuals who had a myocardial infarction ("heart attack") and/or coronary artery bypass graft surgery ("bypass surgery").

The aftermath of a cardiac event is a useful situation in which to further our understanding of enacted support and communal coping (Goldsmith & Leslie, 2001). There is increasing recognition that successful rehabilitation from a cardiac event includes not only medical treatment but also changes in lifestyle and perspective, adjustment to changes in personal and professional roles, and management of emotional reactions. Interactions between spouses play a crucial role in a patient's success in adjusting to these changes; however, spouses are intimately involved in these same challenges and may experience the same or even greater levels of distress as the patient. The shared stresses and adjustment challenges faced by patients and spouses create an environment in which both social support and communal coping occur and in which the stakes of coping well together are high.

The Illinois Heart Care Project was open to patients who had experienced a heart attack or bypass surgery within the last year and to spouses or partners of patients who fit this description. The analyses that follow are based on a subset of the larger sample, composed of fifteen male patients and their wives. Each participated in a separate, individual interview focused on ways the person's life had changed, followed by a series of specific questions regarding common challenges and adjustments (e.g., dietary changes, restrictions on activity, new priorities, and fears and anxieties) and the ways in which couples did or did not communicate about these challenges and adjustments (see the Appendix for additional information on sample and procedures).

One of the primary goals of the Illinois Heart Care Project was to describe the range of ways couples responded to a cardiac event and to identify strategies that seemed particularly effective at managing the challenges of coping together in this particular context. The interviews did provide examples of one partner providing support to the other and of patients and spouses engaging in communal coping. Also prominent, however, were patterns of interaction in which support or communal coping were disguised or embedded in more mundane kinds of interaction such as dinnertime conversation, making plans, joking around, and the like. In their research on heart patients and spouses, Coyne and his colleagues (1990, p. 145) speculated on the importance of "well-established routines and shared understandings that are relevant to the tasks at hand." The focused attention to communication patterns in the Illinois Heart Care Project produced accounts of these routines and understandings, revealing how social support may be disguised in ordinary conversation. An examination of these patterns further expands our understanding of the relational orientations available to close relational partners as they assist one another with coping.

Routine Talk in Close Relationships

My understanding of routine talk is informed by a series of studies I conducted with Leslie Baxter (reported in Goldsmith & Baxter, 1996), in which we developed a taxonomy of the types of speech events that occurred over several weeks in the personal relationships of a diverse sample of college students. We found that a large proportion of the events our respondents reported were events they characterized as trivial, informal, and lacking a clear task or purpose. Conversations in which participants disclosed deep feelings, argued passionately, or gave focused attention to problem solving occurred much less frequently than the more ordinary events of gossiping, making plans, asking a favor, reminiscing, recapping the day's events, joking around, and the like. Although these routine talk events were not very memorable or involving, they nonetheless made up the everyday living of close relationships and there were systematic differences in the particular pattern of ordinary events in different kinds of close relationships. Our findings were consistent with the observations of other researchers (Coupland, 2000; Dainton & Stafford, 1993; Duck, Rutt, Hurst, & Strejc, 1991) who have remarked on the significance of the ordinary for understanding how close relationships are defined and sustained.

Upon completion of our speech events study, I conceptualized routine talk as distinct from troubles talk and other genres of serious talk. I presumed that routine talk and serious talk each played an important but distinct role in the conduct of satisfying personal relationships. Our findings provided some warrant for this view: In response to sorting and rating tasks, our respondents differentiated important, involving, deep events from superficial, trivial, and quick events; formal and goal-oriented events from informal events that lacked a clear goal; and positively valenced events from negatively valenced events. However, our findings also suggested ways that routine and serious talk were interrelated. For example, conversations might begin with small talk and then transition to serious talk. Everyday interactions also shape the perceptions partners have of one another and of their relationship that may lead, eventually, to episodes of serious conversation such as those in which support is enacted (Barnes & Duck, 1994; Leatham & Duck, 1990). Thus, I had an understanding of routine talk and troubles talk as analytically distinct, though potentially related in a sequential fashion (either in a sequence in a given conversation or in a sequence in the development of a relationship).

The interviews with heart patients and their spouses challenged me to see another set of potential relationships between routine talk and troubles talk. The routine talk category in my qualitative analysis of the heart study interviews referred to instances when patients or spouses described engaging in the types of events categorized in our previous study as superficial and informal; namely, small talk, joking around, catching up, recapping the day's events, morning talk, bedtime chat, gossiping, and making plans. However, because the interviews focused on adjustment to a cardiac event, most mentions of routine talk in these interviews involved ways in which it was directed toward the "trouble" of adjustment to the cardiac event. It seems highly likely that the couples in our sample also engaged in routine talk for routine purposes and in routine ways; however, the particular context of our interviews provided insight into some of the ways in which ordinary routines could also be pressed into the service of meeting extraordinary challenges. In other words, these interviews pointed to a type of hybrid conversation in which troubles talk was disguised or embedded in a more ordinary type of event. Troubles talk was the background of a conversation in which some routine was the foreground.[4] Four categories emerged from this analysis: routine talk as familiar context for troubles talk, routine talk as a substitute for explicit troubles talk, routine talk as indirect troubles talk, and routine talk as familiarized troubles talk.

Routine Talk as Familiar Context

Ordinary routines may serve as a context that is conducive to episodes of enacted support or communal coping. Couples who routinely talk with

---

[4] Dainton and Stafford (1993) make a similar observation about the role of routine behaviors in relational maintenance. They point out that at one point in time (or in a particular couple) a behavior may be simply routine and enacted without a conscious intention to maintain the relationship, whereas at another point in time (or in another couple) the same behavior might be purposefully enacted as a strategy for relational maintenance.

one another about a variety of issues and who routinely do things together may find more opportunities to transition to explicit talk about a problem and may have more experience doing so together. Petronio, Reeder, Hecht, and Ros-Mendoza (1996) suggested that mundane settings and activities could also provide a sense of safety and normalcy in which to address difficult or risky topics.

Phil (age 69) and his wife Marjorie (age 68) had been married for 50 years. He had bypass surgery 3 months prior to our interview. Phil described various ways in which his wife had been "with me the whole way," including changing her own diet along with his, exercising with him, going to doctor's appointments with him, and talking easily with him about all of these issues. When asked how this came about, he replied as follows:

We've been together all our lives ... we walk together, ride bicycles together, and do everything together. ... We have two lawn mowers – she uses one and I use one. I got two big gardens, she helps in the garden, puts everything up. We canned fifty, sixty quarts of tomatoes and forty, fifty-some quarts of strawberries last year, raise sweet corn, fight the raccoons for it. We are both active in church ... we go to church two times a week and walk ... we talk all the time.

He also described how their drive together to his rehabilitation exercise program provided opportunities to talk. They lived in an outlying community and so his rehabilitation session was part of a larger routine of going into town to shop and have lunch together.

The communal orientation Phil and Marjorie took to coping with his heart disease was part of a larger pattern of shared activity across various domains of their life. Talking about diet could occur in the context of a shared gardening hobby. Talking about exercise could be occasioned by a regular trip into town or by their exercising together as they mowed the lawn or walked to church. His wife accompanied him to his doctor's appointments, enabling both partners to feel confident in his normal recovery and to have access to similar information about his treatment regimen. When asked how this came about, he said it seemed natural because they did everything else together.

Ken (age 72) and Rose (age 69), his wife of 49 years, also described a pattern of shared participation in the exercise and diet regimen he adopted following bypass surgery (which occurred 9 months prior to the interview). He explained that "we were walkers before; we'd say in the summertime we would walk out at Meadowbrook [Park], wintertime we would usually go to Lincoln Square [Mall], and we'd done that after the surgery too. I think I very seldom walked when she didn't." In a statement that shared the form and rhythm of Phil's description of a shared life, Ken stated: "We camped together, we exercised, we walked together." He also described how they had "always eaten out quite a bit, particularly since I retired" and how this routine was now more challenging because of his dietary restrictions. However, he quickly added that together they have met that challenge, and he described with enthusiasm several local restaurants and their specific low-fat offerings. Throughout his description of their new going-out-to-eat routine, he used *"we* do that" and *"we* are pretty good at that" in a way that was consistent with a communal orientation.

Larry (age 77) had a heart attack and bypass surgery 3 months prior to his interview. He and his wife Carol (age 73) had known one another since high school and during each of their previous marriages, they and their families had been friends. In the 3 years since Larry and Carol married, they had shared an evening routine:

...every evening at five we have a drink, and then she prepares, we call them "nibblies" – cheese, crackers, things like that. And generally we'll sit until six, six-thirty, talk, talk, talk, about anything and everything. And of course this thing comes up, but there, there might be some day where it's particularly frustrating or else it kind of catches your mind.... I always know in the evenings we're gonna sit down and if you got something to say, say it. And the dog doesn't tell anybody what we say, so it's confidential!

The shared "nibblie" routine in place prior to Larry's heart attack and surgery provided a space in which he and Carol were accustomed to talking about whatever might be on their minds. On those days when his heart condition was something he recognized as a particular problem, he knew there would be a conversational space for troubles talk with Carol.

In these examples, talk about the problem was explicit and it occurred in the framework of enacted support or communal coping. Ordinary routines provided the co-presence and behavioral interdependence that facilitated (and perhaps necessitated) enacted support and communal coping. This is a subtle but important distinction from the notion that routine talk forms the basis for a cognitive or perceptual context of troubles talk (i.e., routine talk builds perceptions of trust, continuity, expertise, etc.; see, for example, Barnes & Duck, 1994; Leatham & Duck, 1990). Everyday routines matter in times of stress, not only because of the ways in which they shape cognition but also because of the ways in which they shape action, opportunity, experience, and habit.

Routine Talk as Substitute

Some routines may obviate the need for enacted social support or communal coping. By providing an opportunity to observe the other's coping first-hand, routines can alleviate concerns about the other's condition, stress, or coping. Roger (age 67) and Lois (also 67) had been married 42 years. His heart attack and bypass surgery occurred 3 months prior to the interview. Lois described how worried she felt the first time Roger mowed the lawn. She was sewing when she heard the mower start and after a while, she went outside to offer her husband a glass of water. Her action could readily be interpreted as a simple act of consideration, but it also gave her a chance to observe for herself his level of exertion and his breathing, which she found reassuring. In his interview, Roger said that he could tell his wife "worried some" about his condition. When asked how he knew of her worries, he said, "well, I can tell, she just comes and checks on me a little more often now than she did before. . . . " Roger and Lois were both aware of her concerns and aware of the dual purpose that was now conveyed when she came outside to offer him a cool drink on a hot day. Her actions were not a new or dramatic departure from their ways of interacting (notice he said she checks on him "a little more often now"). A previous routine now allowed them both to acknowledge concerns and to cope without engaging in an explicit discussion of his activity levels at that particular moment.

Similarly, Ken and Rose (whose shared walking and dining-out routines were described previously) each independently mentioned how she now joins him outside when he needs to be on a ladder cleaning the gutters. In Ken's interview, the stepladder issue came up in response to a question about what happened when she observed him engaging in an activity he was not supposed to do. He said she responded not by questioning the activity or expressing concern but by "coming out to help me then, mainly holding the ladder." Rose independently recounted her concerns about him cleaning the gutters, attributing them not only to his heart condition but to a more general risk of falling "at our stage of life." She says the following:

If he's up on the ladder very much, I'm usually up there with him. [interviewer: Do you say anything?] (Rose laughs) "You're gonna be up on it, I wanna be up there!" . . . He always laughs and he kinda, I think he kind of likes me being out there anyway. He's always encouraging me to be out in the yard with him, when he's working out there, just to be out there. No I don't think [he minds].

Ken and Rose were both aware that his heart condition loomed in the background of her helping with the ladder. However, both also accepted her presence as a mutually acceptable way to cope with her concerns and provide support to him and they were able to frame this as "working together outside."

Another way routines may substitute for explicit talk is by regulating behavior so that stressful, problematic episodes are less likely to occur. For example, several couples described how their grocery shopping routine facilitated adherence to dietary restrictions. Ray (age 60) described as follows how he and his wife of 27 years have coped with the need to make adjustments to his diet since his heart attack and bypass surgery 4 months prior to the interview:

She watches her diet and I watch mine so we kind of help each other out, back and forth . . . we don't have any arguments over food or anything. We just buy what we need for our[selves], go over our list, and we go down and buy what we need for the whole week. Well we basically know what we need and what we don't need. . . . So a lot of times we don't buy that stuff anymore. We don't keep it around the house. If we don't buy it, we don't eat it.

The shared grocery shopping routine was part of this couple's joint efforts to "help each other out" with watching their diets and it prevented trouble from arising later in the week when one or the other of them might explicitly correct or question the other's giving in to temptation.

Ray's wife, Faith (age 54), described another way in which a shared routine obviated a need for explicit talk about his health. Her comments came in the context of describing her own conflicting feelings: On the one hand, she believed he needed to exercise more, but on the other hand, she didn't want him to overexert himself. They had occasionally walked together in the past and she found resuming that practice provided a way to address these concerns without explicit discussion. Their walks together allowed her to observe how

before, I had to walk pretty fast to keep up with him, and now, he has a hard time keeping up with me. . . . I don't say anything to him because I figure he is not able to do it because otherwise he would. He's not able to do it. That's why I know his physical strength is not strong enough yet to do it. But I think he just needs to exercise a little bit more to get more strength. Because he's not at full capacity at all. And I didn't realize that until I started going on walks with him. He made some comment here this week about it too.

Nagging Ray to exercise more, reminding him not to overexert, or otherwise commenting explicitly about recovering his physical stamina would create conversations in which the focus was on Ray's limitations. Even if handled sensitively, these kinds of explicit talk would cast him in the role of vulnerable and her in the role of worried (and perhaps controlling). In contrast, Ray independently described their walks together, saying "yeah, we go for walks and stuff like that, bicycle rides. I think we have more fun with each other than we used to." The action of accompanying him provided encouragement for him and an opportunity for her to observe his condition first hand, all the while framing their interaction as enjoyable companionship.

When partners experience a stressor that affects both parties, one way of addressing the experience of concern, worry, or anxiety is to explicitly talk about the problem that creates the stress or about the distress they experience; however, another alternative is to engage in some other sort of interaction that provides an opportunity to solve the problem, gain information, or alleviate concerns. In this way, routine talk may be recognized as "about" a trouble even though the trouble is not the explicit topic of the talk and coping with the trouble is not the officially recognized purpose of the interaction.

Routine Talk as Indirect Troubles Talk

Routine talk can serve as an indirect way of addressing a problem. For example, engaging in familiar routines can create face-saving, autonomy-preserving openings to talk about a problem and, if the patient passes on the chance to talk about the problem, this provides a basis for the spouse to infer that all is well. Many participants saw this process of inference as quite valuable because it allowed the spouse to obtain reassurance without having to express concern in a way that might make the patient feel vulnerable and monitored.

One routine that is quite useful in this regard is the ordinary practice of recapping the events of the day after having been apart. In everyday life, close partners make polite inquiries about one another's activities: "How did you sleep?" over coffee in the morning, "How was your day?" while preparing dinner, or "How was your meeting?" upon returning home. Sometimes the inquiry may concern an event that the partner knows was potentially problematic, but frequently partners inquire even about routine matters, simply as a way of making conversation (Goldsmith & Baxter, 1996). Several spouses of patients gave examples of routine talk that followed this pattern. For example, Lois mentioned the following:

Oh, I'm always asking how he feels after he exercises, usually after he's taken a shower or after the rehab on our way home, 'cause I don't always make it to the rehab. He'll say "they really worked me out this afternoon."

It is not difficult to imagine spouses who are not coping with cardiac rehabilitation having a similar conversation on the way home from the gym and the similarity in the routine inquiry form is what makes it particularly useful. Lois's husband, Roger, pointed out how these conversations, like so many episodes of small talk, involved talk for talk's sake rather than a true need for information. He commented, "She always asks me what I do in classes but she knows what's going on. She's been there enough." Lois indicated that part of why she asked was because she was concerned about stiffness he experienced in his chest, a concern he shared. So although both partners were aware that routine inquiry about his activities had a deeper meaning in their situation, concern was cloaked in a routine shared by other couples (and likely a part of their interaction before his heart surgery). This enabled her to obtain information that was reassuring and it let him know she was concerned about him without their having to assume the potentially risky identities of worried, meddling spouse or unwell patient.

In some couples in which the patient was experiencing difficulty sleeping, casual conversation over breakfast took on a similar dual quality. Rita (age 76) had been married for 54 years to Mike (also 76). He had a heart attack 1 year prior to the interview, followed by bypass surgery 6 months prior to the interview. Rita commented as follows:

I don't usually ask how he's feeling. Usually when he gets up in the morning, we just make a comment about how long he slept or "what time did you get up?" or "what are you having for lunch?" 'cause he makes his own lunch; "what are we having for dinner?", I make dinner. Usually I don't ask him that, I figured that, I don't know, when somebody is ill like that; I have experience with my sister. She said it really bothered her to have people ask her how she was when there was something wrong. So I'm always kind of leery about that . . . if he has feelings, well, he will tell me. And he has.

Polite inquiries about how one slept and coordinating kitchen duty for the day are ordinary topics of talk at many breakfast tables but they have other potential meanings when one partner is recovering from a cardiac event. Both Rita and Mike mentioned at other points in their respective interviews that his changes in diet had been a real challenge and were sometimes a source of explicit discussion. Although Mike had not experienced difficulty sleeping, Rita had concerns that he might be suffering from depression and this accounted for an interest in his sleep that went beyond simply making conversation. However, Rita clearly differentiated ordinary conversation over breakfast from talk that would have his health problems as its primary and recognized focus. Morning talk and making meal plans together gave him an opportunity to talk about his illness (and sometimes he did) or to treat the inquiry as innocent breakfast talk. When he responded to an inquiry about sleep or lunch or dinner as if it were no more than simply breakfast talk, it allowed Rita to infer "everything must be OK."

Mike concurred that "If we have something to say to each other, we say it" but for the most part, "I think we kinda know each other without talking." He continued, as follows:

After so many years of marriage we breathe pretty easy with each other. And we do look after each other. And maybe through this heart attack I didn't realize how much she thought about me at the time. But if anything, it's probably brought us a little closer.

Rita's care for him came through loud and clear, even when it was not the explicit focus of discussion, and the symmetry that occurred in engaging these issues through ordinary routines was a way of enacting the relational qualities he valued: ease in one another's presence, reciprocal looking after each other, and closeness.

Another example of routine talk addressing problems indirectly is the use of humor. In an example that illustrates both joking and breakfast talk routines, Lois mentioned the following:

I always ask him "how'd you sleep last night?" You know what? When we were getting ready to come this morning I just asked him. I just happened to say it. I don't know why I say these things. I always do that. And he'll say whether he slept good or rather he didn't. He would tease me, "I know you slept all right."

Lois indicated in our interview that she worried about Roger having a heart attack, especially because prior to his bypass surgery, there were no symptoms to indicate that he was developing blockages in his arteries. One way she coped with her worries was to "off and on ask him how he's feeling," to which he jokingly replied, "Oh, my heart's still beating away."

Joking around is a common form of talk in close relationships (Goldsmith & Baxter, 1996) and humor may serve important stress management and comforting functions (Bippus, 2000). When the couples in our study used joking around episodes to address the stresses, worries, and challenges of cardiac rehabilitation, it provided reassurance in two ways. First, treating a serious topic humorously implied that it wasn't as serious as might be thought ("if he really were having angina, we wouldn't be laughing"). Second, treating a serious topic in a familiar frame helped to normalize the experience ("he's back to his old self, teasing and joking around with me"). Similarly, the well spouse's use of humor provided a means of raising topics that were of concern while simultaneously downplaying them. The relational message was one of solidary fun, even as the patient was made aware that the spouse was noticing or thinking about a serious topic.

Routine Talk as Familiarized Troubles Talk

A final facet of routine talk that was apparent in the interviews was the way in which couples' creation of new routines helped to normalize change, loss, and restriction. The previous three categories have focused on how preexisting and socially shared forms of routine talk could serve the purpose of assisted coping. This category focuses on new routines couples develop.

A cardiac event typically initiates a variety of changes in everyday life. Some are temporary self-care procedures or restrictions that are lifted after a period of time. Several couples commented how procedures following surgery had become shared routines. Wives helped their husbands check incisions in their chests and legs (where veins used in the bypass may have been taken) or monitor new medications. Initially framed as heroic actions of care for an incapacitated patient, these eventually became just another part of the daily routine until they were discontinued or unless the patient experienced some additional difficulty.

Other aspects of a patient's treatment regimen are intended to be fundamental changes in lifestyle that will continue for the rest of his or her life. The fact that these changes strike at the core of everyday life, and must be enacted daily if they are to be effective, can be a source of great difficulty but it also offers the prospect of making the changes eventually seem routine. Donna (age 62) had been married for 17 years to George (age 64), who had a heart attack and bypass surgery 2 months prior to the interview. When asked what topics were especially easy to discuss, she mentioned exercise and food, "I guess because they occur everyday! (She laughs) [we talk about them] when it's time to go get groceries and decide what things to get and are we gonna exercise, is it too hot out, what do you think we should do as far as that." In response to the same question about topics that are easy for them to discuss, George independently commented, "The diet. Exercise. When I should go back to work. How much work should I do. How much I should be outside in the heat." The daily need to address these issues gave the couple plenty of practice and helped to normalize these as routine topics of everyday conversation. It is also worth noting that these topics were addressed within daily routines such as making grocery lists and coordinating daily activities.

Some of the restrictions on patients' physical activity led to the development of new shared activities that came to be framed as enjoyable in their own right. In the following excerpt, Donna remarked how George's heart attack and bypass surgery had given her renewed appreciation for simple pleasures:

We have enjoyed so much just in the evening, you know it's been hot, we go out and sit on the patio. We'd done a lot of that anyway but I mean even maybe thinking about it even more, even on hot evenings, and just enjoying that time together doing nothing. (laughs) We just absolutely do nothing.

Restrictions on George's physical activity following surgery seem a likely explanation for why they might be doing nothing more often now than before. However, Donna framed their relaxed evenings spent sitting on the patio not in terms of a temporary restriction but in terms of a new-found enjoyable routine. Likewise, Carol described how "when we started walking, when he started walking outside, he really only could walk when someone went with him. So we just held hands and walked. We went a block and then the next day, we went further. And we were very close in life anyway." In Carol's description, her husband's health-induced restrictions are more explicit than in Donna's example, and yet Carol has also reframed the new walking-together routine in terms of its recreational and relational value. The kind of walking one does when holding hands is not power walking or treadmill time to achieve mere physical outcomes; it suggests instead a leisurely, enjoyable stroll. Their walking together wasn't an imposed regimen or a frustrating demonstration of his vastly reduced capacity but instead "just" another manifestation of their "closeness in life." His limitations (not being able to go alone, not being able to go very far or very fast) were recognized, but they were not foregrounded.

Conclusions From the Routine Talk Study

This analysis suggests yet another set of roles and conversational frames through which married couples may engage in social support and assisted coping. One partner may provide support to another for a problem or both partners may cope together with a shared problem within a conversation in which support and coping are not the officially recognized business that defines the episode. Partners engage in a conversation that has the form of one type of speech event but one or both partners recognize that they do so in the service of their own coping needs and their desire to support their partner. Other researchers have pointed to the significance of invisible support (Bolger et al., 2000), protective buffering (Coyne et al., 1990), and covert support (Gottlieb, 1985b); this analysis contributes a description of the costuming used to enact these various forms of disguised support. The trappings of everyday life and ordinary conversational routines provide repeated, convenient, familiar, and unobtrusive ways for partners to enact their concern for one another as well as their own individual coping needs.

CONCLUSIONS

Observation of couples talking about everyday stresses and interviews with couples in the aftermath of a major life event provide compelling evidence that the dominant provider/recipient conceptualization of social support roles is simply too narrow to encompass the ways in which close relational partners talk about problems. Couples may adopt different interactional roles within an episode of troubles talk (e.g., communal coping) or they may adopt a different conversational frame in which to disguise talk related to the trouble (e.g., routine talk) with corresponding implications for their roles in the conversation.

Previous research has begun to document the different interactional roles that can occur within an episode of troubles talk, including experience swapping (Glidewell et al., 1983; Tannen, 1990) and communal coping (Lyons et al., 1998). The four conversational markers of communal coping identified here complement the analysis of communal coping offered by Lyons and her colleagues (Lyons et al., 1998). They say communal coping is defined by at least one party's orientation to the stressor as shared, by communication about the stressor, and by collaboration in adaptation and problem solving. The descriptive analysis provided here shows how a communal orientation is acted out in the details of a conversation and shows not only *that* partners communicate but also *how*. It also demonstrates how partners may differ in the degree to which they share this orientation and how they may attempt to influence one another toward a more or less communal orientation to a problem.

In provider/recipient, experience swapping, and communal coping patterns, talking about a trouble is still the recognized topic of talk and facilitating coping is still a recognized purpose. In contrast, couples may talk about a problem and facilitate their own or the other's coping indirectly, through a conversation disguised as something ordinary and nonproblematic.

Although at least one participant recognizes the dual nature of the conversation, the coping purpose of the conversation is not the officially recognized point of interaction and the trouble with which the couple is coping may not be explicitly mentioned.[5] Both partners engage in some other type of interaction, such as the ordinary, everyday speech events that were described by participants in the Illinois Heart Care Project. Familiar routines take on new functionality, providing ways of coping that need not be officially recognized as such. New practices become routine, normalizing the coping that is occurring so that the coping agenda begins to fade. Previous research has indicated that this territory exists; the analysis offered here helps to map some of the different types of activities therein.

It is both useful and challenging to study how these different possibilities are enacted in talk. Although I have identified prototypical patterns, the examples provided in this chapter should make clear that interactive roles and episodic frames are matters that may be worked out within the conversation itself. In some of the conversations in the first study, communal coping was enacted seamlessly, whereas in others it appeared to be contested in the different styles of talk that partners employed. In some of the interviews in the second study, each spouse spontaneously mentioned the same routine practice as supportive or useful for coping, whereas in other interviews, what one partner saw fit for comment was not mentioned by the other. Sometimes when heart patients and their spouses go for a walk together, the heart condition lies near to the surface, whereas at other times, it may be nearly or completely forgotten as they enjoy being together on a beautiful day. Studying how these alternative roles are manifest in the features of conversations helps to direct our attention to the possibility that partners may disagree about or negotiate what they are doing (and who

---

[5] Readers who recall my definition of troubles talk conversation (in the introduction and Chapter 2 of the book) may question whether these routine conversations should still be characterized as troubles talk. I have defined troubles talk conversations as those in which the topic of conversation was a trouble experienced by one or both of the participants and in which assistance in coping was a purpose of talking about the trouble. Do my analyses of routine conversation fall outside this scope and stretch the concept of troubles talk too far to make it useful? The attribution of coping purpose by one or both of the participants provides a useful criterion that enables me to examine conversations that lie at the boundaries between prototypical troubles talk and other kinds of conversations. Further, this ambiguity is precisely what makes these cases so important. Ambiguity in the nature of the event may be advantageous. By putting the trouble in the background, participants may take other preferred identities even as one or both realize that the interaction serves a dual purpose. Conversely, this ambiguity may reveal the degree to which an illness or other major life stressor may pervasively contaminate one's identity and interactions. For heart patients and their spouses, the patient's condition may lurk in the corner of even the most ordinary conversations, ready to leap out as a possible interpretation of what is going on in the interaction. It seems plausible that this could also be a deterrent to recovery and rehabilitation.

they are as they do it). The degree to which one partner's orientation to a conversation does not preclude the other's seems a likely determinant of satisfaction and success. Couples who repeatedly find themselves at odds may experience additional stress.

In discussing these alternative orientations, I have drawn again on the assumption (introduced in Chapter 2) that in any conversation, the way partners go about talking has implications for the identities they project and for the kind of relational definitions they enact. This theoretical orientation offers an account for the risks and benefits of the various patterns: Different ways of framing what partners are doing (providing and receiving support, working together to cope with a problem, engaging in some other kind of activity) suggest different kinds of identities (worried provider, ill recipient, members of a team, people who enjoy walking, a guy with a sense of humor and his wife who likes to be teased) and relationships (caregiver/care receiver, peers in this together, close partners who enjoy one another's company). These identities and relationships that are enacted in doing social support, communal coping, or ordinary talk may provide a link between what happens in particular conversations and the maintenance or change of important beliefs and perceptions such as self-efficacy, self-worth, validation, acceptance, caring, inequality, reciprocity, and the like.

It seems quite likely that these different configurations have different costs and benefits in different kinds of situations. To the extent that enacted support has risks that derive from the asymmetry of partners' roles and the explicit recognition of one person's need for help, then ways of interacting that enable coping assistance to occur without asymmetry or explicit coping may offer useful alternatives. Although I did not measure stress-related outcomes in either of the two studies I describe in this chapter, other studies suggest that the kinds of interaction patterns documented here may benefit their participants (Bolger et al., 2000; Glidewell et al., 1983). Conversely, to the extent that coping is implicit it may make it difficult for partners to diagnose or correct problematic patterns. The analyses offered here point to a range of alternatives, but the conditions under which they may be functional remains to be demonstrated.

The different roles from which coping assistance flows may have implications for participants' interpretations and evaluations of the support that is enacted. For example, speaking little and just listening may be desirable in a conversation in which I expect to be the recipient of empathy you provide. However, it probably would have seemed oddly uninvolved and distant to our couples who presumed a shared problem with which they were coping and problem solving together. Another example: Much of the social support literature cautions against minimizing or making light of another person's problem as a way of providing social support (for example, see the studies of unhelpful support reviewed in Chapter 1). Likewise,

Jefferson's research (1984b) discusses the potential danger in introducing laughter or humor into troubles talk. Yet couples in both studies provide examples of how humorous diversion can be a shared coping strategy. Brashers and colleagues (in press) found that persons with HIV/AIDS remarked on the relief they experienced among peers with the disease when laughing about their condition or ignoring it all together became options that were seen as less viable when they were among those who did not have HIV/AIDS. An understanding of the different frames within which troubles talk may occur suggests one way of differentiating those occasions when it is ill-advised to make light of another's problem (within provider/recipient roles) from those in which it may be experienced as supportive (within communal coping roles or everyday talk frames). Making light of a problem you do not share may have greater potential for face threat and offense than making a joke at one's own expense regarding a problem you also experience. Similarly, partners who acknowledge that they share a problem may derive some comfort from knowing they can laugh about it together. These are but two examples of a larger issue raised by this analysis: The enactment of support that is perceived to facilitate one's coping efforts is contingent on the enactment of identity and relational definitions that are acceptable to participants and conducive to the coping assistance that is offered. The interpretation of the same action may differ, depending on whether it is performed in the role of "support provider," "communal coper," or "ordinary spouse making small talk."

A recognition of the various interactive roles couples may adopt as they talk (or avoid talking or hint at talking) about troubles is especially important if we seek to provide practical advice for couples or for professionals who seek to develop effective interventions. The existence of multiple frames for engaging in troubles talk should lead us to question the notion that the most effective recommendation for couples undergoing stress is to improve or increase the support provided by one person to the other or to encourage partners to openly discuss all their needs and concerns. To focus attention on improving support provision is to overlook the interdependence between partners' needs and the potential benefits of symmetrical roles. To encourage explicit talk about problems and coping is to underestimate the potential utility of implicit ways in which support and coping may occur. Nor does it seem realistic or effective to simply train couples in the full range of patterns revealed in these analyses (e.g., "when you talk about problems, try to use 'we' instead of 'I'" or "when you get up in the morning, ask your husband how he slept"). Documenting some of the ways in which support is enacted among couples who appear to be coping well does not necessarily mean that encouraging other couples to engage in the same behaviors will result in better coping. To the extent that routines might help couples, it may well be because they are already a part of their ongoing relationship rather than something intentionally undertaken to improve the situation. The intent of my analyses is not to make causal claims but to lead us to ask more useful questions about the range of possibilities. My findings challenge the dominant theoretical conceptualization of social support as providers giving something to receivers. These findings also suggest we proceed cautiously in recommending that individuals under stress need to improve skill at support provision or employ more open, explicit communication. In Chapter 6 I have more to say about new kinds of research on the enactment of social support in close relationships and different approaches to improving communication in close relationships.

6

Conclusions and Implications

The preceding chapters have demonstrated the value in attending to communication processes to understand when and why close relational partners will evaluate enacted social support as helpful, supportive, and sensitive. This is important for understanding social support and its effects on coping as well as for understanding the conduct of close relationships. Participants' interpretations and positive evaluations of troubles talk conversations are a key link in the processes that enable individuals to cope more effectively with stressors and sustain satisfying relationships.

The social support that is enacted in the troubles talk conversations of close relational partners is socially situated, meaningful, and rhetorical activity. This helps explain why previous research focused on the sheer frequency or amount of social support a person reports has seldom yielded consistent or powerful effects. Although most researchers agree that enacted social support is conceptually different from social network structures, social integration, or the perceived availability of support, we have not always fully recognized one of the implications of this distinction; namely, that the ways we have conceptualized and measured other facets of support may not be the most useful ways to study enacted support. In this book I have proposed that, because enacted social support is a communicative phenomenon, it is useful to study it with a set of assumptions, concepts, and methods that are suited to capturing communicative processes and their associations with participants' evaluations of support. I have demonstrated the usefulness of this approach by showing how it can account for puzzles and shortcomings in the enacted social support literature.

Previous research showed that although advice is one of the most frequent ways of responding to a close relational partner under stress, it is often unappreciated. In Chapter 3, I showed how it is possible to explain when advice will be evaluated positively by taking into account communicative features such as what is said and how. A series of studies I have conducted shows that to be effective, advice must be adapted to the situation in which it is given. This involves appropriate selection of advice as a form of support (instead of concern or tangible aid, etc.) as well as the substantive quality of the advice that is offered and its utility for facilitating coping with some problem. In addition, the evaluation of advice is based not only on its usefulness for solving a problem but also on what it implies about identities and relationships. The concept of face is a useful way of capturing some of these implications: Advice that is seen as honoring face is typically evaluated more positively than advice that threatens face. Similarly, diverse features of messages and conversations that shape interpretations of face are predictably associated with evaluations of advice, including the language style used to communicate advice, the other content that accompanies advice, and the sequence through which advice is introduced into a conversation.

Previous research has struggled to explain mixed findings regarding the buffering effects of enacted social support, even when researchers have adopted matching models that identify the type or source of support thought to be most appropriate for some stressor. In Chapter 4, I showed how matching models underestimate the complexity of stressful situations and the rhetorical power of conversation to selectively and creatively portray stressful demands and coping options. Although intuitively appealing, matching models do not go far enough in exploring how relational partners work together (or fail to do so) in fitting support to the situation. Social support that is appreciated by recipients and contributes to adaptive coping is not simply matched to objective and preexisting features of a situation. Instead, participants in troubles talk must construct together a vision of the situation and coping options that is coherent – internally, externally, and between partners. Internal coherence refers to the symbolic plausibility of the situation as it is represented in talk and the types of social support that are offered. External coherence refers to whether the types of coping that are encouraged in troubles talk are responsive to the demands of the environment. Between-partner coherence refers to the degree to which partners in a conversation develop a coordinated version of the situation. What partners say, how they say it, and how they coordinate the tone and form of their talk contribute to achieving coherence.

Previous research has been dominated by a vision of social support as transacted between a provider and a recipient and scholars have recently begun to recognize limitations in this view when it is applied to the interactions of interdependent relational partners. In Chapter 5, I demonstrated how close relational partners seeking to cope with a problem may adopt not only provider/recipient roles but also other interactive roles and conversational frames. Other researchers have suggested that these processes occur and my examination of talk in close relationships provides a description of what it looks like when partners engage in communal coping as a way of doing troubles talk or when social support is disguised in the frame of ordinary talk. Communal coping is not simply an orientation that one or both partners take but also an observable feature of their talk, and one that may be contested in the way partners approach troubles talk. In addition, explicit talk about a trouble is not the only way that partners may communicate to facilitate their coping. Ordinary routines may provide a less threatening set of interactive roles within which to covertly assist one another with coping and adaptation to life events. The degree to which partners coordinate their choice of conversational frames and the different risks and benefits of dealing with a problem in these alternative frames suggest both greater complexity and greater opportunity in how close relational partners can help one another in stressful times.

In addition to the relevance of these findings for particular topics and problems of research, there is also a larger significance to the studies as a set. Taken together, the analyses in Chapters 3, 4, and 5 suggest a different way of thinking about enacted social support. Rather than picturing enacted support as a resource that is handed over unproblematically from one person to another, we should see enacted social support as a process through which conversational partners construct together a view of the situation, including the nature of the problem, the options for coping, the implications for valued images of self, and the significance for the relationship. If and when social support facilitates coping, it is not only by virtue of having advised, informed, complimented, assured, or aided but also by virtue of having created (or sustained) an understanding of the task, identities, and relationship involved. If we fail to consider how well enactments of support are adapted to these symbolic purposes, we miss critical features that make some enactments of support better than others (Goldsmith, 1995; Goldsmith & Fitch, 1997).

To this point, then, I have shown how a communication approach problematizes some of the assumptions and procedures that are common in the literature on enacted social support. In that literature, the actual talk that occurs between partners is nearly always represented by self-report instruments or coding schemes that accomplish data reduction by a focus on frequencies of behaviors and generic types of support. By descending into the details of messages and conversations, we begin to see what these research practices obscure and from that vantage point, we can see why these previous approaches have frequently turned up puzzling, weak, and/or inconsistent results.

In this chapter, I climb up out of the conversational trenches to discuss three broader implications of my work. First, my work provides a basis for two complementary types of generalizations about the relationship between features of troubles talk conversations and their evaluation by close relational partners. Second, an understanding of the link between features of talk and participant evaluations has implications for how we go about detecting relationships between enacted support and outcomes such as individual coping or relational satisfaction. Finally, my findings sound cautionary notes for those who develop social support interventions.

GENERALIZATIONS ABOUT THE EVALUATION OF ENACTED SOCIAL SUPPORT

For scholars who are centrally interested in the communication of social support, this book yields two kinds of useful generalizations: (1) predictions about features of talk that are associated with positive evaluations of talk and (2) descriptions of the opportunities, challenges, and resources involved in conducting troubles talk. The first type of generalization is most evident in my research on advice, summarized in Chapter 3. The second type of generalization is illustrated in my qualitative analyses of messages, conversations, and interviews in Chapters 3, 4, and 5.

Predicting Evaluations

We have seen that it is possible to identify some systematic patterns in the features of conversations that produce positive evaluations. Delving into the *quality* of enacted support is not a hopeless exercise in individual subjectivity. Although there are most certainly individual factors that shape interpretations and evaluations of support, there are also commonalities. These enable prediction of what is likely to be evaluated positively for many people in many situations. This is most evident in my research on advice summarized in Chapter 3, where I showed systematic relationships of advice style, content, and sequence with judgments of face with corresponding implications for evaluations that advice is helpful, sensitive, and supportive. Burleson and his colleagues (see Burleson, 2003, for a review) have similarly documented features of comforting messages that predict recipients' reactions to the emotional support they receive.

The analyses of situation definition (Chapter 4) and relational roles (Chapter 5) do not provide quantitative tests of the link between message features and evaluation but a similar approach could be applied. For example, in Chapter 4 I describe several features of messages that might contribute to a hearer's perception of a situation as more or less controllable, including the degree of elaboration of themes that say or imply the problem is controllable, the amount of detail given in describing a course of action, stylistic features that convey enthusiasm and confidence, and content relevant to establishing the speaker's credibility. These features could be coded or manipulated to test their association with hearers' (or observers') perceptions of problem controllability. Like perceived regard for face, perceived controllability of the problem might be a mediating interpretation that accounts for why some message features predict a more positive evaluation of problem-solving forms of support. Similarly, in Chapter 5 I identified four features of conversation that enact communal coping. One could envision a study in which these markers were coded and tested for their association with a couple's self-reported communal coping orientation or studies in which some of the sociocultural and relational factors that are thought to predict communal coping (Lyons et al., 1998) are examined for their association with these conversational markers.

It is possible, then, to see something in troubles talk conversations that goes beyond the frequency of generic types of support (i.e., informational, emotional, tangible, etc.). By attending to various aspects of what is said and how it is said, we can develop a more theoretically sophisticated and potentially powerful understanding of the first link in the chain of phenomena I proposed in Chapter 2: the relationships between enacted social support behaviors and their evaluation by participants in a conversation. Although it is becoming more common to see conversational data in studies of social support, the data are nearly always immediately reduced to codings of the frequency with which various types of social support occur. I hope to have offered a broader range of relevant features of talk that might be explored and to have modeled a way of using descriptive research and theory to select features of talk and mediating processes that can help predict and explain participant reactions (see also O'Keefe's 1994 comparison of strategy-based versus feature-based analysis).

Describing Challenges, Resources, and Principles

A second type of generalization that emerges from the work reported in Chapters 3, 4, and 5 is the identification of challenges, resources, and reasoning principles that are evident in the practice of enacted social support. Rather than predicting when support will be evaluated positively, this research agenda focuses on illuminating the *constraints and challenges* close relational partners face as they attempt to enact social support, the features of talk that may serve as *resources* for managing these challenges, and the rational *principles* that underlie adaptation. For example, in architecture, structural principles constrain what is possible, and a knowledge of styles and conventions plays a role in seeing possibilities and anticipating their evaluation, but skill consists in adapting to these parameters in ways suited to a specific site and client. Some sites and clients may be addressed with straightforward textbook solutions but in many cases, multiple requirements for building use, time and budget constraints, differences in the architect's and client's sense of style, and other factors may pose challenging dilemmas. The descriptive analyses in this book focus closely on the architecture of talk: How are features of the talk well- or ill-suited to the sometimes complicated and competing demands posed by the adaptational requirements of a stressful situation as well as by the personal identities and relational dynamics of the participants? Rather than trying to create a blueprint that could be widely reproduced, the goal of this type of analysis is to identify types of goals and constraints that interactants may encounter, a variety of design resources available for meeting these challenges, and the principles that provide a basis for judging some performances as better designed to achieve goals and overcome constraints than other performances (for additional elaboration of this approach see Brashers et al., in press; Goldsmith & Fitch, 1997; Goldsmith, 2001).

The goal of this agenda is not statistical generalization and these methods are not appropriate for making claims about how frequently some pattern occurs or for establishing cause and effect.[1] The goal is not to reproduce the same behavior on identical occasions but to sharpen understanding of the multiple purposes that are relevant to the enactment of social support (facilitating coping in some way while enacting valued identities and relational definitions), to heighten awareness of the ways of talking that are relevant to these purposes, and thereby to cultivate the practical art of performing (see Sanders, 2003, pp. 232–234, on the difference between training someone to perform a skill versus cultivating greater proficiency in achieving multiple goals).

So, for example, the ethnographic study of advice reported in Chapter 3 identified dilemmas of seeking, giving, and receiving advice as well as some of the contextual factors that shape participants' interpretations of how well these dilemmas are addressed. Chapter 4 identified three requirements for developing coherence between the support that is enacted in a troubles talk conversation and the adaptational needs of the person experiencing stress. My analyses also pointed to a wide variety of features of talk that were pressed into service in constructing these kinds of coherence in various conversations. In Chapter 5 I observed that when close relational partners face a stressor experienced by one or both persons, there are multiple possible configurations of task, identity, and relationship that they can take up in their talk together. Analyses of conversations in which these different configurations were evident suggested features of talk that differentiated one frame from another as well as potential advantages and disadvantages to adopting one or another of these frames.

---

[1] It is important to note that this is not the same as making claims about principles or mechanisms of message production. My claims concern message architecture, not cognitive architecture. Regardless of how a message came to be produced (accident, thoughtful planning, overlearned skill, routine), what features and principles account for its suitability? O'Keefe (1992) provides an especially useful discussion of the points of difference and contact between the two areas of study.

Complementary Results

These two kinds of generalizations (predictive and descriptive) have typically emerged in different areas of the communication field and are sometimes seen as antithetical to one another (or, more charitably, as irrelevant to one another). In contrast, I hope to have illustrated how these two kinds of generalizations are complementary to our understanding of broader issues such as the ways in which close relational partners engage in troubles talk conversations. Generalizations of the first sort provide baseline predictions about how some features of talk are typically interpreted and what types of interpretations (e.g., interpretations of face threat) play a role in judgments of the effectiveness of talk. Predictive research also provides means of testing the claim that features of talk do make a difference to participant evaluations and for testing some of the mediating interpretations. The generalizations that emerge from this type of research seem to be especially useful for avoiding poor performance – for example, my series of studies on advice suggest would-be support providers will usually want to avoid blunt unsolicited indiscriminate advice giving and instead identify face-saving ways of directing others' behavior.

The kinds of predictions we can make about what message features are positively evaluated will always have an "all-other-things-being-equal" caveat or a stipulation of certain boundary conditions. Even blunt, unsolicited advice has its place. It would be impossible, and not all that productive, to try to specify all the possible contextual factors that might moderate the patterns identified in these baseline predictions. A general trend in the data does not describe every individual case equally well and in any particular situation, all other things are seldom, in fact, equal. Consequently, it is also useful to explore the relevant features, constraints, and principles that must be creatively marshaled in particular enactments. Descriptive research is well-suited not only for identifying candidate features and processes for quantitative testing but also important in its own right as a demonstration of adaptation and coordination processes and as a reminder that life is not lived in the statistical aggregate. This type of research sensitizes us to constraints, opportunities, and resources.

These kinds of generalizations about features of talk and their relationship to participant evaluations are likely most appealing to communication researchers, for whom the relationship between message or conversation features and effects is a central disciplinary problem. My findings also have implications for those within and outside the communication discipline whose research questions focus on what comes after a participant has evaluated troubles talk, that is, on the links between enacted support and other outcomes. What do these analyses suggest for those whose primary interest is in how communication processes shape individual coping or relational satisfaction?

LINKING EVALUATIONS OF SUPPORT TO INDIVIDUAL AND
RELATIONAL WELL-BEING

In Chapter 2, I presented a figure showing how features of enacted support were linked to participant evaluations of enacted support with subsequent effects on individual coping. There are also good reasons to explore how enacted social support, and participant evaluations of it, contribute to relational satisfaction. By now, I hope to have made a clear case for refocusing attention on the quality of enacted social support and not simply its quantity. So, as we move outward from enacted support in these chains of relationships, we need to ask, "what ways of assessing participant evaluations of enacted social support will reflect the occurrence of high quality enacted social support?"[2] Two common themes recur throughout the analyses reported in Chapters 3, 4, and 5: a need for domain-specific assessment of the content (and not just the form) of enacted social support and a need for multifaceted assessment of the extent to which enacted support has successfully addressed task, identity, and relational implications of troubles talk.

Domain-Specific Content

When people engage in successful coping, or in successful assisted coping, it is not by employing just any behavior that happens to fit a broad meta-strategy type. What they say – the content or substance – matters. It is not simply the act of giving information that helps someone cope; the information must be relevant, accurate, and so on if it is to make a positive difference. Similarly, it is not simply the act of offering an alternative problem appraisal that helps; some alternative appraisals might be quite dysfunctional. Just as there are adaptive and maladaptive ways of managing one's own emotions, there are more and less useful ways of reassuring or responding to another's emotions. Assessments of the quality of support must take into account not only generic forms or types of support

---

[2] I would not advocate that scholars interested in looking at the effects of enacted support on coping or relational satisfaction should attempt to link these directly to microscopic details of a particular conversation or self-reports of those details. For example, I doubt that it would be useful or plausible to ask individuals to self-report on the kinds of features of style, form, content, and sequence that I have focused on in explaining the link between features of talk and participant evaluations. Although these features do shape participant evaluations, that does not necessarily mean that all participants are highly or equally aware of the features or inclined to recall them accurately. However, I think it is quite possible that individuals can report on domain-specific content (e.g., What advice were you given? and What did they say to try to cheer you up?) and the interpretations they reach based on conversations that exhibit various features (e.g., face threat, control of the situation, instrumental utility, sensitivity to feelings, and relational loyalty and caring). In this way, research on the message features that reliably yield those interpretations can dovetail with research that shows the broader individual and relational significance of those interpretations.

(informational, emotional, tangible) but also their content. Although the widely used scales and coding schemes for assessing types of support have the advantage of widespread application across support sources, problems, and situations, they are limited in what they can tell us about the suitability of support for assisting coping or building a relationship.

Probably few researchers will argue against the notion that content is of variable quality; the challenge is in developing useful ways of representing something so varied and situation-specific as content. A parallel critique has emerged in the coping literature, where it is common to use generic types or forms of coping to characterize the particular ways people interact with their environments. For example, DeRidder and Schreurs (1996) reviewed research on coping with chronic illness, concluding that it would be useful to "map the adaptive tasks confronting the chronically ill" for different diseases and stages rather than relying on measures that conceptualize coping as "an isolated bundle of metastrategies" (p. 79). Similarly, Coyne and Gottlieb (1996) discuss how the necessarily broad descriptions of coping strategies that are used in generic checklist measures may mean different things in different contexts or at different points in the coping process.

In their work with caregivers of persons with dementia, Gottlieb and his colleagues demonstrate an alternative way of studying coping that is sensitive to the particular domain of study. Through content analysis of interviews with caregivers, they develop a classification scheme of caregiver coping efforts (Gottlieb & Gignac, 1996). For example, one of the most powerful types of coping is a category entitled "making meaning," which includes the specific strategies of developing causal attributions for symptoms or events, causal attributions for the disease, reading cognitions or internal states of the care recipient, searching for meaning in adversity, and normalizing experiences and feelings. The general strategy of "making meaning" and some of the component strategies within this category (e.g., meaning in adversity and normalizing) likely apply to a wide variety of stressful situations and this classification scheme helps researchers identify how these more general processes unfold with respect to a particular stressor. However, the category is also well-grounded in some of the distinctive ways that dementia caregivers make meaning (e.g., attributions for symptoms, events, and disease and reading a care recipient whose capabilities have diminished). Another category, "symptom management," includes seventeen different verbal and behavioral strategies for coping with the demanding symptoms exhibited by care recipients with dementia; some are quite specific to dementia, whereas others bear some similarity to strategies that might be used in other difficult interpersonal situations.

Gignac and Gottlieb (1996) also develop a typology of twelve different appraisals caregivers gave in their evaluations of their coping efforts (e.g., efficacious outcomes, no coping options, improved ability to cope, and less stressor reactivity). Their research demonstrates that within a particular common type of problem, it is possible to develop domain-specific measures of coping efforts and evaluations of coping efforts. Their research also indicates that these content- and domain-specific measures enable better prediction of distress and well-being than generic measurement approaches. To the extent that we conceptualize enacted social support as assisted coping, this work provides an important model: Within a particular domain of stressful event, we can identify specific things others say and do to help us cope as well as multifaceted ways of assessing those forms of support.

Studies that have employed domain-specific measures of social support have shown promising results and provide insight into practical ways of taking into account the content of support. For example, Fenlason and Beehr (1994) found that different contents of supportive conversations with supervisors, coworkers, friends, and family had different kinds of effects on the strains experienced in the workplace. Talking about positive aspects of the job with supervisors, family, or friends buffered the effects of work stress on strain. In contrast, griping about the job with coworkers or diversionary talk about other topics with family or friends were associated with reverse buffering effects. They also found that the content-specific measures of support were stronger predictors of effects than traditional, global indices of received emotional and instrumental support.

LaGreca and Bearman (2002) used interviews with diabetic adolescents to identify five domains of family support for diabetes management (e.g., insulin administration, blood glucose testing, meals, exercise, and emotional support). This formed the basis for the Diabetes Social Support Questionnaire, an instrument that measures the frequency of various supportive behaviors (How often does a family member ... ?) as well as satisfaction (How does this make you feel? *not supportive/neutral/a little supportive/ supportive/very supportive*). They found an index formed by weighting the frequency of supportive behaviors by their perceived supportiveness predicted additional variance in adherence to diabetes care over and above general measures of family support and cohesion. In addition, differentiating among the five domains yielded more powerful prediction than aggregating across domains.

Multidimensional Assessment of Evaluations

The other theme that is supported by all of the analyses I report is the significance of considering how ways of talking about a problem and enacting support implicate ways of viewing the persons involved and their relationship. Further, these interrelated purposes of talk may be mutually reinforcing or working at cross-purposes: there is informational support that is helpful but insensitive and there are expressions of concern that are supportive but maladaptive. Consequently, deeming troubles talk between close relational partners a "success" is a multifaceted judgment and global reports of satisfaction with support are insufficiently precise to capture the power of enacted support to shape subsequent effects.

The imprecision that is involved in global judgments of support satisfaction can be illustrated by considering the interpretation of a moderate amount of satisfaction with enacted support. It could reflect that the support was mediocre across the board – its accuracy or utility for solving a problem was moderate, its responsiveness to emotion and identity was so-so, and its expression of a caring and concerned relationship was just OK. Alternatively, it could reflect that support was fine in some respects but not in others; for example, the support was quite helpful but conveyed in a way that was insensitive or unsupportive. Global ratings of satisfaction with support may adequately represent the very best support (very well adapted to task, identity, and relational issues) and the very worst support (poorly adapted across these dimensions) but for interactions that fall in between, we will have more precise measurement and better explanations for what goes wrong if we consider multiple ways of evaluating support.

Studies that have taken a multidimensional approach to assessing participants' evaluations of conversations have shown the usefulness of doing so. Clark and her colleagues (1997) found that different types of support were differentially associated with various evaluations of support. For example, a message that offered a distressed other an optimistic reappraisal of the situation was the most successful type of support for making the other feel better and among the most successful in displaying concern; however, it was also considered one of the most irritating messages. Jones and Burleson (1997) found that in some situations messages judged as sensitive were not necessarily viewed as helpful, effective, or appropriate. Conversely, their respondents said an insensitive message might nonetheless be helpful, effective, and appropriate in some instances.

My colleagues and I have proposed three types of evaluations that may be broadly applicable to participants' judgments of the quality of enacted social support. Virginia McDermott and I reviewed studies that measured participant evaluations of conversations (Goldsmith & McDermott, 1997). Measures used the adjectives *helpful, sensitive,* and *supportive* widely and interchangeably as indicators of the overall goodness or badness of enacted social support; however, we suspected that these adjectives might have different connotations and so we asked the participants in the Community Conversation Study (see Appendix) to respond to open-ended questions about what these terms meant to them. Their responses provided a basis for proposing three interrelated criteria by which participants might judge a troubles talk conversation.

One way of evaluating the social support one has provided or received is with reference to its instrumental or problem-solving utility. Our respondents talked about whether a partner's actions were helpful, useful, and generous and contributed to solving a problem, making things better, or clarifying ideas. Another criterion for evaluating a conversation is the degree to which partners showed relational assurance. This notion was related to terms and ideas, including supportiveness, loyalty, agreement, availability, encouragement, and reassurance. Finally, participants evaluated conversations for the sensitivity that was shown to emotional experiences and outcomes. A judgment of sensitivity was associated with being gentle, perceptive, considerate, caring, understanding, and compassionate as well as with risks such as being vulnerable or upset. Using the terms generated by our respondents, Virginia McDermott, Stewart Alexander, and I (Goldsmith et al., 2000, Study 2) developed a set of twelve semantic-differential-type scales for measuring judgments of problem-solving utility (helpful/hurtful, useful/useless, knowledgeable/ignorant, generous/selfish), relational assurance (supportive/unsupportive, reassuring/upsetting, comforting/distressing, encouraging/discouraging), and emotional awareness (sensitive/insensitive, compassionate/heartless, considerate/inconsiderate, understanding/misunderstanding).

These scales proved useful in detecting mixed evaluations of advice (Goldsmith et al., 2000, Study 3). We examined the ratings given to advice messages in the Advice Sequence Study (see the Appendix) and found that some advice messages were seen as uniformly strong or weak across all three dimensions. For example, the advice "you should go talk to the professor" given to a friend who has failed an exam was seen as equally helpful, sensitive, and supportive. However, most of the other advice messages were seen as more supportive than helpful or more sensitive than supportive and so on. For example, one of the advice messages occurred in a hypothetical situation in which a friend complained about gaining weight. The advice "you need to start exercising more" was rated as more helpful than sensitive or supportive, likely because the scenario pointed to an objective need to lose weight but the advice to exercise was given rather bluntly. In a scenario in which two friends were leaving the library at night, the advice "you shouldn't walk by yourself on this campus at night" was seen as more helpful and sensitive than supportive, likely because it was not accompanied by an offer to walk together. These differential evaluations were seen in response to messages that were all of one type (advice) and were all posed in a direct fashion. We expect there to be even more variability in ratings as we compare different types of support given in different styles (e.g., solidary, deferential, and indirect as well as direct).

My review of previous research in Chapter 1 and my own research in Chapters 3, 4, and 5 make it quite clear that interpretations of what enacted support means for autonomy, reciprocity, closeness, similarity, and the like are significant for the experience of support as useful for coping and satisfying for relationships. Global assessments of overall satisfaction with support obscure the more complex judgments that may occur as individuals respond to support attempts that are not fatally flawed but are still less than or different from what they might have liked to hear. Our scales are but one illustration of a kind of assessment approach that is sensitive to these nuances. A domain-specific approach to support evaluations (parallel to Gignac and Gottlieb's 1996 study of caregiver coping appraisals, summarized above, for example) is another way to develop multidimensional asssessments. Multidimensional measures of participant satisfaction with support provide a more informative measure of how and when enacted social support will predict various kinds of coping. For example, support that simply agrees with an irrational friend's appraisal of a situation might be seen as quite supportive but not all that helpful; such a pattern might actually contribute to forms of coping that are diversionary and avoidant. In contrast, it might take support that is both sensitive and helpful for participants to achieve new insight into their responsibility for a situation or the options for taking action. These multidimensional assessments are likely to be particularly important if we wish to explore not only individual coping but also relational satisfaction. For example, a friend's blunt advice to exercise more might solicit grudging compliance with actions that have problem-solving utility but it might also create relational resentment and a reluctance to share other personal concerns in the future.

Not only is it important to assess multiple dimensions of a support recipient's evaluations of support; it is also important to solicit evaluations from multiple perspectives. Consistent with my focused interest in the link between features of conversations and participant evaluations, most of my analyses focus on messages, conversations, and participant or reader reactions to them. However, my analysis of external coherence in Chapter 4 and my juxtaposition of patient and spouse perspectives in Chapter 5 point to the importance of incorporating multiple perspectives of evaluation. This is especially important if we seek to use these evaluations as a basis for predicting outcomes beyond the evaluation of support (such as coping or relational satisfaction). If we are to understand how evaluations of enacted support develop, sustain, or threaten a relationship, it will be useful to assess both partners in a close relationship (or, in some cases, multiple members of a family or network who may be providing complementary or contradictory forms of support). To predict how support shapes coping and well-being, we will also need to compare the support and coping that are evaluated positively by participants with standards for evaluation that are external to the conversation, such as normative beliefs about the best ways to cope or expert opinion about adaptative and maladaptive patterns.

IMPROVING TROUBLES TALK

Although research on social support and research on close relationships have strong traditions of theory testing and development, both areas also have a history of intervention-based research. The idea that improvement in social skills may be an efficient way of alleviating individual distress and improving relationships is widespread and includes programs more comprehensive in scope than those that focus specifically on social support (for example, see Segrin & Givertz, 2003, for a review). Similarly, the kinds of interventions that seek to improve social support include a variety of programs aimed at individual, dyadic, system, and community change, both through altering existing ties and through the creation of new ties (Gottlieb, 1992).

My work is of greatest relevance to social support interventions that target improvement of interactions in which close relational partners attempt to assist one another with coping. These types of program aim to improve skill in seeking and using support for some at-risk population and/or improve skill in providing support among close relational partners of individuals undergoing some stressful experience. The ability to teach individuals how to participate more effectively in troubles talk offers hope of empowering them to take better advantage of the potential for assisted coping and to feel greater satisfaction in relationships. Improving the ways individuals seek, offer, provide, and use support is one concrete point of contact for intervention. The communication approach developed in this book has some potentially disturbing yet innovative ramifications for those who wish to improve their own or others' troubles talk conversations.

First, it should be apparent from my theoretical framework and empirical findings that successful troubles talk conversations can take a wide variety of forms adapted to particular problems, participants, and relationships. Under some circumstances, blunt advice is warranted and gains force and credibility from the directness with which it is expressed; however, in most situations, effective advice is couched in a style, substance, and sequence that are best suited to the existing or desired relationship between the parties. We have seen transcripts of conversations in which partners laid their problems out and engaged in problem-solving or comforting in rather straightforward ways but we have also seen transcripts in which partners shared in humorous diversion or fantasy or reports of conversational patterns in which problems were addressed covertly and anxieties allayed by inference rather than discussion. It is also evident that sometimes partners' ways of proceeding are in synch, sometimes they are not, and there are various things they do to try to achieve alignment.

In the theory and data I have presented there are no one-size-fits-all behaviors that are uniformly supportive across contexts. Open, clear, direct support seeking is but one mode of conduct, with both risks and advantages. Nondirective ways of responding are not necessarily the expected or appropriate response in all situations. As Heller and Rook (2001) have observed, many support interventions proceed from an untested assumption that the kinds of unfettered communication and empathic listening that characterize clinical practice and therapeutic helping traditions set the standard for what we hope to achieve in social support interventions with naturally occurring social ties. They conclude that this is too simple and potentially harmful, a conclusion shared with Gottlieb's (1992) review of interventions. Recommendations to individuals to communicate their needs more openly or to listen and respond more empathically likely do have some utility as new options for individuals who may not have previously practiced these behaviors. Many of us probably do go it alone when we could benefit from help or unrealistically expect our partners to know and do what we need without our having to ask. Many of us probably do talk too much and listen not enough when others close to us are in distress. However, most social skills-based approaches fail to capture the potential utility of indirectness and overlook how individual behavior (skilled or not) must be coordinated with a partner in the context of an ongoing relationship (Röhrle & Sommer, 1994).

A second implication of my work is to acknowledge that even if we were to mount an intervention that does justice to the variety and complexity of abilities involved in enacted social support, we would need to do so with a recognition that seeking and providing support are but one of the ways in which close relational partners may cope effectively. Seeking and providing support imply a corresponding set of identities and relational definitions that may be desirable in some circumstances but undesirable in others. Coping assistance can also flow from other configurations of interactive roles, including experience swapping, communal coping, and support disguised as ordinary routine. As Coyne and his colleagues (1990) have observed, in long-term close relationships, seeking and providing support may represent a breakdown of the normal interactions through which support is perceived and needs are met without asking or telling. Any intervention designed to improve skill in seeking and giving support must be accompanied by an appreciation for when this is most appropriate and when other kinds of routines might serve better. Alternatively, a focus on improving support skills might be more usefully targeted toward individuals for whom communal coping or routine ways of interacting have broken down rather than a program offered universally to high and low functioning relationships alike.

Changing communication patterns is not a quick fix for individuals or relationships and even when there is reason to believe that improving interaction patterns is an appropriate type of intervention, communication patterns exist in a complex relationship to dispositions, current and past relationships, and mental health (Mallinckrodt, 2000). Similarly, the communication behaviors we might seek to develop are intimately connected with motivational, cognitive, and emotional aptitudes. As Burleson (2003) observed with reference to improving emotional support skills, the ability to provide effective emotional support depends not only on communication skill but also on fundamental social perception skills and on the motivation to assist.

Nonetheless, my theoretical framework and findings suggest that one way to approach the formidable task of improving troubles talk is to sensitize participants to the challenges of conducting troubles talk and engage them in reflecting on how different ways of responding accomplish different tasks, identities, and relationships. This is likely to be most feasible when the focus is on assisted coping with particular stressors in particular relationships. For particular stressors, it is possible to identify a range of common difficulties and normatively adaptive appraisals and behaviors. For particular relationships, it is possible to delve into existing patterns of interaction as well as individual preferences. For example, in the Illinois Heart Care Project (Goldsmith & Leslie, 2001), we are focusing on some of the common health and communication problems that occur in the context of recovery from a cardiac event. Instead of attempting to cultivate general skill in "seeking or providing support," we have the more modest goal of helping partners reflect on ways of implementing specific changes such as maintaining the dietary and exercise changes that are normative for individuals facing this particular coping challenge (see also Sher & Baucom, 2001, whose Partners for Life program focuses on a couples intervention for improving adherence to cardiac risk reduction). We are also focusing on a particular relationship so that couples can reflect on what existing patterns of interaction are serving them well and which ones are serving them poorly. We seek to normalize some of the dilemmas individuals experience and encourage them to realize their own and partner's preferences and options for negotiating these dilemmas (see Brashers et al., in press, for a discussion of some similar issues among persons with HIV/AIDS).

CONCLUSION

Both as scholars of social interaction and as participants in social life, we know that enacted social support matters. What we say and do in our close relationships to help one another cope with daily stresses and significant crises shapes the decisions we make, the joy and sorrow we feel, and the people we become. The conduct of troubles talk is a crucible for individual and relational development as well as for theoretical development. If we can find ways to capture and account for what goes on in these conversations, we contribute not only to understanding this aspect of our close relationships but also our ability to penetrate other complex types of interactions where multiple goals, interpretations, evaluations, and outcomes come together.

Appendix

Here I provide additional information about the participants, procedures, and measures employed in various studies that are reported in this book. For the reader's ease of reference, I have listed the studies alphabetically according to the label given in the text (rather than chronologically).

ADVICE CONTENT STUDY

A sample of 233 University of Illinois undergraduate students completed a questionnaire during the last 10 minutes of their speech communication class or during a meeting at their fraternity. Some questionnaires were incomplete and others were randomly discarded to achieve an equal number of men and women in each of the cells of the study design. Results were based on 186 participants. Our sample included 66.5% European Americans, 15.5% African Americans, and 8.6% Asian Americans. The remaining students were members of other racial-ethnic groups or declined to indicate their racial-ethnic identity. The mean age of respondents was 19.6 years. Most students were sophomores or juniors and half were speech communication majors.

Each student read a narrative about a student named Pat whose sex varied to match the respondent's sex. In the story, Pat was very nervous about giving a speech in class the next day. He/she encountered a friend in the library and mentioned being nervous about the speech. In the course of their conversation, the friend delivered the message that respondents were then asked to rate. Each respondent read a single message, selected from messages produced by a different sample of students in the Naturalistic Experiment study. The sample of messages included all responses to the speech anxiety scenario that included one or more statements of advice. Immediately following the message, students were asked to complete Likert-type rating scales to indicate their agreement with a variety of statements about the message, including ratings of perceived regard for positive and negative face. This study is described in greater detail in Goldsmith (1999; Study 2).

ADVICE FOLLOW-UP STUDY

A sample of 407 University of Illinois undergraduate students completed a questionnaire during the first or last 15 minutes of a speech communication course. Questionnaires with missing data were discarded and an identical questionnaire was given to another student until 384 questionnaires were completed (the number needed to fill all cells in the study design with equal numbers of men and women). Respondents ranged in age from 17 to 29 ($M = 20.26$, $SD = 1.45$) and most were juniors or seniors. Our sample included 66.7% European Americans, 15.1% African Americans, 6.8% Asian or Asian Americans, 5.5% Hispanics or Latino/as; the remaining respondents either indicated some other racial-ethnic identity or declined to respond to this question. Most respondents were speech communication majors (53.1%), though a variety of other majors were represented.

Respondents read a narrative in which a person named Chris disclosed a problem to another person, who then gave Chris advice (the sex of both characters was the same as that of the respondent). Scenarios included a brief description of the relationship between Chris and the adviser and a brief description of what Chris said about his or her problem. Then, the respondents read a single advice message given to Chris by the other person in the scenario. Immediately following the message, respondents were asked to complete semantic-differential-type scales anchored by effective/ineffective, helpful/unhelpful, appropriate/inappropriate, and sensitive/insensitive. Respondents then rated the message on a series of Likert-type scales measuring perceived regard for positive and negative face and perceptions of the power and closeness of the two characters in the narrative. This study is described in greater detail in Goldsmith and MacGeorge (2000).

ADVICE PILOT STUDY

Participants were twenty-nine undergraduate students at the University of Maryland, College Park (I did not solicit demographic information). Each student read twelve different messages a person might say in one of two situations: "Upon hearing that a close friend has failed an important exam in his or her major and is very upset" or "If a close friend called to tell you he or she has just been dumped by his or her girlfriend or boyfriend." The twelve messages represented three types of supportive acts (advice, offer, expression of concern) in four different face work styles (direct, solidary, deferential, indirect). Students rated each of the twelve messages on a scale anchored by *not at all helpful* and *very helpful*. For the messages they identified as most and least helpful, students also explained why they rated the message that way. They also completed measures designed to assess whether they correctly perceived each message as advice, offer, or concern and to assess their perception of the degree to which each message honored or threatened positive and negative face. Additional details of this study are reported in Goldsmith (1994b).

ADVICE SEQUENCE STUDY

Participants were 420 University of Illinois undergraduate students who completed a questionnaire in response to a request by a student taking a speech communication course. Participants ranged in age from 17 to 29 ($M = 20.66$ years, $SD = 1.53$). Just over half of the sample were women (57.6%). Most participants were European American (62.2%); 21.1% were African American; and 4.5% were Asian or Asian American, and 4.5% were Hispanic or Latino/a. Although questionnaires were distributed by students from speech communication courses, study participants came from a wide variety of academic majors. Most were juniors or seniors.

Each participant read one of sixty dialogues. Each dialogue represented one of ten different advice message scenarios (e.g., one friend giving another advice about studying for an exam or one friend giving another advice about walking home after dark) embedded in one of six ways of introducing advice into a conversation. After reading the dialogue, participants responded to a series of Likert-type scales designed to measure the perceived realism of the conversation, the degree to which advice was solicited by the advice recipient, the degree to which the advice giver showed regard for the recipient's positive and negative face, and the effectiveness of the support provided. Additional information about this study appears in Goldsmith (2000, Study 2) and Goldsmith et al. (2000, Study 3).

COMMUNITY ADVICE STUDY

This study is based on participant observation and ethnographic interview data collected by a research team of five women and one man, aged 20 to 38. Four team members were undergraduate speech communication majors at the University of Maryland, College Park; one was a faculty member who taught at University of Maryland, College Park; University of Iowa; and University of Illinois at Urbana–Champaign during the period of data collection; and one was a faculty member who taught at the University of Colorado at Boulder and University of Iowa. Thus, data collection occurred in a western university community, two different midwestern university communities, and a large eastern metropolitan area.

The members of the research team kept field notes of advice episodes they observed or in which they participated in the course of their everyday life. In addition to reconstructing the dialogue we also took detailed notes on the context in which the episode occurred. The 112 episodes on which our analyses were based took place in a variety of settings and relationships. We also conducted interviews with eleven women and seven men; eight of our interviewees were college students and the other ten were adults ranging in age from 32 to 81. All interviewees were European American. The interviews asked participants to whom they gave advice, from whom they received advice, why they gave advice, why others gave advice to them, and under what circumstances advice was given and received. We also asked participants to recall the best and worst advice they had received recently and reasons why the advice was well- or ill-received. Additional information about this study appears in Goldsmith and Fitch (1997).

COMMUNITY CONVERSATION STUDY

Adult residents of Urbana–Champaign, Illinois, and surrounding communities brought a friend, romantic partner, family member, or acquaintance for participation in a study of everyday conversation. Sixty-one pairs participated, forty-two-males and eighty females, aged 18–66 years ($M = 34.5$, $SD = 12.2$). Most participants were European American (71.3%); 14.8% were African American and 4.1% were Hispanic or Latino/a. Our participants came from a variety of occupations, including blue collar work, skilled trades, clerical work, professional work, and academic employment. The highest level of schooling completed was also variable, including some who had not completed high school (2.3%); high school graduates (7.7%); those who had completed some college, trade, or professional school (36.1%); graduates of trade or professional school (4.6%); college graduates (16.2%); those who had completed some graduate school (15.4%); and those who held a postgraduate degree (15.4%; the remaining 2.3% declined to answer this item or fell into some other category).

The analyses reported in Chapter 5 are based on the seventeen married couples in our sample. These married participants ranged in age from 20 to 51 and had known one another, on average, for 8.52 years ($SD = 7.70$ years, range = 6 months to 29.83 years). A single item measure of relational satisfaction indicated the married couples in our sample were generally quite satisfied with their relationships ($M = 5.53$ on a 7-point scale, $SD = 2.12$). Most of the participants (85.3%) were European American, two individuals were African American (5.9%), and three designated some other category or declined to indicate their racial/ethnic identity (8.8%).

Conversations between partners lasted approximately 20 to 30 minutes. Prior to the conversation, our contact person in each dyad was asked to list three "stresses, hassles, or problems in your life right now." At the bottom of the page was a short paragraph asking the participant to "select the one problem that is most pressing to you at the moment" and to "try to bring this problem up as you normally would in conversation with your partner." At the same time, the conversational partner was responding to a similar sheet that asked them to "please list below three good things or happy events in your life right now." This partner was told that they should try to have a normal, everyday conversation and that these topics might be discussed if they became "stuck" for something to talk about. The researcher then took both partners to a classroom with audio and video equipment, started the equipment, and left the participants to hold their conversation. Our procedures were successful in eliciting conversations that were perceived as natural by the participants: In response to a single-item scale measuring the degree to which the conversation seemed natural, the mean rating was 5.18 on a 7-point scale ($SD = 1.42$).

Following their conversation, partners completed a questionnaire regarding their impressions of the conversation. Among the scales we used were the Iowa Communication Record (Duck et al., 1996); the various change items reported in Chapter 4 (e.g., change in attitude and change in behavior) are from the ICR. We also used semantic-differential-type scales to measure participants' evaluation of the social support they received (helpful/harmful, sensitive/insensitive, effective/ineffective, support-ive/unsupportive, liked/disliked, accepted/criticized, more calm/less calm).

The conversations were transcribed verbatim and then rechecked against the original tapes for accuracy. Then, an independent listener returned to tapes and transcripts to refine our representation of pausing and turn taking. In transcripts, italicized material in brackets indicates overlapping speech and equal signs indicate when two speaker's utterances followed closely with no pausing (latched speech). Punctuation is used to mark intonation: A period indicates falling intonation and pausing as at the end of a thought or sentence, a comma indicates a less dramatic fall in intonation and a brief pause as is typical in the middle of a thought or sentence, and a question mark indicates rising intonation.

ILLINOIS HEART CARE PROJECT

Forty-one adults from Urbana–Champaign, Illinois, and surrounding communities participated in 60- to 90-minute interviews about their experiences as patients or spouses of patients who had experienced a heart attack or bypass surgery in the last year. The analyses reported in Chapter 5 are based on the fifteen married couples who participated together in the study; in all of these couples, the husband was the heart patient. The couples had been married 3 to 55 years ($M = 34.53$, $SD = 16.34$); their responses to an eleven-item measure of marital satisfaction (Huston, McHale, & Crouter, 1986) indicated most were quite satisfied with their relationship

($M = 5.58$ on a 7-point scale, $SD = 1.21$). These thirty individuals were European American, aged 37 to 77 ($M = 63.57$, $SD = 10.97$). Their education varied: 36.67% had a high school education, 26.67% had completed some college, 10% held a college degree, and 26.67% held graduate degrees. A variety of present and preretirement occupations were represented, including farmers, engineers, homemakers, teachers, factory line workers, secretaries, and owners of small businesses. Seventeen were retired.

Interviews were conducted individually: One interviewer spoke with the husband at the same time another interviewer in a separate room spoke with the wife. Immediately prior to the interview, participants completed a measure of marital satisfaction, a measure of distress, and a measure of relational coping strategies. The interviews began by asking individuals to describe some of the changes they had observed following the cardiac event, including changes in one's own life and priorities, changes in one's spouse's life, and changes in their relationship. We asked them to describe topics related to their (or their partner's) heart condition that were easy to discuss with their spouse, topics that were difficult to discuss, and topics that were a source of disagreement or argument. We then asked a series of specific questions regarding common challenges and adjustments, including changes in diet, level of activity, fears about recurrence, depression, changes in relational roles, changes in priorities, concerns about recovery, avoiding conflict, expressing affection, and sharing information with their social network. For each of these topics, we asked them if this was an area of concern and, if it was, whether and how they had communicated about this issue with their spouse. Finally, we asked participants to recall and describe a conversation with their spouse that was especially pleasing as well as one that they wished they could do over. Tapes of the interviews were transcribed verbatim.

NATURALISTIC EXPERIMENT

Participants were 119 undergraduates at the University of Maryland, College Park and the University of Illinois at Urbana–Champaign. Participants were predominantly white and between the ages of 18 and 22 years (in the first wave of data collection at University of Maryland, the only demographic information I obtained from respondents was their sex, so the preceding characterization of race and age is based on my firsthand observation of students during data collection at Maryland and on demographic information collected in the second wave of data collection at Illinois). Most participants were speech communication majors; however, students from a variety of majors were represented. Equipment malfunction and failure to follow instructions resulted in incomplete data for nineteen participants; the analyses presented in Chapters 3 and 4 are based on the 109 participants from whom we had complete responses to three scenarios described below.

Participants were taken to a lab or classroom with a tape recorder and asked to read and respond to each of nine situations in which another person had disclosed some problem and appeared upset. Students were assured that there were no right or wrong answers and were instructed to "speak into the tape recorder as if the other person were sitting here in the room. Say into the tape recorder the actual words you would say." The nine scenarios were selected from a larger sample of twenty-four scenarios that had been pretested with a separate sample of fifty-one students. We selected our nine scenarios on the basis of pretest ratings of realism and relevance of a helping response and to obtain scenarios that varied in pretest ratings of power and closeness in the relationship between characters. In Chapters 3 and 4, I report on data from three of the nine scenarios: a best friend who has failed an important exam, a friend who is anxious about giving a speech, and a close friend who has been dumped by her boyfriend. All responses were transcribed verbatim, preserving colloquial language (e.g., "gotta" and "you know") but without attempting to represent nonword fillers (e.g., "uh") or nonstandard pronunciation.

References

Abbey, A., Andrews, F. M., & Halman, L. J. (1995). The provision and receipt of social support and disregard: What is their impact on the marital life quality of infertile and fertile couples? *Journal of Personality and Social Psychology, 68,* 455–469.

Abdel-Halim, A. A. (1982). Social support and managerial affective responses to job stress. *Journal of Occupational Behavior, 3,* 281–295.

Abel, E. K. (1989). The ambiguities of social support: Adult daughters caring for frail elderly parents. *Journal of Aging Studies, 3,* 211–230.

Acitelli, L. K. (1996). The neglected links between marital support and marital satisfaction. In G. R. Pierce, B. R. Sarason, & I. G. Sarason (Eds.), *Handbook of social support and the family* (pp. 83–103). New York: Plenum.

Albrecht, T. L., & Goldsmith, D. J. (2003). Social support, social networks, and health. In T. L. Thompson, A. M. Dorsey, K. I. Miller, & R. Parrott (Eds.), *Handbook of health communication* (pp. 263–284). Mahwah, NJ: Erlbaum.

Aldwin, C. M. (1994). *Stress, coping, and development: An integrative perspective.* New York: Guilford Press.

Aneshensel, C. S., & Frerichs, R. R. (1982). Stress, support, and depression: A longitudinal causal model. *Journal of Community Psychology, 10,* 363–376.

Antonucci, T. C. (1985). Personal characteristics, social networks, and social behavior. In R. H. Binstock & E. Shanas (Eds.), *Handbook of aging and the social sciences* (2nd ed., pp. 94–128). New York: Van Nostrand Reinhold.

Antonucci, T. C., & Israel, B. (1986). Veridicality of social support: A comparison of principal and network members' responses. *Journal of Consulting and Clinical Psychology, 54,* 432–437.

Antonucci, T. C., & Jackson, J. S. (1987). Social support, interpersonal efficacy, and health: A life course perspective. In L. Carstensen & B. A. Edelstein (Eds.), *Handbook of clinical gerontology* (pp. 291–311). New York: Pergamon.

Baker, J. M. (1997). *Social support and academic persistence: A test of the optimal-matching model.* Unpublished dissertation, Arizona State University, Tempe, AZ.

Bakhtin, M. M. (1986). The problem of speech genres. In C. Emerson & M. Holquist (Eds.), *M. M. Bakhtin: Speech genres and other late essays* (pp. 60–102). (V. W. McGee, Trans.). Austin: University of Texas Press.

Barbee, A. P., & Cunningham, M. (1995). An experimental approach to social support communications: Interactive coping in close relationships. In B. R. Burleson (Ed.), *Communication yearbook 18* (pp. 381–413). Thousand Oaks, CA: Sage.

Barker, C., & Lemle, R. (1984). Informal helping in partner and stranger dyads. *Journal of Marriage and the Family, 49,* 541–547.

Barnes, M. K., & Duck, S. (1994). Everyday communicative contexts for social support. In B. R. Burleson, T. L. Albrecht, & I. G. Sarason (Eds.), *Communication of social support: Messages, interactions, relationships, and community* (pp. 175–194). Thousand Oaks, CA: Sage.

Barnet, M. A., & Harris, R. J. (1984). Peer counselors and friends: Expected and preferred responses. *Journal of Counseling Psychology, 31,* 253–261.

Barrera, M. (1980). A method for the assessment of social support networks in community survey research. *Connections, 3,* 8–13.

Barrera, M. (1981). Social support in the adjustment of pregnant adolescents. In B. H. Gottlieb (Ed.), *Social networks and social support* (pp. 69–96). Beverly Hills, CA: Sage.

Barrera, M. (1986). Distinctions between social support concepts, measures, and models. *American Journal of Community Psychology, 14,* 413–445.

Barrera, M. (1988). Models of social support and life stress. In L. H. Cohen (Ed.), *Life events and psychological functioning: Theoretical and methodological issues* (pp. 211–236). Thousand Oaks, CA: Sage.

Barrera, M., & Ainlay, S. L. (1983). The structure of social support: A conceptual and empirical analysis. *Journal of Community Psychology, 11,* 133–143.

Bates, D. B., & Toro, P. A. (1999). Developing measures to assess social support among homeless and poor people. *Journal of Community Psychology, 27,* 137–156.

Baxter, L. A. (1987). Symbols of relationship identity in relationship culture. *Journal of Social and Personal Relationships, 4,* 261–280.

Baxter, L. A. (1993). The social and the personal of close relationships. In S. Duck (Ed.), *Social contexts of relationships* (pp. 139–165). Newbury Park, CA: Sage.

Belsher, G., & Costello, C. G. (1991). Do confidants of depressed women provide less social support than confidants of nondepressed women? *Journal of Abnormal Psychology, 100,* 516–525.

Berkman, L. F. (1985). The relationship of social networks and social support to morbidity and mortality. In S. Cohen & S. L. Syme (Eds.), *Social support and health* (pp. 241–262). New York: Academic Press.

Berman, S. L., Kurtines, W. M., Silverman, W. K., & Serafini, L. T. (1996). The impact of exposure to crime and violence on urban youth. *American Journal of Orthopsychiatry, 66,* 329–336.

Bippus, A. M. (2000). Humor usage in comforting episodes: Factors predicting outcomes. *Western Journal of Communication, 64,* 359–384.

Bippus, A. M. (2001). Recipients' criteria for evaluating the skillfulness of comforting communication and the outcomes of comforting interactions. *Communication Monographs, 68,* 301–313.

Bishop, S. J., & Leadbeater, B. J. (1999). Maternal social support patterns and child maltreatment: Comparison of maltreating and nonmaltreating mothers. *American Journal of Orthopsychiatry, 69,* 172–181.

Bodenmann, G. (1997a). Dyadic coping: A systemic-transactional view of stress and coping among couples: Theory and empirical findings. *Revue Europeenne de Psychologie Appliquee, 47*, 137–140.

Bodenmann, G. (1997b). The influence of stress and coping on close relationships: A two-year longitudinal study. *Swiss Journal of Psychology, 56*, 156–164.

Bolger, N., Foster, M., Vinokur, A. D., & Ng, R. (1996). Close relationships and adjustment to a life crisis: The case of breast cancer. *Journal of Personality and Social Psychology, 70*, 283–294.

Bolger, N., Zuckerman, A., & Kessler, R. C. (2000). Invisible support and adjustment to stress. *Journal of Personality and Social Psychology, 79*, 953–961.

Brashers, D. E., Neidig, J. L., & Goldsmith, D. J. (in press). Social support and the management of uncertainty for people living with HIV or AIDS. *Health Communication.*

Broadhead, W. E., Kaplan, B. H., James, S. A., Wagner, E. H., Schoenbach, V. S., Grimson, R., et al. (1983). The epidemiologic evidence for a relationship between social support and health. *American Journal of Epidemiology, 117*, 521–537.

Brown, P., & Levinson, S. C. (1987). *Politeness: Some universals in language usage.* Cambridge: Cambridge University Press.

Buhrmeister, D., Furman, W., Wittenberg, M. T., & Reis, H. T. (1988). Five domains of interpersonal competence in peer relationships. *Journal of Personality and Social Psychology, 55*, 991–1008.

Burleson, B. R. (1994). Comforting messages: Significance, approaches, and effects. In B. R. Burleson, T. L. Albrecht, & I. G. Sarason (Eds.), *Communication of social support: Messages, interactions, relationships, and community* (pp. 3–28). Thousand Oaks, CA: Sage.

Burleson, B. R. (2003). Emotional support skill. In J. O. Greene & B. R. Burleson (Eds.), *Handbook of communication and social interaction skills* (pp. 551–594). Mahwah, NJ: Erlbaum.

Burleson, B. R., Albrecht, T. L., Sarason, I. G., & Goldsmith, D. J. (1994). Introduction: The communication of social support. In B. R. Burleson, T. L. Albrecht, & I. G. Sarason (Eds.), *Communication of social support: Messages, interactions, relationships, and community* (pp. xi–xxx). Thousand Oaks, CA: Sage.

Burleson, B. R. & Goldsmith, D. J. (1998). How comforting messages work: Some mechanisms through which messages may alleviate emotional distress. In P. A. Anderson & L. K. Guerrero (Eds.), *Handbook of communication and emotion: Research, theory, applications, and contexts* (pp. 245–280). Orlando, FL: Academic Press.

Burleson, B. R., & MacGeorge, E. (2002). Supportive communication. In M. L. Knapp & J. A. Daly (Eds.), *Handbook of interpersonal communication* (3rd ed., pp. 374–424). Thousand Oaks, CA: Sage.

Burleson, B. R., & Samter, W. (1985). Consistencies in theoretical and naive evaluations of comforting messages. *Communication Monographs, 52*, 103–123.

Buttny, R. (1996). Clients' and therapist's joint construction of the clients' problems. *Research on Language and Social Interaction, 29*, 125–153.

Buunk, B. P., & Hoorens, V. (1992). Social support and stress: The role of social comparison and social exchange processes. *British Journal of Clinical Psychology, 31*, 445–457.

Caplan, S. E., & Samter, W. (1999). The role of facework in younger and older adults' evaluations of social support messages. *Communication Quarterly, 47*, 245–264.

Carbaugh, D. (1988). *Talking American: Cultural discourses on Donahue*. Norwood, NJ: Ablex.

Carels, R. A., & Baucom, D. H. (1999). Support in marriage: Factors associated with on-line perceptions of support helpfulness. *Journal of Family Psychology, 13*, 131–144.

Carkhuff, R. R. (1969). *Helping and human relations*. New York: Holt, Rinehart, & Winston.

Cassel, J. (1976). The contribution of the social environment to host resistance. *American Journal of Epidemiology, 104*, 107–123.

Cauce, A. M. (1986). Social networks and social competence: Exploring the effects of early adolescent friendships. *American Journal of Community Psychology, 14*, 607–628.

Caughlin, J. P. (2003). Family communication standards: What counts as excellent family communication and how are such standards associated with family satisfaction? *Human Communication Research, 29*, 5–40.

Chesler, M. A., & Barbarin, O. A. (1984). Dilemmas of providing help in a crisis: The role of friends with parents of children with cancer. *Journal of Social Issues, 41*, 47–63.

Cheuk, W. H., Swearse, B., Wong, K. W., & Rosen, S. (1998). The linkage between spurned help and burnout among practicing nurses. *Current Psychology, 17*, 188–196.

Clark, M. S. (1983). Some implications of close social bonds for help-seeking. In B. M. DePaulo, A. Nadler, & J. D. Fisher (Eds.), *New directions in helping: Vol. 2. Help seeking* (pp. 205–229). New York: Academic Press.

Clark, R. A., & Delia, J. G. (1979). *Topoi* and rhetorical competence. *The Quarterly Journal of Speech, 65*, 187–206.

Clark, R. A., Pierce, A. J., Finn, K., Hsu, K., Toolsey, A., & Williams, L. (1997, May). *The impact of alternative comforting messages, closeness of relationship, and gender on multiple measures of effectiveness*. Paper presented at the annual meeting of the International Communication Association, Montreal, Quebec.

Clark, S. L., & Stephens, M. A. P. (1996). Stroke patients' well-being as a function of caregiving spouse's helpful and unhelpful actions. *Personal Relationships, 3*, 171–184.

Cobb, S. (1976). Social support as a moderator of life stress. *Psychosomatic Medicine, 38*, 300–314.

Cohen, S. (1988). Psychosocial models of the role of social support in the etiology of physical disease. *Health Psychology, 7*, 269–297.

Cohen, S., Gottlieb, B. H., & Underwood, L. G. (2000). Social relationships and health. In S. Cohen, L. G. Underwood, & B. H. Gottlieb (Eds.), *Social support measurement and intervention: A guide for health and social scientists* (pp. 3–25). Oxford University Press.

Cohen, S., & Hoberman, H. M. (1983). Positive events and social supports as buffers of life change stress. *Journal of Applied Social Psychology, 13*, 99–125.

Cohen, S., & McKay, G. (1984). Social support, stress and the buffering hypothesis: A theoretical analysis. In A. Baum, S. E. Taylor, & J. E. Singer (Eds.), *Handbook of psychology and health: Vol. IV. Social psychological aspects of health* (pp. 253–267). Hillsdale, NJ: Erlbaum.

Cohen, S., & Wills, T. A. (1985). Stress, social support, and the buffering hypothesis. *Psychological Bulletin, 98*, 310–357.

Collins, N. L., & Feeney, B. C. (2000). A safe haven: An attachment theory perspective on support seeking and caregiving in intimate relationships. *Journal of Personality and Social Psychology, 78*, 1053–1073.

Colvin, C. R., & Block, J. (1994). Do positive illusions foster mental health? An examination of the Taylor and Brown formulation. *Psychological Bulletin, 116*, 3–20.

Colvin, C. R., Block, J., & Funder, D. C. (1995). Overly positive self-evaluations and personality: Negative implications for mental health. *Journal of Personality and Social Psychology, 65*, 1224–1236.

Cooper, M. L. (1986). *The role of supportive transactions and perceived functional support as stress buffers.* Unpublished dissertation, University of California, Santa Cruz.

Coriell, M., & Cohen, S. (1995). Concordance in the face of a stressful event: When do members of a dyad agree that one person supported the other? *Journal of Personality and Social Psychology, 69*, 289–299.

Coupland, J. (2000). *Small talk.* Harlow, England: Longman.

Coupland, N., Coupland, J., & Giles, H. (1991). *Language, society, and the elderly: Discourse, identity, and aging.* Oxford, UK: Blackwell.

Coyne, J. C., Aldwin, C., & Lazarus, R. S. (1981). Depression and coping in stressful episodes. *Journal of Abnormal Psychology, 90*, 439–447.

Coyne, J. C., & DeLongis, A. (1986). Going beyond social support: The role of social relationships in adaptation. *Journal of Counseling and Clinical Psychology, 54*, 454–460.

Coyne, J. C., Ellard, J. H., & Smith, D. (1990). Social support, interdependence, and the dilemmas of helping. In B. R. Sarason, I. G. Sarason, & G. R. Pierce (Eds.), *Social support: An interactional view* (pp. 129–149). New York: Wiley.

Coyne, J. C., & Fiske, V. (1992). Couples coping with chronic and catastrophic illness. In T. J. Akamatsu, M. A. P. Stephens, S. E. Hobfoll, & J. H. Crowther (Eds.), *Family health psychology* (pp. 129–149). Washington, DC: Hemisphere.

Coyne, J. C., & Gottlieb, B. H. (1996). The mismeasure of coping by checklist. *Journal of Personality, 64*, 959–991.

Coyne, J. C., & Smith, D. A. F. (1994). Couples coping with a myocardial infarction: Contextual perspective on patient self-efficacy. *Journal of Family Psychology, 8*, 43–54.

Coyne, J. C., Wortman, C. B., & Lehman, D. R. (1988). The other side of support: Emotional overinvolvement and miscarried helping. In B. H. Gottlieb (Ed.), *Marshaling social support; Formats, processes, and effects* (pp. 305–330). Newbury Park, CA: Sage.

Cramer, D. (1987). Self-esteem, advice-giving, and the facilitative nature of close personal relationships. *Person-centered Review, 2*, 99–110.

Cramer, D. (1990). Helpful actions of close friends to personal problems and distress. *British Journal of Guidance and Counseling, 18*, 281–293.

Cummins, R. C. (1988). Perceptions of social support, receipt of supportive behaviors, and locus of control as moderators of chronic stress. *American Journal of Community Psychology, 16*, 685–700.

Cutrona, C. E. (1986). Objective determinants of perceived social support. *Journal of Personality and Social Psychology, 50*, 349–355.

Cutrona, C. E. (1990). Stress and social support – In search of optimal matching. *Journal of Social and Clinical Psychology, 9,* 3–14.

Cutrona, C. E. (1996a). Social support as a determinant of marital quality. In G. R. Pierce, B. R. Sarason, & I. G. Sarason (Eds.), *Handbook of social support and the family* (pp. 173–194). New York: Plenum.

Cutrona, C. E. (1996b). *Social support in couples.* Thousand Oaks, CA: Sage.

Cutrona, C. E., Cole, V., Colangelo, N., Assouline, S. G., & Russell, D. W. (1994). Perceived parental social support and academic achievement: An attachment theory perspective. *Journal of Personality and Social Psychology, 66,* 396–378.

Cutrona, C. E., & Russell, D. W. (1990). Type of social support and specific stress: Toward a theory of optimal matching. In B. R. Sarason, I. G. Sarason, & G. R. Pierce (Eds.), *Social support: An interactional view* (pp. 319–366). New York: Wiley.

Cutrona, C. E., & Suhr, J. A. (1992). Controllability of stressful events and satisfaction with spouse support behaviors. *Communication Research, 19,* 154–174.

Cutrona, C. E., & Suhr, J. A. (1994). Social support communication in the context of marriage: An analysis of couples' supportive interactions. In B. R. Burleson, T. L. Albrecht, & I. G. Sarason (Eds.), *Communication of social support: Messages, interactions, relationships, and community* (pp. 113–135). Thousand Oaks, CA: Sage.

Cutrona, C. E., Suhr, J. A., & MacFarlane, R. (1990). Interpersonal transactions and the psychological sense of support. In S. Duck with R. Cohen-Silver (Eds.), *Personal relationships and social support* (pp. 30–45). London: Sage.

Dainton, M., & Stafford, L. (1993). Routine maintenance behaviors: A comparison of relationship type, partner similarity, and sex differences. *Journal of Social and Personal Relationships, 10,* 255–271.

Dakof, G. A., & Taylor, S. E. (1990). Victim's perceptions of social support: What is helpful from whom? *Journal of Personality and Social Psychology, 58,* 80–89.

Danish, S. J., & D'Augelli, A. R. (1976). Rationale and implementation of a training program for paraprofessionals. *Professional Psychology, 7,* 38–46.

D'Augelli, A. R., & Levy, M. (1978). The verbal helping skills of trained and untrained human service paraprofessionals. *American Journal of Community Psychology, 6,* 23–31.

D'Augelli, A. R., & Vallance, T. R. (1982). The helping community: Issues in the evaluation of a preventive intervention to promote informal helping. *Journal of Community Psychology, 10,* 199–209.

D'Augelli, A. R., Vallance, T. R., Danish, S. J., Young, C. E., & Gerdes, J. L. (1981). The community helpers project: A description of a prevention strategy for rural communities. *Journal of Prevention, 1,* 209–224.

Davidowitz, M., & Myrick, R. D. (1984). Responding to the bereaved: An analysis of "helping" statements. *Death Education, 8,* 1–10.

Davis, R. C., & Brickman, E. (1996). Supportive and unsupportive aspects of the behavior of others toward victims of sexual and nonsexual assault. *Journal of Interpersonal Violence, 11,* 250–262.

Dean, A., Kolody, B., Wood, P., & Ensel, W. M. (1989). The effects of types of social support from adult children on depression in elderly persons. *American Journal of Community Psychology, 17,* 341–355.

Dehle, C., Larsen, D., & Landers, J. E. (2001). Social support in marriage. *The American Journal of Family Therapy, 29,* 307–324.

DePaulo, B. M. (1982). Social psychological processes in informal help-seeking. In T. A. Wills (Ed.), *Basic processes in helping relationships* (pp. 255–279). New York: Academic Press.

DePaulo, B. M., & Fisher, J. D. (1980). The costs of asking for help. *Basic and Applied Psychology, 1*, 23–35.

Depner, C. E., Wethington, E., & Ingersoll-Dayton, B. (1984). Social support: Methodological issues in design and measurement. *Journal of Social Issues, 40*, 37–54.

DeRidder, D., & Schreurs, K. (1996). Coping, social support and chronic disease: A research agenda. *Psychology, Health, & Medicine, 1*, 71–82.

DiMatteo, M. R., & Hays, R. (1981). Social support and serious illness. In B. H. Gottlieb (Ed.), *Social networks and social support* (pp. 117–148). Beverly Hills, CA: Sage.

Doeglas, D., Suurmeijur, T., Briancon, S., Moum, T., Krol, B., Bjelle, E., et al. (1996). An international study on measuring social support: Interactions and satisfaction. *Social Science and Medicine, 43*, 1389–1397.

Duck, S., Rutt, D. J., Hurst, M. H., & Strejc, H. (1991). Some evident truths about conversations in everyday relationships: All communications are not created equal. *Human Communication Research, 18*, 228–267.

Dunkel-Schetter, C. (1984). Social support and cancer: Findings based on patient interviews and their implications. *Journal of Social Issues, 40*, 77–98.

Dunkel-Schetter, C., & Bennett, T. L. (1990). Differentiating the cognitive and behavioral aspects of social support. In B. R. Sarason, I. G. Sarason, & G. R. Pierce (Eds.), *Social support: An interactional view* (pp. 267–296). New York: Wiley.

Dunkel-Schetter, C., Blasband, D., Feinstein, L., & Herbert, T. (1992). Elements of supportive interactions: When are attempts to help effective? In S. Spacapan & S. Oskamp (Eds.), *Helping and being helped: Naturalistic studies* (pp. 83–114). Newbury Park, CA: Sage.

Dunkel-Schetter, C., & Wortman, C. B. (1982). The interpersonal dynamics of cancer: Problems in social relationships and their impact on the patient. In H. S. Friedman & M. R. DiMatteo (Eds.), *Interpersonal issues in health care* (pp. 69–100). New York: Academic Press.

Duranti, A., & Goodwin, C. (1992). *Rethinking context: Language as interactive phenomenon.* Cambridge: Cambridge University Press.

Eckenrode, J., & Wethington, E. (1990). The process and outcome of mobilizing support. In S. Duck with R. Cohen-Silver (Eds.), *Personal relationships and social support* (pp. 83–103). London: Sage.

Emmons, R. A., & Colby, P. M. (1995). Emotional conflict and well-being: Relation to perceived availability, daily utilization, and observer reports of social support. *Journal of Personality and Social Psychology, 68*, 947–959.

Erickson, R. J. (1993). Reconceptualizing family work: The effect of emotion work on perceptions of marital quality. *Journal of Marriage and the Family, 55*, 888–900.

Fenlason, K. J., & Beehr, T. A. (1994). Social support and occupational stress: Effects of talking to others. *Journal of Organizational Behavior, 15*, 157–175.

Fiore, J., Becker, J., & Coppel, B. (1983). Social network interactions: A buffer or a stress. *American Journal of Community Psychology, 11*, 432–440.

Fiore, M. C., Bailey, W. C., Cohen, S. J., Dorfman, S. F., Fox, B. J., Goldstein, M. J., et al. (2000). A clinical practice guideline for treating tobacco use and dependence: A US public health service report. *Journal of the American Medical Association, 283,* 3244–3254.

Fisher, J. D., Goff, B. A., Nadler, A., & Chinsky, J. M. (1988). Social psychological influences on help seeking and support from peers. In B. H. Gottlieb (Ed.), *Marshaling social support* (pp. 267–304). Newbury Park, CA: Sage.

Fitch, K. (1998). *Speaking relationally: Culture, communication, and interpersonal connection.* New York: Guilford.

Folkman, S. (1984). Personal control and stress and coping processes: A theoretical analysis. *Journal of Personality and Social Psychology, 46,* 839–852.

Folkman, S., & Lazarus, R. S. (1985). If it changes it must be a process: Study of emotion and coping during three stages of a college examination. *Journal of Personality and Social Psychology, 48,* 150–170.

Ford, E. S., Ahluwalia, I. B., & Galuska, D. A. (2000). Social relationships and cardiovascular disease risk factors: Findings from the third national health and nutrition examination survey. *Preventive Medicine, 30,* 83–92.

Ford, L. A., & Ellis, B. H. (1998). A preliminary analysis of memorable support and nonsupport messages received by nurses in acute care settings. *Health Communication, 10,* 37–63.

Forgas, J. P. (1979). *Social episodes: The study of interaction routines.* New York: Academic Press.

Frazier, P. A., Tix, A. P., & Barnett, C. L. (2003). The relational context of social support: Relationship satisfaction moderates the relations between enacted support and distress. *Personality and Social Psychology Bulletin, 29,* 1133–1146.

Garbarino, J., & Kostelny, K. (1997). Coping with the consequences of community violence. In A. P. Goldstein & J. C. Conoley (Eds.), *School violence intervention: A practical handbook* (pp. 366–387). New York: Guilford Press.

Gignac, M. A. M., & Gottlieb, B. H. (1996). Caregivers' appraisals of efficacy in coping with dementia. *Psychology and Aging, 11,* 214–225.

Glidewell, J. C., Tucker, S., Todt, M., & Cox, S. (1983). Professional support systems: The teaching profession. In A. Nadler, J. D. Fisher, & B. M. DePaulo (Eds.), *New directions in helping: Vol. 3. Applied perspectives on help-seeking and receiving* (pp. 189–212). New York: Academic Press.

Goffman, E. (1967). *Interaction ritual.* Garden City, NY: Anchor Books.

Goldsmith, D. (1988). *To talk or not to talk: The flow of information between romantic dyads and members of their communication networks.* Unpublished master's thesis. University of Washington, Seattle, WA.

Goldsmith, D. (1992). Managing conflicting goals in supportive interaction: An integrative theoretical framework. *Communication Research, 19,* 264–286.

Goldsmith, D. J. (1993, November). *Considering culture in interpersonal communication theory.* Paper presented at the meeting of the Speech Communication Association, Miami, FL.

Goldsmith, D. J. (1994a, July). *Messages that define situations: An alternative to matching models of supportive communication.* Paper presented at the meeting of the International Communication Association, Sydney, Australia.

Goldsmith, D. J. (1994b). The role of face work in supportive communication. In B. R. Burleson, T. L. Albrecht, & I. G. Sarason (Eds.), *The communication of support: Messages, interactions, relationships, and community* (pp. 29–49). Newbury Park, CA: Sage.

Goldsmith, D. J. (1995). Commentary on Barbee & Cunningham: The communicative microdynamics of support. In B. R. Burleson (Ed.), *Communication yearbook 18* (pp. 414–433). Newbury Park, CA: Sage.

Goldsmith, D. J. (1999). Content-based resources for giving face-sensitive advice in troubles talk episodes. *Research on Language and Social Interaction, 32*, 303–336.

Goldsmith, D. J. (2000). Soliciting advice: The role of sequential placement in mitigating face threat. *Communication Monographs, 67*, 1–19.

Goldsmith, D. J. (2001). A normative approach to the study of uncertainty and communication. *Journal of Communication, 51*, 514–533.

Goldsmith, D. J. (in press). Politeness theory. In B. Whaley & W. Samter (Eds.), *Explaining communication: Contemporary theories and exemplars*. Mahwah, NJ: Erlbaum.

Goldsmith, D. J., & Baxter, L. A. (1996). Constituting relationships in talk: A taxonomy of speech events in social and personal relationships. *Human Communication Research, 23*, 87–114.

Goldsmith, D. J., & Dun, S. (1997). Sex differences in the provision of support. *Journal of Social and Personal Relationships, 14*, 317–337.

Goldsmith, D. J., & Fitch, K. (1997). The normative context of advice as social support. *Human Communication Research, 23*, 454–476.

Goldsmith, D. J., & Fulfs, P. A. (1999). "You just don't have the evidence": An analysis of claims and evidence in Deborah Tannen's *You Just Don't Understand*. In M. E. Roloff (Ed.), *Communication yearbook 22* (pp. 1–49). Thousand Oaks, CA: Sage.

Goldsmith, D. J., & Leslie, K. B. (2001, November). *Negotiating identity and relationship during recovery from a coronary incident*. Paper presented at the meeting of the National Communication Association, Atlanta, GA.

Goldsmith, D. J., & MacGeorge, E. L. (2000). The impact of politeness and relationship on perceived quality of advice about a problem. *Human Communication Research, 26*, 234–263.

Goldsmith, D. J., & McDermott, V. M. (1997, November). *Helpful, supportive, and sensitive: Interpreting outcomes of social support in personal relationships*. Paper presented at the meeting of the National Communication Association, Chicago, IL.

Goldsmith, D. J., & McDermott, V. M. (1998, November). *Identifying "troubles talk" in conversations of close relational partners*. Paper presented at the meeting of the National Communication Association, New York, NY.

Goldsmith, D. J., & McDermott, V. M. (2000, November). *The discursive negotiation of social support in troubles talk conversations*. Paper presented at the meeting of the National Communication Association, Seattle, WA.

Goldsmith, D. J., McDermott, V. M., & Alexander, S. C. (2000). Helpful, supportive, and sensitive: Measuring the evaluation of enacted social support in personal relationships. *Journal of Social and Personal Relationships, 17*, 369–391.

Gore, S., & Aseltine, R. H. (1995). Protective processes in adolescence: Matching stressors with social resources. *American Journal of Community Psychology, 23,* 301–327.

Gottlieb, B. H. (1974). Re-examining the preventive potential of mental health consultation. *Canada's Mental Health, 22,* 4–6.

Gottlieb, B. H. (1978). The development and application of a classification scheme of informal helping behaviors. *Canadian Journal of Behavioral Science, 10,* 105–115.

Gottlieb, B. H. (1985a). Social support and community mental health. In S. Cohen & L. S. Syme (Eds.), *Social support and health* (pp. 303–326). New York: Academic Press.

Gottlieb, B. H. (1985b). Social support and the study of personal relationships. *Journal of Social and Personal Relationships, 2,* 351–375.

Gottlieb, B. (1985c). Theory into practice: Issues that surface in planning interventions which mobilize support. In I. G. Sarason & B. R. Sarason (Eds.), *Social support: Theory, research, and applications* (pp. 417–437). Dordrecht, The Netherlands: Martinus Nijhoff.

Gottlieb, B. H. (1992). Quandaries in translating support concepts to intervention. In H. O. F. Veiel & U. Baumann (Eds.), *The meaning and measurement of social support* (pp. 293–309). New York: Hemisphere.

Gottlieb, B. H. (1996). Theories and practices of mobilizing support in stressful circumstances. In G. L. Cooper (Ed.), *Handbook of stress, medicine, and health* (pp. 339–356). Boca Raton, FL: CRC Press.

Gottlieb, B. H., & Gignac, M. A. M. (1996). Content and domain specificity of coping among family caregivers of persons with dementia. *Journal of Aging Studies, 10,* 137–155.

Gottlieb, B. H., & Wagner, F. (1991). Stress and support processes in close relationships. In J. Eckenrode (Ed.), *The social context of coping* (pp. 165–188). New York: Plenum.

Grant, D. A. (1990). *Person–environment fit and stressor-support specificity models of the stress-buffering hypothesis.* Unpublished dissertation, York University, North York, Ontario.

Greenberg, M. S., & Shapiro, S. P. (1971). Indebtedness: An adverse aspect of asking for and receiving help. *Sociometry, 34,* 290–301.

Greenglass, E., Fiksenbaum, L., & Burke, R. J. (1996). Components of social support, buffering effects and burnout: Implications for psychological functioning. *Anxiety, Stress, & Coping: An International Journal, 9,* 185–197.

Gross, A., Wallston, B. S., & Piliavin, I. M. (1979). Reactance, attribution, equity, and the help recipient. *Journal of Applied Social Psychology, 9,* 297–313.

Gurowka, K. M., & Lightman, E. S. (1995). Supportive and unsupportive interactions as perceived by cancer patients. *Social Work in Health Care, 21,* 71–88.

Gurung, R. A. R., Sarason, B. R., & Sarason, I. G. (1997). Personal characteristics, relationship quality, and social support perceptions and behavior in young adult romantic relationships. *Personal Relationships, 4,* 319–339.

Harre, R., & Secord, P. F. (1972). *The explanation of social behavior.* Oxford, UK: Basil Blackwell.

Harris, T. O. (1992). Some reflections on the process of social support and nature of unsupportive behaviors. In H. O. F. Veiel & U. Baumann (Eds.), *The meaning and measurement of social support* (pp. 171–190). New York: Hemisphere.

Hatfield, E., Utne, M. K., & Traupmann, J. (1979). Equity theory and intimate relationships. In R. L. Burgess & T. L. Huston (Eds.), *Social exchange in developing relationships* (pp. 99–133). New York: Academic Press.

Hays, R. B., Magee, R. H., & Chauncey, S. (1994). Identifying helpful and unhelpful behaviours of loved ones: The PWA's perspective. *AIDS Care, 6*, 379–392.

Helgeson, V. S. (1993). Two important distinctions in social support: Kind of support and perceived versus received. *Journal of Applied Social Psychology, 23*, 825–845.

Heller, K., & Rook, K. S. (1997). Distinguishing the theoretical functions of social ties: Implications for support interventions. In S. Duck (Ed.), *Handbook of personal relationships* (2nd ed., pp. 649–670). New York: Wiley.

Heller, K., & Rook, K. S. (2001). Distinguishing the theoretical functions of social ties: Implications for support interventions. In B. R. Sarason & S. Duck (Eds.), *Personal relationships: Implications for clinical and community psychology* (pp. 119–139). Chichester, UK: Wiley.

Heller, K., & Swindle, R. W. (1983). Social networks, perceived social support and coping with stress. In R. D. Felner, L. A. Jason, J. Moritsugu, & S. S. Farber (Eds.), *Preventive psychology: Theory, research, and practice in community intervention* (pp. 87–103). New York: Pergamon.

Heller, K., Swindle, R. W., & Dusenbury, L. (1986). Component social support processes: Comments and integration. *Journal of Consulting and Clinical Psychology, 54*, 466–470.

Henderson, M., & Argyle, M. (1985). Source and nature of social support given to women at divorce/separation. *British Journal of Social Work, 15*, 57–65.

Hobfoll, S. E. (1989). Conservation of resources: A new attempt at conceptualizing stress. *American Psychologist, 44*, 513–524.

Hobfoll, S. E., Nadler, A., & Leiberman, J. (1986). Satisfaction with social support during crisis: Intimacy and self-esteem as critical determinants. *Journal of Personality and Social Psychology, 51*, 296–304.

Hobfoll, S. E., & Stokes, J. P. (1988). The process and mechanics of social support. In S. W. Duck (Ed.), *Handbook of personal relationships* (pp. 497–517). London: Wiley.

Holahan, C. J., Moos, R. H., & Bonin, L. (1997). Social support, coping, and psychological adjustment: A resources model. In G. R. Pierce, B. Lakey, I. G. Sarason, & B. R. Sarason (Eds.), *Sourcebook of social support and personality* (pp. 169–186). New York: Plenum.

Holahan, C. J., Moos, R. H., Holahan, C. K., & Brennan, P. L. (1997). Social context, coping strategies and depressive symptoms: An expanded model with cardiac patients. *Journal of Personality and Social Psychology, 72*, 918–928.

Horowitz, L. M., Krasnoperova, E. N., Tatar, D. G., Hansen, M. B., Person, E. A., Galvin, K. L., et al. (2001). The way to console may depend on the goal: Experimental studies of social support. *Journal of Experimental Social Psychology, 37*, 49–61.

Hosley, C. A. (1999). *Social support in parent-adolescent relationships: Variation in support provision and the impact of support on adolescent psychological health.* Unpublished dissertation, The Ohio State University, Columbus, OH.

House, J. S. (1981). *Work stress and social support*. Reading, MA: Addison-Wesley.

House, J. S., & Kahn, R. L. (1985). Measures and concepts of social support. In S. Cohen & S. L. Syme (Eds.), *Social support and health* (pp. 83–108). Orlando, FL: Academic Press.

House, J. S., Landis, K. R., & Umberson, D. (1988). Social relationships and health. *Science, 241*, 540–544.

House, J. S., Umberson, D., & Landis, K. R. (1988). Structures and processes of social support. *Annual Review of Sociology, 14*, 293–318.

Hummert, M. L., & Ryan, E. B. (2001). Patronizing. In W. P. Robinson & H. Giles (Eds.), *The new handbook of language and social psychology* (pp. 253–269). London: Wiley.

Husaini, B. A., Neff, J. A., Newbrough, J. R., & Moore, M. (1982). The stress-buffering role of social support and personal competence among the rural married. *Journal of Community Psychology, 10*, 409–426.

Huston, T. L., McHale, S. M., & Crouter, A. C. (1986). When the honeymoon's over: Changes in the marriage relationship over the first year. In R. Gilmour & S. Duck (Eds.), *The emerging field of personal relationships* (pp. 109–131). Hillsdale, NJ: Erlbaum.

Hymes, D. (1972). Models of the interaction of language and social life. In J. Gumperz & D. Hymes (Eds.), *Directions in socio-linguistics: The ethnography of communication* (pp. 35–71). New York: Holt, Rinehart, & Winston.

Ingram, K. M., Betz, N. E., Mindes, E. J., Schmitt, M. M., & Smith, N. G. (2001). Unsupportive responses from others concerning a stressful life event: Development of the unsupportive social interactions inventory. *Journal of Social and Clinical Psychology, 20*, 173–207.

Jacobson, D. E. (1986). Types and timing of social support. *Journal of Health and Social Behavior, 27*, 250–264.

Jefferson, G. (1980). On "trouble-premonitory" response to inquiry. *Sociological Inquiry, 50*, 153–185.

Jefferson, G. (1984a). On stepwise transition from talk about a trouble to inappropriately next-positioned matters. In J. M. Atkinson & J. Heritage (Eds.), *Structures of social action: Studies in conversation analysis* (pp. 191–222). Cambridge University Press.

Jefferson, G. (1984b). On the organization of laughter in talk about troubles. In J. M. Atkinson & J. Heritage (Eds.), *Structures of social action: Studies in conversation analysis* (pp. 346–367). Cambridge University Press.

Jefferson, G. (1988). On the sequential organization of troubles talk in ordinary conversation. *Social Problems, 35*, 418–441.

Jefferson, G., & Lee, J. R. E. (1992). The rejection of advice: Managing the problematic convergence of a "troubles telling" and a "service encounter." In P. Drew & J. Heritage (Eds.), *Talk at work: Interaction in institutional settings* (pp. 521–548). Cambridge University Press.

Jones, S. M., & Burleson, B. R. (1997, May). *The impact of situational variables on the perception of comforting messages*. Paper presented at the annual meeting of the International Communication Association, Montreal, Quebec.

Jung, J. (1989). Social support rejection and reappraisal by providers and recipients. *Journal of Applied Social Psychology, 19*, 159–173.

Kaniasty, K., & Norris, F. H. (1992). Social support and victims of crime: Matching event, support, and outcome. *American Journal of Community Psychology, 20*, 211–241.

Katriel, T. (1991). *Communal webs: Communication and culture in contemporary Israel.* Albany: State University of New York Press.

Kessler, R. C., & McLeod, J. D. (1985). Social support and mental health in community samples. In S. Cohen & S. L. Syme (Eds.), *Social support and health* (pp. 219–240). New York: Academic Press.

Kitson, G. C., & Holmes, W. M. (1992). *Portrait of divorce: Adjustment to marital breakdown.* New York: Guilford Press.

Kliewer, W., Lepore, S. J., Oskin, D., & Johnson, P. D. (1998). The role of social and cognitive processes in children's adjustment to community violence. *Journal of Consulting and Clinical Psychology, 66*, 199–209.

Knapp, M. L., Stohl, C., & Reardon, K. (1981). "Memorable" messages. *Journal of Communication, 31*, 27–41.

Krause, N. (1986). Social support, stress, and well-being among older adults. *Journal of Gerontology, 41*, 512–519.

Krause, N. (1987). Chronic financial strain, social support, and depressive symptoms among older adults. *Psychology and Aging, 2*, 185–192.

LaGreca, A. M., & Bearman, K. J. (2002). The diabetes social support questionnaire-family version: Evaluating adolescents' diabetes specific support from family members. *Journal of Pediatric Psychology, 27*, 665–676.

Laireiter, A. R., Baumann, U., Perkonigg, A., & Himmelbauer, S. (1997). Social support resources in interpersonal relationships (social networks) during stressful life conditions: Results from two pilot studies. *Revue Europeenne de Psychologie Appliquee, 47*, 123–128.

Lakey, B., Adams, K., Neely, L., Rhodes, G., Lutz, C. J., & Sielky, K. (2002). Perceived support and low emotional distress: The role of enacted support, dyad similarity, and provider personality. *Personality and Social Psychology Bulletin, 28*, 1546–1555.

Lakey, B., & Cassady, P. (1990). Cognitive processes in perceived social support. *Journal of Personality and Social Psychology, 59*, 337–343.

Lakey, B., & Drew, J. B. (1997). A social-cognitive perspective on social support. In G. R. Pierce, B. Lakey, I. G. Sarason, & B. R. Sarason (Eds.), *Sourcebook of social support and personality* (pp. 107–140). New York: Plenum.

Lakey, B., Drew, J. B., & Sirl, K. (1999). Clinical depression and perceptions of supportive others: A generalizability analysis. *Cognitive Therapy and Research, 23*, 511–533.

Lakey, B., McCabe, K., Fisicaro, S. A., & Drew, J. B. (1996). Environmental and personal determinants of support perceptions: Three generalizability studies. *Journal of Personality and Social Psychology, 70*, 1270–1280.

Lakey, B., Moineau, S., & Drew, J. B. (1992). Perceived social support and individual differences in the interpretation and recall of supportive behaviors. *Journal of Social and Clinical Psychology, 11*, 336–348.

Lakey, B., Ross, L. T., Butler, C., & Bentley, K. (1996). Making social support judgments: The role of similarity and conscientiousness. *Journal of Social and Clinical Psychology, 15*, 283–304.

Lam, J. A., & Rosenheck, R. A. (2000). Correlates of improvement in quality of life among homeless persons with serious mental illness. *Psychiatric Services, 51,* 116–118.

Lanza, A. F., Cameron, A. E., & Revenson, T. A. (1995). Perceptions of helpful and unhelpful support among married individuals with rheumatic diseases. *Psychology and Health, 10,* 449–462.

LaRocco, J. R., House, J. S., & French, J. R. P. (1980). Social support, occupational stress, and health. *Journal of Health and Social Behavior, 21,* 202–218.

Lazarus, R. S. (1991). *Emotion and adaptation.* New York: Oxford University Press.

Lazarus, R. S., & Folkman, S. (1984). *Stress, appraisal, and coping.* New York: Springer-Verlag.

Leatham, G., & Duck, S. (1990). Conversations with friends and the dynamics of social support. In S. Duck with R. Cohen-Silver (Eds.), *Personal relationships and social support* (pp. 1–29). London: Sage.

Lee, F. (1997). When the going gets tough, do the tough ask for help? Help seeking and power motivation in organizations. *Organizational Behavior and Human Decision Processes, 72,* 336–363.

Lehman, D. R., Ellard, J. H., & Wortman, C. B. (1986). Social support for the bereaved: Recipients' and providers' perspectives on what is helpful. *Journal of Consulting and Clinical Psychology, 54,* 438–446.

Lehman, D. R., & Hemphill, K. J. (1990). Recipients' perceptions of support attempts and attributions for support attempts that fail. *Journal of Social and Personal Relationships, 7,* 563–574.

Leppin, A., & Schwarzer, R. (1990). Social support and physical health: An updated meta-analysis. In L. R. Schmidt, P. Schwenkmezger, J. Weinman, & S. Maes (Eds.), *Theoretical and applied aspects of health psychology* (pp. 185–202). London: Harwood.

Lesser, E. K., & Comet, J. J. (1987). Help and hindrance: Parents of divorcing children. *Journal of Marital and Family Therapy, 13,* 197–202.

Levinson, S. C. (1995). Interactional biases in human thinking. In E. N. Goody (Ed.), *Social intelligence and interaction* (pp. 221–260). Cambridge: Cambridge University Press.

Liang, J., Krause, N. M., & Bennett, J. M. (2001). Social exchange and well-being: Is giving better than receiving? *Psychology and Aging, 16,* 511–523.

Lieberman, M. A. (1986). Social supports – the consequences of psychologizing: A commentary. *Journal of Consulting and Clinical Psychology, 54,* 461–465.

Lim, V. K. G. (1996). Job insecurity and its outcomes: Moderating effects of work-based and nonwork-based social support. *Human Relations, 49,* 171–194.

Lin, N., Woelfel, M. W., & Light, S. C. (1985). The buffering effect of social support subsequent to an important life event. *Journal of Health and Social Behavior, 26,* 247–263.

Littrell, P. C., Billingsley, B. S., & Cross, L. H. (1994). The effects of principal support on special and general educators' stress, job satisfaction, school commitment, health, and intent to stay in teaching. *Rase: Remedial & Special Education, 15,* 297–310.

Luckmann, T. (1995). Interaction planning and intersubjective adjustment of perspectives by communicative genres. In E. N. Goody (Ed.), *Social intelligence and interaction* (pp. 175–186). Cambridge: Cambridge University Press.

Lydon, J. E., & Zanna, M. P. (1992). The cost of social support following negative life events: Can adversity increase commitment to caring in close relationships? In L. Montada, S. H. Filipp, & M. J. Lerner (Eds.), *Life crises and experiences of loss in adulthood* (pp. 461–475). Hillsdale, NJ: Erlbaum.

Lyons, R. G., Mickelson, K. D., Sullivan, M. J., & Coyne, J. C. (1998). Coping as a communal process. *Journal of Social and Personal Relationships, 15,* 579–605.

Ma, X., & Kishor, N. (1997). Attitude toward self, social factors, and achievement in mathematics: A meta-analytic review. *Educational Psychology Review, 9,* 89–120.

MacGeorge, E. L., Lichtman, R. M., & Pressey, L. C. (2002). The evaluation of advice in supportive interactions. *Human Communication Research, 28,* 451–463.

Malkinson, R. (1987). Helping and being helped: The support paradox. *Death Studies, 11,* 205–219.

Mallinckrodt, B. (2000). Attachment, social competencies, social support, and interpersonal process in psychotherapy. *Psychotherapy Research, 10,* 239–266.

Mankowski, E. S., & Wyer, R. S. (1996). Cognitive processes in perceptions of social support. *Personality and Social Psychology Bulletin, 22,* 894–905.

Manne, S., & Schnoll, R. (2001). Measuring supportive and unsupportive responses during cancer treatment: A factor analytic assessment of the partner responses to cancer inventory. *Journal of Behavioral Medicine, 24,* 297–321.

Manne, S. L., & Zautra, A. J. (1989). Spouse criticism and support: Their association with coping and psychological adjustment among women with rheumatoid arthritis. *Journal of Personality and Social Psychology, 56,* 608–617.

Martin, R., Davis, G. M., Baron, R. S., Suls, J., & Blanchard, E. B. (1994). Specificity in social support: Perceptions of helpful and unhelpful provider behaviors among irritable bowel syndrome, headache, and cancer patients. *Health Psychology, 13,* 432–439.

McCaskill, J. W., & Lakey, B. (2000). Perceived support, social undermining, and emotion: Idiosyncratic and shared perspectives of adolescents and their families. *Personality and Social Psychology Bulletin, 26,* 820–832.

McLeroy, K. R., Devellis, R., Devellis, B., Kaplan, B., & Toole, J. (1984). Social support and physical recovery in a stroke population. *Journal of Social and Personal Relationships, 1,* 395–413.

Metts, S., Backhaus, S., & Kazoleas, D. (1995, February). *Social support as problematic communication.* Paper presented at the meeting of the Western States Communication Association, Portland, OR.

Meyerowitz, B. E., Levin, K., & Harvey, J. H. (1997). On the nature of cancer patients' social interactions. *Journal of Personal and Interpersonal Loss, 2,* 49–69.

Mikulincer, M., & Florian, V. (1997). Are emotional and instrumental supportive interactions beneficial in times of stress? The impact of attachment style. *Anxiety, Stress, and Coping, 10,* 109–127.

Miller, P. J., & Goodnow, J. J. (1995). Cultural practices: Toward an integration of culture and development. In J. J. Goodnow, P. J. Miller, & F. Kessel (Eds.), *Cultural practices as contexts for development* (pp. 5–16). San Francisco, CA: Jossey-Bass.

Moncher, F. J. (1995). Social isolation and child-abuse risk. *Families in Society, 76,* 421–433.

Neuling, S. J., & Winefield, H. R. (1988). Social support and recovery after surgery for breast cancer: Frequency and correlates of supportive behaviors by family, friends, and surgeon. *Social Science and Medicine, 27*, 385–392.

Newsom, J. T. (1999). Another side to caregiving: Negative reactions to being helped. *Current Directions in Psychological Science, 8*, 183–187.

Notarius, C. I., & Herrick, L. R. (1988). Listener response strategies to a distressed other. *Journal of Social and Personal Relationships, 5*, 97–108.

O'Brien, T. B., & DeLongis, A. (1997). Coping with chronic stress: An interpersonal perspective. In B. H. Gottlieb (Ed.), *Coping with chronic stress* (pp. 161–190). New York: Plenum.

O'Keefe, B. J. (1988). The logic of message design: Individual differences in reasoning about communication. *Communication Monographs, 55*, 80–103.

O'Keefe, B. J. (1990). The logic of regulative communication: Understanding the rationality of message designs. In J. P. Dillard (Ed.), *Seeking compliance: The production of interpersonal influence messages* (pp. 87–104). Scottsdale, AZ: Gorsuch Scarisbrick.

O'Keefe, B. J. (1992). Developing and testing rational models of message design. *Human Communication Research, 18*, 637–649.

O'Keefe, B. J., & Delia, J. G. (1988). Communicative tasks and communicative practices: The development of audience-centered message production. In B. A. Rafoth & D. L. Rubin (Eds.), *The social construction of written communication* (pp. 70–98). Norwood, NJ: Ablex.

O'Keefe, B. J., & McCornack, S. A. (1987). Message design logic and message goal structure: Effects on perceptions of message quality in regulative communication situations. *Human Communication Research, 14*, 68–92.

O'Keefe, B. J., & Shepherd, G. J. (1987). The pursuit of multiple objectives in face-to-face persuasive interactions: Effects of construct differentiation on message organization. *Communication Monographs, 54*, 396–419.

O'Keefe, D. J. (1987, November). *Message description.* Paper presented at the annual meeting of the Speech Communication Association, Boston, MA.

O'Keefe, D. J. (1994). From strategy-based to feature-based analyses of compliance-gaining message classification and production. *Communication Theory, 4*, 61–69.

Okun, M. A., Sandler, I. N., & Baumann, D. J. (1988). Buffer and booster effects as event-support transactions. *American Journal of Community Psychology, 16*, 435–449.

O'Reilly, P., & Thomas, H. E. (1989). Role of support networks in maintenance of improved cardiovascular health status. *Social Science and Medicine, 28*, 249–260.

Pakenham, K. I. (1998). Specification of social support behaviors and network dimensions along the HIV continuum for gay men. *Patient Education and Counseling, 34*, 147–157.

Pasch, L. A., & Bradbury, T. N. (1998). Social support, conflict, and the development of marital dysfunction. *Journal of Consulting and Clinical Psychology, 66*, 219–230.

Pasch, L. A., Bradbury, T. N., & Sullivan, K. T. (1997). Social support in marriage: An analysis of intraindividual and interpersonal components. In G. R. Pierce, B. Lakey, I. G. Sarason, & B. R. Sarason (Eds.), *Sourcebook of social support and personality* (pp. 229–256). New York: Plenum.

Patterson, J. M., Garwick, A. W., Bennett, F. C., & Blum, R. W. (1997). Social support in families of children with chronic conditions: Supportive and nonsupportive behaviors. *Developmental and Behavioral Pediatrics, 18,* 13–21.

Pearlin, L. I. (1985). Social structure and processes of social support. In S. Cohen & S. L. Syme (Eds.), *Social support and health* (pp. 43–60). New York: Academic Press.

Pearlin, L. I., & McCall, M. E. (1990). Occupational stress and marital support: A description of microprocesses. In J. Eckenrode & S. Gore (Eds.), *Stress between work and family* (pp. 39–60). New York: Plenum.

Peirce, R. S., Frone, M. R., Russell, M., & Cooper, M. L. (1996). Financial stress, social support, and alcohol involvement: A longitudinal test of the buffering hypothesis in a general population survey. *Health Psychology, 15,* 38–47.

Pennix, B. W. J. H., Van Tilburg, T., Deeg, D. J. H., Kriegsman, D. M. W., Boeke, J. P., & Van Eijk, J. T. M. (1997). Direct and buffer effects of social support and personal coping resources in individuals with arthritis. *Social Science and Medicine, 44,* 393–402.

Petronio, S., Reeder, H. M., Hecht, M. L., & Ros-Mendoza, T. M. (1996). Disclosure of sexual abuse by children and adolescents. *Journal of Applied Communication Research, 24,* 181–199.

Peyrot, M., McMurry, J. F., & Hedges, R. (1988). Marital adjustment to adult diabetes: Interpersonal congruence and spouse satisfaction. *Journal of Marriage and the Family, 50,* 363–376.

Philipsen, G. (1992). *Speaking culturally: Explorations in social communication.* Albany: State University Press of New York.

Picard, M., Lee, C. M., & Hunsley, J. (1997). Social supports received and desired: The experiences of recently divorced parents with their parents and parents-in-law. *Journal of Divorce and Remarriage, 27,* 57–69.

Pierce, G. R., Lakey, B., Sarason, I. G., Sarason, B. R., & Joseph, H. J. (1997). Personality and social support processes: A conceptual overview. In G. R. Pierce, B. Lakey, I. G. Sarason, & B. R. Sarason (Eds.), *Sourcebook of social support and personality* (pp. 3–18). New York: Plenum.

Pierce, G. R., Sarason, B. R., & Sarason, I. G. (1992). General and specific support expectations and stress as predictors of perceived supportiveness: An experimental study. *Journal of Personality and Social Psychology, 63,* 297–307.

Pierce, G. R., Sarason, I. G., & Sarason, B. R. (1996). Coping and social support. In M. Zeidner & N. S. Endler (Eds.), *Handbook of coping: Theory, research, applications* (pp. 434–451). New York: Wiley.

Pistrang, N., & Barker, C. (1998). Partners and fellow patients: Two sources of emotional support for women with breast cancer. *American Journal of Community Psychology, 26,* 439–456.

Pistrang, N., Barker, C., & Rutter, C. (1997). Social support as conversation: Analysing breast cancer patients' interactions with their partners. *Social Science and Medicine, 45,* 773–782.

Pistrang, N., Clare, L., & Barker, C. (1999). The helping process in couples during recovery from heart attack: A single case study. *British Journal of Medical Psychology, 72,* 227–237.

Pistrang, N., Picciotto, A., & Barker, C. (2001). The communication of empathy in couples during the transition to parenthood. *Journal of Community Psychology, 29,* 615–636.

Pistrang, N., Solomons, W., & Barker, C. (1999). Peer support for women with breast cancer: The role of empathy and self-disclosure. *Journal of Community and Applied Social Psychology, 9,* 217–229.

Pomerantz, A. (1984). Agreeing and disagreeing with assessments: Some features of preferred/dispreferred turn shapes. In J. M. Atkinson & J. Heritage (Eds.), *Structures of social action: Studies in conversation analysis* (pp. 57–101). Cambridge University Press.

Power, M. J. (1988). Stress-buffering effects of social support: A longitudinal study. *Motivation and Emotion, 12,* 197–204.

Ptacek, J. T., Pierce, G. R., Ptacek, J. J., & Nogel, C. (1999). Stress and coping processes in men with prostate cancer: The divergent views of husbands and wives. *Journal of Social and Clinical Psychology, 18,* 299–324.

Range, L. M., Walston, A. S., & Pollard, P. M. (1992). Helpful and unhelpful comments after suicide, homicide, accident, or natural death. *Omega, 25,* 25–31.

Rankin, S. H. (1992). Psychosocial adjustments of coronary artery disease patients and their spouses: Nursing implications. *Nursing Clinics of North America, 27,* 271–284.

Ratcliff, K. S., & Bogdan, J. (1988). Unemployed women: When "social support" is not supportive. *Social Problems, 35,* 54–63.

Rawlins, W. K. (1983). Openness as problematic in ongoing friendships: Two conversational dilemmas. *Communication Monographs, 50,* 1–13.

Ray, E. B. (1987). Supportive relationships and occupational stress in the workplace. In T. L. Albrecht & M. B. Adelman (Eds.), *Communicating social support* (pp. 172–191). Newbury Park, CA: Sage.

Reich, J. W., Zautra, A. J., & Manne, S. (1993). How perceived control and congruent spouse support affect rheumatoid arthritis patients. *Journal of Social and Clinical Psychology, 12,* 148–163.

Reis, H. T., & Collins, N. (2000). Measuring relationship properties and interactions relevant to social support. In S. Cohen, L. G. Underwood, & B. H. Gottlieb (Eds.), *Social support measurement and intervention: A guide for health and social scientists* (pp. 136–192). Oxford, UK: Oxford University Press.

Reisman, J. M., & Shorr, S. (1980). Developmental changes in friendship-related communication skills. *Journal of Clinical Child Psychology, 36,* 67–69.

Reisman, J. M., & Yamokoski, T. (1974). Psychotherapy and friendship: An analysis of the communications of friends. *Journal of Counseling Psychology, 21,* 269–273.

Revenson, T. A., & Majerovitz, D. (1990). Spouses' support provision to chronically ill patients. *Journal of Social and Personal Relationships, 7,* 575–586.

Robertson, E. B., Elder, G. H., Skinner, M. L., & Conger, R. D. (1991). The costs and benefits of social support in families. *Journal of Marriage and the Family, 53,* 403–416.

Rogers, C. R. (1957). The necessary and sufficient conditions of therapeutic personality change. *Journal of Consulting Psychology, 21,* 95–103.

Röhrle, B., & Sommer, G. (1994). Social support and social competencies: Some theoretical and empirical contributions to their relationship. In F. Nestmann &

K. Hurrelmann (Eds.), *Social networks and social support in childhood and adolescence* (pp. 111–129). Berlin: Walter de Gruyter.

Rook, K. S. (1990). Social relationships as a source of companionship: Implications for older adults' psychological well-being. In B. R. Sarason, I. G. Sarason, & G. R. Pierce (Eds.), *Social support: An interactive view* (pp. 219–250). New York: Wiley.

Rook, K., & Dooley, D. (1985). Applying social support research: Theoretical problems and future directions. *Journal of Social Issues, 41,* 5–28.

Rook, K. S., & Underwood, L. G. (2000). Social support measurement and interventions: Comments and future directions. In S. Cohen, L. G. Underwood, & B. H. Gottlieb (Eds.), *Social support measurement and intervention: A guide for health and social scientists* (pp. 311–334). Oxford, UK: Oxford University Press.

Rosen, S., Mickler, S. E., & Collins, J. E. (1987). Reactions of would be helpers whose offer of help is spurned. *Journal of Personality and Social Psychology, 53,* 288–297.

Rosenberg, M. R. (1985). *Social support: Mechanisms of action and stressor support specificity.* Unpublished dissertation, Southern Illinois University, Carbondale, IL.

Rosenfeld, L. B., Richman, J. M., & Bowen, G. L. (2000). Social support networks and school outcomes: The centrality of the teacher. *Child and Adolescent Social Work Journal, 17,* 205–226.

Sanders, R. E. (2003). Applying the social skills concept to discourse and conversation: The remediation of performance defects in talk-in-interaction. In J. O. Greene & B. R. Burleson (Eds.), *Handbook of communication and social interaction skills* (pp. 221–256). Mahwah, NJ: Erlbaum.

Sandler, I. N., & Barrera, M., Jr. (1984). Toward a multimethod approach to assessing the effects of social support. *American Journal of Community Psychology, 12,* 37–52.

Sandler, I. N., & Lakey, B. (1982). Locus of control as a stress moderator: The role of control perceptions and social support. *American Journal of Community Psychology, 10,* 65–80.

Sarason, B. R., Pierce, G. R., & Sarason, I. G. (1990). Social support: The sense of acceptance and the role of relationships. In B. R. Sarason, I. G. Sarason, & G. R. Pierce (Eds.), *Social support: An interactive view* (pp. 97–128). New York: Wiley.

Sarason, B. R., & Sarason, I. G. (1994). Assessment of social support. In S. A. Shumaker & S. M. Czajkowski (Eds.), *Social support and cardiovascular disease* (pp. 41–63). New York: Plenum.

Sarason, B. R., Sarason, I. G., & Gurung, R. A. R. (1997). Close personal relationships and health outcomes: A key to the role of social support. In S. Duck (Ed.), *Handbook of personal relationships* (2nd ed., pp. 547–573). New York: Wiley.

Savelkoul, M., Post, M. W. M., de Witte, L. P., & van den Borne, H. G. (2000). Social support, coping, and subjective well-being in patients with rheumatic diseases. *Patient Education and Counseling, 39,* 205–218.

Schaefer, C., Coyne, J. C., & Lazarus, R. S. (1981). The health related functions of social support. *Journal of Behavioral Medicine, 4,* 381–406.

Schieman, S., & Turner, H. A. (2001). "When feeling other people's pain hurts": The influence of psychosocial resources on the association between self-reported empathy and depressive symptoms. *Social Psychology Quarterly, 64,* 376–389.

Schreurs, K. M. G., & DeRidder, D. T. D. (1997). Integration of coping and social support perspectives: Implications for the study of adaptation to chronic diseases. *Clinical Psychology Review, 17*, 89–112.

Schwarzer, R., & Leppin, A. (1989). Social support and health: A meta-analysis. *Psychology and Health: An International Journal, 3*, 1–15.

Schwarzer, R., & Leppin, A. (1991). Social support and health: A theoretical and empirical overview. *Journal of Social and Personal Relationships, 8*, 99–127.

Searcy, E., & Eisenberg, N. (1992). Defensiveness in response to aid from a sibling. *Journal of Personality and Social Psychology, 62*, 422–433.

Seeman, T. E. (2000). Health promoting effects of friends and family on health outcomes in older adults. *American Journal of Health Promotion, 14*, 362–370.

Segrin, C., & Givertz, M. (2003). Methods of social skills training and development. In J. O. Greene & B. R. Burleson (Eds.), *Handbook of communication and social interaction skills* (pp. 135–176). Mahwah, NJ: Erlbaum.

Sher, T. G., & Baucom, D. H. (2001). Mending a broken heart: A couples approach to cardiac risk reduction. *Applied and Preventive Psychology, 10*, 125–133.

Shinn, M., Lehmann, S., & Wong, N. W. (1984). Social interaction and social support. *Journal of Social Issues, 40*, 55–76.

Shumaker, S. A., & Brownell, A. (1984). Toward a theory of social support: Closing conceptual gaps. *Journal of Social Issues, 40*, 11–36.

Smith, C. E., Fernengel, K., Holcroft, C., Gerald, K., & Marien, L. (1994). Meta-analysis of the associations between social support and health outcomes. *Annals of Behavioral Medicine, 16*, 352–362.

Smith, J., & Goodnow, J. J. (1999). Unasked-for support and unsolicited advice: Age and the quality of social experience. *Psychology and Aging, 14*, 108–121.

Snyder, C. R., & Higgins, R. L. (1988). Excuses: Their effective role in the negotiation of reality. *Psychological Bulletin, 104*, 23–35.

Sprecher, S., Metts, S., Burleson, B., Hatfield, E., & Thompson, A. (1995). Domains of expressive interaction in intimate relationships: Associations with satisfaction and commitment. *Family Relations, 44*, 203–210.

Stokes, J. P. (1983). Predicting satisfaction with social support from social network structure. *American Journal of Community Psychology, 11*, 141–152.

Swanson-Hyland, E. F. (1996). *The influence of spousal social support on psychological and physical health among persons with type II diabetes mellitus: A test of the optimal matching model of social support.* Unpublished dissertation, University of Iowa, Iowa City, IA.

Swindle, R., Heller, K., Pescosolido, B., & Kikuzawa, S. (2000). Responses to nervous breakdowns in America over a 40-year period. *American Psychologist, 55*, 740–749.

Tannen, D. (1990). *You just don't understand: Women and men in conversation.* New York: Ballantine Books.

Tannen, D. (1993). *Framing in discourse.* New York: Oxford University Press.

Taylor, S. E., & Armor, D. A. (1996). Positive illusions and coping with adversity. *Journal of Personality, 64*, 873–898.

Taylor, S. E., Falke, R. L., Mazel, R. M., & Hilsberg, B. L. (1988). Sources of satisfaction and dissatisfaction among members of cancer support groups. In B. H. Gottlieb (Ed.), *Marshaling social support* (pp. 187–208). Newbury Park, CA: Sage.

Taylor, S. E., Kemeny, M. E., Reed, G. M., Bower, J. E., & Gruenewald, T. L. (2000). Psychological resources, positive illusions, and health. *American Psychologist, 55,* 99–109.

Thoits, P. A. (1985). Social support and psychological well-being: Theoretical possibilities. In I. G. Sarason & B. R. Sarason (Eds.), *Social support: Theory, research, and application* (pp. 51–72). Dordrecht: Martinus Nijhoff.

Thoits, P. A. (1986). Social support as coping assistance. *Journal of Consulting and Clinical Psychology, 54,* 416–423.

Thoits, P. A. (1995). Stress, coping, and social support processes: Where are we? What next? *Journal of Health and Social Behavior, Extra Issue,* 53–79.

Thompson, K. E., & Range, L. M. (1992). Bereavement following suicide and other deaths: Why support attempts fail. *Omega, 26,* 61–70.

Tijhuis, M. A. R., Flap, H. D., Foets, M., & Groenewegen, P. P. (1995). Social support and stressful life events in two dimensions: Life events and illness as an event. *Social Science & Medicine, 40,* 1513–1526.

Timmerman, I. H. G., Emanuels-Zuurveen, E. S., & Emmelkamp, P. M. G. (2000). The Social Support Inventory (SSI): A brief scale to assess perceived adequacy of social support. *Clinical Psychology and Psychotherapy, 7,* 401–410.

Tracy, K. (1989). Conversational dilemmas and the naturalistic experiment. In B. Dervin, L. Grossberg, B. J. O'Keefe, & E. Wartella (Eds.), *Rethinking communication: Vol. 2. Paradigm exemplars* (pp. 411–423). Newbury Park, CA: Sage.

Tracy, K. (1990). The many faces of face work. In H. Giles & W. P. Robinson (Eds.), *Handbook of language and social psychology* (pp. 209–226). New York: Wiley.

Tracy, K. (1998). Analyzing context: Framing the discussion. *Research on Language and Social Interaction, 31,* 1–28.

Tripathi, R., Caplan, R., & Naidu, R. (1986). Accepting advice: A modifier of social support's effect on well-being. *Journal of Social and Personal Relationships, 3,* 213–228.

Tucker, M. B., & Johnson, O. (1989). Competence-promoting versus competence inhibiting social support for mentally retarded mothers. *Human Organization, 48,* 95–107.

Uchino, B. N., Cacioppo, J. T., Malarkey, W., Glaser, R., & Kiecolt-Glaser, J. K. (1995). Appraisal support predicts age-related differences in cardiovascular function in women. *Health Psychology, 14,* 556–562.

Uehara, E. S. (1995). Reciprocity reconsidered: Gouldner's 'moral norm of reciprocity' and social support. *Journal of Social and Personal Relationships, 12,* 483–502.

Ugolini, K. A. (1998). *The effects of social support type on psychosocial adjustment to low back pain: Testing the optimal matching model.* Unpublished dissertation, University of Iowa, Iowa City, IA.

Umberson, D. (1987). Family status and health behaviors: Social control as a dimension of social integration. *Journal of Health and Social Behavior, 28,* 306–319.

Vachon, M. L. S., & Stylianos, S. K. (1988). The role of social support in bereavement. *Journal of Social Issues, 44,* 175–190.

Vangelisti, A. L., Crumley, L. P., & Baker, J. L. (1999). Family portraits: Stories as standards for family relationships. *Journal of Social and Personal Relationships, 4,* 203–219.

Vaux, A., & Harrison, D. (1985). Social network characteristics associated with support satisfaction and perceived support. *American Journal of Community Psychology, 13,* 245–267.

Veiel, H. O. F. (1992). Some cautionary notes on buffer effects. In H. O. F. Veiel & U. Baumann (Eds.), *The meaning and measurement of social support* (pp. 273–289). New York: Hemisphere.

Veroff, J., Douvan, E., & Kulka, R. A. (1981). *The inner American: A self-portrait from 1957 to 1976.* New York: Basic Books, Inc.

Vinokur, A., Schul, Y., & Caplan, R. D. (1987). Determinants of perceived social support: Interpersonal transactions, personal outlook, and transient affective states. *Journal of Personality and Social Psychology, 53,* 1137–1145.

Viswesvaran, C., Sanchez, J. I., & Fisher, J. (1999). The role of social support in the process of work stress: A meta-analysis. *Journal of Vocational Behavior, 54,* 314–334.

Wade, C. K., Howell, F. M., & Wells, J. G. (1994). Turning to family, friends, or others: A model of social network usage during stressful events. *Sociological Spectrum, 14,* 385–407.

Wade, T. D., & Kendler, K. S. (2000). Absence of interactions between social support and stressful life events in the prediction of major depressive symptomatology in women. *Psychological Medicine, 30,* 965–974.

Wallsten, S. M., Tweed, D. L., Blazer, D. G., & George, L. K. (1999). Disability and depressive symptoms in the elderly: The effects of instrumental support and its subjective appraisal. *International Journal of Aging and Human Development, 48,* 145–159.

Walster, E. G., Walster, W., & Berscheid, E. (1978). *Equity: Theory and research.* Boston, MA: Allyn & Bacon.

Wan, C. K., Jaccard, J., & Ramey, S. L. (1996). The relationship between social support and life satisfaction as a function of family structure. *Journal of Marriage and the Family, 58,* 502–513.

Wellman, B., & Wortley, S. (1990). Different strokes from different folks: Community ties and social support. *American Journal of Sociology, 96,* 558–588.

Wenz-Gross, M., Siperstein, G. N., Untch, A. S., & Widaman, K. F. (1997). Stress, social support, and adjustment of adolescents in middle school. *Journal of Early Adolescence, 17,* 129–151.

Werner, T. A., & Monsour, M. (1997). Resocialization of the bereaved via interpersonal communication techniques. *Journal of Personal and Interpersonal Loss, 2,* 345–366.

Westman, M., & Vinokur, A. D. (1998). Unraveling the relationship of distress levels within couples: Common stressors, empathic reactions, or crossover via social interaction? *Human Relations, 51,* 137–156.

Wethington, E., & Kessler, R. C. (1986). Perceived support, received support, and adjustment to stressful life events. *Journal of Health and Social Behavior, 27,* 78–89.

Wheaton, B. (1985). Models for the stress-buffering functions of coping resources. *Journal of Health and Social Behavior, 26,* 352–364.

Wiesenfeld, A. R., & Weis, H. M. (1979). Hairdressers and helping: Influencing the behavior of informal caregivers. *Professional Psychology, 10,* 786–792.

Wilcox, B. L., & Vernberg, E. M. (1985). Conceptual and theoretical dilemmas facing social support research. In I. G. Sarason & B. R. Sarason (Eds.), *Social support:*

Theory, research, and applications (pp. 3–20). Dordrecht, The Netherlands: Martinus Nijhoff.

Wills, T. A. (1983). Social comparison in coping and help-seeking. In B. M. DePaulo, A. Nadler, & J. D. Fisher (Eds.), *New directions in helping: Vol. 2. Help-seeking* (pp. 109–141). New York: Academic Press.

Wills, T. A. (1990). Multiple networks and substance use. *Journal of Social and Clinical Psychology, 9*, 78–90.

Wills, T. A. (1992). The helping process in the context of personal relationships. In S. Spacapan & S. Oskamp (Eds.), *Helping and being helped: Naturalistic studies* (pp. 17–48). Newbury Park, CA: Sage.

Wills, T. A., & Shinar, O. (2000). Measuring perceived and received social support. In S. Cohen, L. G. Underwood, & B. H. Gottlieb (Eds.), *Social support measurement and intervention: A guide for health and social scientists* (pp. 86–135). Oxford, UK: Oxford University Press.

Wilson, S. R., Aleman, C. B., & Leatham, G. B. (1998). Identity implications of influence goals: A revised analysis of face-threatening acts and application to seeking compliance with same-sex friends. *Human Communication Research, 25*, 64–96.

Winemiller, D. R., Mitchell, M. E., Sutliff, J., & Cline, D. J. (1993). Measurement strategies in social support: A descriptive review of the literature. *Journal of Clinical Psychology, 49*, 638–648.

Wortman, C. B., & Conway, T. (1985). The role of social support in adaptation and recovery from physical illness. In S. Cohen & S. L. Syme (Eds.), *Social support and health* (pp. 281–302). New York: Academic Press.

Wortman, C. B., & Dunkel-Schetter, C. (1979). Interpersonal relationships and cancer: A theoretical analysis. *Journal of Social Issues, 35*, 120–155.

Yates, B. C. (1995). The relationships among social support and short- and long-term recovery outcomes in men with coronary heart disease. *Research on Nursing and Health, 18*, 193–203.

Ybema, J. F., Kuijer, R. G., Buunk, B. P., DeJong, G. M., & Sanderman, R. (2001). Depression and perceptions of inequity among couples facing cancer. *Personality and Social Psychology Bulletin, 27*, 3–13.

Young, C. E., Giles, D. E., & Plantz, M. C. (1982). Natural networks: Help-giving and help-seeking in two rural communities. *American Journal of Community Psychology, 10*, 457–469.

Zich, J., & Temoshok, L. (1987). Perceptions of social support in men with AIDS and ARC: Relationships with distress and hardiness. *Journal of Applied Social Psychology, 17*, 193–215.

Author Index

Ingersoll-Dayton, B., 12
Ingram, K. M., 19
Israel, B., 36

Jaccard, J., 80
Jackson, J. S., 12
Jacobson, D. E., 80
James, S. A., 12
Jefferson, G., 4, 5, 75, 120, 147
Johnson, O., 21
Johnson, P. D., 10
Jones, S. M., 159
Joseph, H. J., 18, 37
Jung, J., 22

Kahn, R. L., 12
Kaniasty, K., 83
Kaplan, B., 22
Kaplan, B. H., 12
Katriel, T., 42
Kazoleas, D., 5
Kemeny, M. E., 115
Kendler, K. S., 83
Kessler, R. C., 12, 15, 16–17, 36, 37, 117–118,
    144, 146
Kiecolt-Glaser, J. K., 5
Kikuzawa, S., 6
Kishor, N., 11
Kitson, G. C., 7, 49
Kliewer, W., 10
Knapp, M. L., 78
Kolody, B., 17
Kostelny, K., 10
Krasnoperova, E. N., 52, 55, 56
Krause, N., 22, 83
Kriegsman, D. M. W., 17–18
Krol, B., 33
Kuijer, R. G., 22
Kulka, R. A., 6
Kurtines, W. M., 10

LaGreca, A. M., 158
Laireiter, A. R., 52, 53
Lakey, B., 18–19, 34, 35, 36, 37, 38, 41
Lam, J. A., 10
Landers, J. E., 7
Landis, K. R., 12
Lanza, A. F., 21, 80
LaRocco, J. R., 80
Larsen, D., 7
Lazarus, R. S., 15, 80, 84
Leadbeater, B. J., 10

Leatham, G., 4, 59, 119, 135, 137
Lee, C. M., 53, 54
Lee, F., 21
Lee, J. R. E., 75
Lehman, D. R., 5, 8, 20, 21, 52, 53, 117
Lehmann, S., 80
Leiberman, J., 44
Lemle, R., 53
Lepore, S. J., 10
Leppin, A., 10, 12, 16, 18
Leslie, K. B., 133, 164
Lesser, E. K., 21
Levin, K., 20
Levinson, S. C., 40, 59–60, 70–71
Levy, M., 52
Liang, J., 22
Lichtman, R. M., 67, 68
Lieberman, M. A., 118
Light, S. C., 15, 17
Lightman, E. S., 20
Lim, V. K. G., 17
Lin, N., 15, 17
Littrell, P. C., 11
Luckmann, T., 40
Lutz, C. J., 18–19, 36, 38
Lydon, J. E., 7, 117
Lyons, R. G., 117, 122, 144, 153

Ma, X., 11
MacFarlane, R., 36
MacGeorge, E., 2, 24, 39, 66, 67, 68, 71–72
Magee, R. H., 21
Majerovitz, D., 7
Malarkey, W., 5
Malkinson, R., 20
Mallinckrodt, B., 163
Mankowski, E. S., 35
Manne, S., 20, 26, 115
Marien, L., 23
Martin, R., 21, 80
Mazel, R. M., 20
McCabe, K., 35, 41
McCall, M. E., 21, 44, 52, 53, 54, 75
McCaskill, J. W., 36
McCornack, S. A., 46
McDermott, V. M., 1, 4, 32, 66, 67, 120,
    122–132, 159–160
McHale, S. M., 169
McKay, G., 55, 80, 81
McLeod, J. D., 12, 15
McLeroy, K. R., 22
McMurry, J. F., 7

Subject Index

adaptation, communication to situation. *See* communication, multiple purposes of
adaptation, person to stressor, 90–93, 156–157
advice, 47, 52–79, 121, 149–150
  evaluation of, 39, 44, 49–50
  effects of, 49
  interpretation of, 38–39, 41, 46
  style of giving, 39–40
agreement, between partner, 36–38, 93, 113, 144, 145–146, 161
appraisal, 26, 30, 84–85, 91, 157. *See also* coherence
assessments, 40
attachment styles, 18, 34
autonomy. *See* face, negative

cardiac recovery, support for, 67, 133–144, 164
close relationships
  communication in, 2, 134, 163
  compared to therapy, 54–55
  distinctive features of, 44–45, 60, 76, 97, 116–117, 150–151
  effects of support from, 17
  as source of support, 5–8
  see also family, support from; friends, support from; spouse, support from
closeness. *See* intimacy
coding
  compared to participant ratings, 36
  interpretive processes in, 33, 35
  limitations of, 33, 47–48, 57, 83, 114, 151, 157

cognition
  and interpretation of support, 34–36
  study of, compared to communication approach, 29, 31, 46, 137, 154, 163–164
comforting, 2, 39, 56, 57, 117, 152. *See also* empathy
communal coping, 120–133, 136–137, 144–146, 150–151, 153, 163. *See also* communication, coordination of
confidants, 4–5
control, 22, 115, 117
  construction of, 84, 86–93, 152–153
  locus of, 18
  of others' behavior, 138–139
  of problem, 2, 52, 55–56, 82
  see also face, negative; power
coherence, 113, 150
communication, 13, 23–24, 26, 29, 30–31
  coordination of
    conversation, 39, 41, 108–109, 145–146, 151, 162
    problem representation, 93, 105, 113, 150
  content of, 39, 83, 91–92, 112, 150, 156–158
    and advice, 57, 66–68, 72–75
  effectiveness of, 46–49, 50
  evaluation of, 26, 29, 31–41, 152–153
    advice, 52–56, 66–68, 71–72, 77
    and interactional roles, 146–147
    measurement of, 97, 156–161
    and message features, 48–49, 71–72
  interpretation of, 31–41, 45, 60, 146–147
  multiple purposes of, 23, 45, 46–50, 62–79, 151, 153–154, 158–161